IRELAND'S ECONOMIC SUCCESS
REASONS AND PROSPECTS

Paul Sweeney

NEW
ISLAND

IRELAND'S ECONOMIC SUCCESS
First published 2008
by New Island
2 Brookside
Dundrum Road
Dublin 14

www.newisland.ie

© Paul Sweeney 2008

The author has asserted his moral rights.

ISBN 978-1-905494-71-2

British Library Cataloguing in Publication Data. A CIP catalogue record for this book is available from the British Library.

Typeset by TypeIT, Dublin
Cover design by Inka Hagen
Printed in the UK by Mackays

10 9 8 7 6 5 4 3 2 1

CONTENTS

For Anne

PREFACE

I had been out visiting factories and offices in the late 1990s and noticed a palpable change for the better throughout Ireland. It was radically better than the 1980s, which were utterly depressing in every way. I began to check the data and found that all the economic fundamentals, especially jobs were positively humming.

As nobody had written a book on the subject, I decided to do so. I wrote one in 1997 and when it was being launched in December, I was terrified that the boom might not last and I'd look like a fool! At the time, most Irish people knew there was a boom, that the Celtic Tiger existed, but were also worried that it would not last. The boom has continued for ten more years. Ireland has been transformed, utterly. And Irish people have also changed – become more confident, enterprising and sometimes brash.

What are the reasons for Ireland's phenomenal success? I decided to ask a number of people from differing backgrounds and this book is the result. There is a broad consensus on the reasons for the Irish economic success but some sharp differences of opinion and outlook.

I wish to thank the seven people who gave time for the interviews and follow ups from extraordinarily busy lives. Thanks to the Taoiseach, Bertie Ahern; David Begg; Gary McGann; Joe Macri; Olivia O'Leary; Frances Ruane and Peter Sutherland. I trust that I have accurately reflected their views, especially in the analysis. I hope the book helps in explaining to the average reader why Ireland has had such astonishing economic success over the twenty years from 1987. My thanks also to the others who gave me time, including Peter Cassells, Bill Attley, and Jack O'Connor. Thanks also to Professor David Jacobson and Rafique Mottiar who commented on some chapters. Anne Butler yet again put up with me as I worked on this book over 2007 and give me the usual superb advice! Thanks also to Edwin Higel and Deirdre Nolan of New Island.

Paul Sweeney,
December 2007
Dublin

INTRODUCTION
All's Changed, Changed Utterly

Ireland, a 'basket case economy',[1] was dramatically transformed in little more than a decade. Employment soared, incomes roared and economic growth reached world-record levels. Unemployment collapsed, mass emigration turned into rapid immigration, the population grew and a monoculture was transformed into diversity in no time. Productivity boomed, exceeding the US and virtually all other countries. Most new jobs were higher skilled and better paid and there was a rapid increase in the number of women in the workforce. 'For more than a decade now, Ireland has been the OECD's star performer.'[2]

Ireland, the most globalised economy in the world, became one of the most competitive. In just over a decade, one of Europe's poorest countries was turned into one of the highest-income countries in the world. Massive national debt was eliminated, though personal debt soared. Taxes on companies and on incomes were cut to near the lowest levels in the advanced world. On the other side of the coin, public spending as a percentage of Gross Domestic Product (GDP) was slashed to one of the lowest levels in the developed world. Yet, paradoxically, public spending grew well above inflation each year, in absolute terms, as the economy grew.

Profits soared and while wages also grew substantially in real terms, the share of the national cake going to profits grew substantially. Wages' share of national income fell from 67.2 per cent in 1994 to 55.5 per cent in 2005. A much, much bigger cake was being baked. However, take-home earnings of average workers grew even faster than gross pay, due to large income-tax cuts. Average industrial workers saw real living standards, measured by earnings, rise by over 80 per cent in twenty years. For some top earners and business owners, real incomes grew tenfold in ten years. Wealth, which was in only a few pockets in Ireland twenty-five years ago, was amassed in serious amounts by some, but also in varying amounts by a rapidly increasing and much more prosperous middle class. House prices soared, making paper millionaires out of many home owners, some of whom were on relatively modest incomes. Many households which had had several unemployed members saw household income rise rapidly as work became available. For pensioners and others on welfare, things were not so hot, yet their living standards improved in real terms and by more than at any other time in history.

The turnaround in Ireland began in 1987 and rapid economic and employment growth began in 1994 (see Appendix 1). The economy was still humming twenty years after the turnaround began. There have been three distinct periods in the twenty-year boom. The take-off period saw jobless growth from 1987 to 1993. There was a small increase of 93,000 net new jobs by the end of 1993 on 1987.

Table 1: Ireland's three growth phases

	Take-off 1987–93	Celtic Tiger 1994–2000	Domestic boom 2001–7
Average percentage rise GNP per annum	3.40 %	8.90 %	4.50 %
Rise in jobs (total in period)	93,000	450,000	400,000

Source: CSO, ESRI forecast for 2007

In the Celtic Tiger phase, from 1994 to 2000 inclusive, there were seven years of phenomenal economic and employment growth based on strong exports and productivity growth. There was a net increase of 450,000 new jobs and growth averaged a very high 8.9 per cent as Table 1 shows. The third phase, the domestic boom, from 2001 to 2007 inclusive, saw surprisingly strong employment growth, but it was based on domestic consumer demand, construction and strong borrowings.[3] Economic growth was still fairly strong at 4.5 per cent a year. Exports were lower in this period and the rapid rise in productivity growth also slowed. But the number of those at work doubled in the twenty years to 2007, to over two million, and economic growth was very, very strong.

This book will explain how Ireland moved from 'basket case' to world leader in a relatively short period of time. It will be seen that there was no single factor, but a multiple of reasons which came together. **Chapter One** provides an outline of Ireland's economic history to set the context for the success, and gives a brief introduction to the twenty-year boom. The following seven chapters comprise the views, laid out in structured interviews, of seven people from diverse backgrounds and with a range of experiences, on how economic success was achieved. Several have been key players in Ireland's economic success and the others are perceptive observers. A broad consensus emerges, though there are some sharp differences of opinion.

Bertie Ahern has been Taoiseach (Prime Minister) for over ten years at time of writing. He was elected for a third term in June 2007. He has led the country in a period of great growth in incomes and employment. **Peter Sutherland**, a former member of the Irish cabinet as Attorney General, is chair of one of the world's largest companies, BP, the oil multinational. He also chairs one of the world's leading financial companies, Goldman Sachs International, and has been a European Commissioner. In fact, he was the first Competition Commissioner and he has an unique insight into the Irish economy from the international business perspective. **David Begg**, General Secretary of the Irish Congress of Trade Unions (ICTU), one of the social partners, gives a unique view of Ireland's success. Begg was the innovator behind the employee share trust in Eircom, which grew to become one of Ireland's unusual, if somewhat controversial, corporate successes[4]. **Professor Frances Ruane**, Director of the Economic and Social Research Institute (ESRI), Ireland's premier research body, and former Professor of Economics at Trinity College Dublin, gives an expert and thoughtful observer's view of the reasons for Ireland's success. **Gary McGann**, CEO of Smurfit Kappa, Ireland's first truly multinational company, was CEO of Aer Lingus when it was a state-owned airline. In 2005/6 as President of IBEC, the Irish Business and Employers' Confederation, one of the social partners, he led that organisation in the negotiations which resulted in the eighth national agreement, Towards 2016. Investment by foreign multinationals in Ireland has been a key driver in the success. One of the biggest companies in the world, Microsoft, has a major facility in Ireland. Its Irish CEO, **Joe Macri**, gives his insights into Ireland's success from the perspective of a foreign direct investor. Mr Macri is also on the IBEC council and chaired the government Forum on Small Business. Finally, one of Ireland's leading broadcasters, writers and observers, **Olivia O'Leary**, gives her views on the reasons for the success, how it has changed Irish society and issues which we still need to address.

Chapter Nine draws together and analyses the views of the interviewees and of other economists on the external and internal reasons for Ireland's economic success. **Chapter Ten** outlines the hard facts of the success and **Chapter Eleven** sets out the building blocks of economic success and the lessons from Ireland for other countries. A critical view of what yet remains to be achieved, especially on the social front, is also examined. While nobody, least of all economists, knows the future, a stab can be made at it, based on existing trends.

This book is about the reasons for the Irish economic success. It is not about social success, which lags considerably behind the economic success. The economic success is an undoubted, superb actuality. Yet more remains to be done. Assessing the task of what remains to be done, particularly on the social side, and how to do it, is a contested area. Yet the economic success lays a wonderful basis for greater social development.

In the early years of the Celtic Tiger, the question on many Irish people's lips was 'Yeah, but will it last?' People seemed to fear that the success was temporary and would be taken away from them, in the way that a farmer knows that a bumper crop is too often followed by falling prices. There was both a religious guilt and a farmer's inherent pessimism about the boom for many Irish. Today they are more sanguine on the economic success, but the question is still lurking in many minds.

Thus the future outlook is discussed. It is shown that Ireland has a very good chance of maintaining its high living standards, relatively low unemployment and strong public finances, if it pursues reasonable economic policies and of course, if there is not a major shock in the big, bad world, which is no longer outside, but within the globalised Irish economy.

After the 1916 Rising which led to Irish Independence, the great Irish poet, W. B. Yeats[6] said that 'all's changed, changed utterly. A terrible beauty is born.' With the Irish economic boom, all's changed utterly. While the outcome is greatly celebrated by virtually everyone, the beauty is far from terrible. How was this superb economic success achieved? How did this 'basket case', this total laggard of Europe, this sick economy, this incubator of labour for export, bleeding its children onto the world's labour markets, suddenly break out of its vicious circle of decline? The following chapters are dedicated to answering this question.

CHAPTER ONE

A Brief Economic History of Ireland

A historical context gives important background to the modern story of the Irish success. It also shows how spectacular it has been. Few countries have had such sad economic histories and for so long. Strong emigration began well before the Great Famine of 1845–8. Ireland was a densely populated and very poor country then. Most Irish people subsisted in abject poverty in the early nineteenth century, in spite of Ireland's being an integral part of the world's greatest power, Great Britain.

The nineteenth century was one of population and industrial decline in the twenty-six counties which make up today's Republic. Industry was not strong and what there was declined in that century. On the other hand, the North East, around Belfast, had strong industrial development. Yet Ireland's twenty-six counties had one of the strongest per capita rises in incomes in the late nineteenth and early twentieth centuries – largely due to the emigration of poorer people.[1] The rise in living standards for those who remained was due not to any technological improvement, but to the large decline in population. By the eve of the First World War, Irish living standards, while well below those of Britain, were comparable with the rest of Europe. In contrast, the North East had industrialised, with export-orientated shipbuilding, textile-machinery manufacturing, boilermaking, etc. What industry there was in the South, such as brewing, distilling and biscuit-making, was aimed largely at the domestic market.

Independence

In 1922 Ireland was the first British colony to break away from Britain since the US in 1776. Like many new states, it began with a bitter civil war. Yet good political institutions were established which were free of corruption. Thus one of the first cornerstones of economic prosperity was laid – a system of good governance. As well as inheriting the British system of administration at both central and local government levels, the new state inherited well-structured legal, media, banking and insurance sectors; further building blocks of a modern economy.

Irish living standards per capita, which were higher than many Western European countries at independence, were to fall relative to most of Europe over the next forty-five years from 1922. Globalisation, a greater integration with trade investment and migration, had ceased with the First World War and Ireland, along with the international trend, adopted protectionism and self-sufficiency in the 1930s. It banned majority foreign control of manufacturing from 1932 to 1958 and engaged in and lost a trade war with Britain in the 1930s – 'burn everything British except its coal'. Yet protectionism was the mood in the 1930s in most countries and the smaller ones were to suffer more because they were small. Emigration was low in the decade of the 1930s, because there were few places to go during the Depression. As part of the programme of self-sufficiency, the government had established many state-owned enterprises in areas where the private sector did not invest due to scale or uncertain returns. These companies were to be important in the delivery of many goods and services and were incubators of talent in the lean years.

Ireland was to remain isolated in trade and also in its culture until the late 1950s, to the great intellectual and material impoverishment of its citizens. Most of Europe opened up to trade after the Second World War, but Ireland was slow to do so, setting itself back awhile. It missed an important decade of the post-war boom.

After the Anglo-Irish Free Trade Agreement in 1965, Ireland began to open up. The 1960s saw economic growth reach its highest levels up to then, averaging 4.4 per cent a year between 1960 and 1973, well above Britain and many European countries. There was indicative economic planning with the first Programme for Economic Expansion (1959–63), which was quite successful, but the Second Programme (1964–70) was largely abandoned as it was predicated on European Economic Community (EEC) membership, which did not materialise because of de Gaulle's refusal to admit the British (and Irish) into the six member states of the Common Market. The third Programme (1969–72) failed to meet its targets, especially on employment.

Recession
By 1972, manufacturing exports finally exceeded those of agriculture, and unemployment was fairly low at 7 per cent, or under 100,000 people. Industrial policy was heavily interventionist and the state gave generous grants, had set up the first tax-free zone in the world at Shannon and established the Industrial Development Authority (IDA)[2] to encourage

local and foreign firms to invest in manufacturing. While most countries were hit by the oil crisis in 1973, Ireland enjoyed strong growth until 1979 due to public spending, favourable demand from abroad and membership of the Common Agricultural Policy (CAP). Growth averaged 4.1 per cent of GDP, not much below the 4.4 per cent of 1960 to 1973. However, there was a prolonged recession with growth averaging only 1.5 per cent of GDP between 1979 and 1986, though this was similar to that of most Organisation for Economic Co-operation and Development (OECD) countries. The Depression was more severe than the GDP figures indicate because of massive outflows of interest on the public debt and because of the repatriation of profits by multinationals.[3] The oil price rise hit Ireland hard and a changing demographic profile reduced per capita income.

The 1980s were a very bleak decade, with large-scale emigration and with national income actually falling in some years. Taxes were very high, evasion was widespread and much public spending was going to repay the soaring national debt, due to the implementation of increased public spending *and* tax cuts after the 1977 general election.

The European Economic Community

After its independence in 1922, Ireland's economy did not take off. It was tied to its old colonial master, Britain, until it joined the EEC in 1973. Britain had declined relative to most other European countries in the twentieth century, many of which really took off after the Second World War. In the words of Kieran Kennedy, former director of the Economic and Social Research Institute (ESRI), its performance was 'very mediocre'. He said that the rise in real product per capita in the seventy years since the First World War was much the same as in the preceding seventy years or so.

With Britain, Ireland had applied to join the EEC in 1961 but both were turned down. Until Ireland joined the Community, it suffered, because of its dependent economic relationship with a declining UK, through trade, its currency and its labour market.

At independence Ireland was well endowed with the building blocks for economic success, but protectionism damaged Ireland's development and strong links with the UK did not help. However, Irish politicians and policy-makers were also to make a number of policy mistakes which held back the Irish economy for many years.

Mistakes

The first policy mistake was to provoke the 'economic war' with Britain,[4] which Ireland lost. The second was the experiment in protectionism in general, which was greatly flawed. While this anti-globalisation era was international (Ireland was simply following a trend) the tariffs imposed by Ireland were inconsistent and discouraged firms from exporting, which resulted in their being very weak when tariffs were dismantled and they faced stronger competition.

The third mistake was the delay of a decade in abandoning the policies of protection and self-sufficiency in favour of outward-looking trade policies, which was the only way forward for a small economy, especially when it was clear that the rest of Europe was booming after the Second World War.

A fourth error was that the policy recommendations of the various thoughtful economic reports on twenty-six sectors, including the tripartite Committee on Industrial Organisation established in 1961, were not followed immediately and vigorously to address the problems of indigenous industry. The fifth major policy mistake was governments' failure to invest in education far earlier than they did.

Finally, the spending spree and tax cuts following the 1977 election were to constrain the economy for around fifteen years and to delay the take-off to success. It could perhaps be argued that the take-off would have occurred sooner and it may have been less dramatic, but no one will ever know for sure.

1987 – year one of the turnaround

The seeds of Irish economic success were sown in the 1960s but the turnaround began in 1987. The 1980s were a period of high unemployment, mass emigration, high inflation, fiscal crisis, soaring taxes on reducing incomes and falling profits. Average incomes of industrial workers fell by 8 per cent in the years to 1987. The economy shrank for a few years. In a modern economy, people are used to some economic growth and a level of around 2 per cent is average for an advanced economy, so when an economy shrinks, people really feel the pinch. They cut back on spending, businesses slow down, some close and people lose their jobs.

In 1987, the government, led by Charles Haughey, invited employers and unions, which were to become the social partners, to attempt to build a consensus on economic and to a lesser degree, social policy. An economic programme, the Programme for National Recovery (PNR), was agreed and put into effect, providing the basis for dramatic recovery.

The management of an economy and government's relationship with business, unions and other stakeholders can ensure that an economy and society can be generally successful, in spite of the inevitable downturns in the business cycle. The Nordic countries, Switzerland and a few others have shown that it is possible to ensure a high level of economic and social development every year. This is partly due to their form of social partnership. Ireland's economic success may be interrupted by a cyclical economic downturn, or worse, by a major international event. Yet the recent Irish economic success is such that it has lifted the economy onto a new plane, where there are new levels of economic performance, expertise, skills and competences and new firms and institutions, largely underpinned by a different, modern structure.

The service sector, employing 67 per cent of the workforce, is potentially very modern and export-orientated, with a good mixture of international and domestic ownership, innovation and confidence. Manufacturing, while suffering recent job losses, had bucked the international decline in the 1990s with expanding employment, and is still highly productive with increasing output. Construction employs too many people to be sustainable and will shrink in time. Farming is negligible in employment size and while still declining, what is left is modern and its productivity is rising.

Twenty years agrowing – rapidly!
While Ireland had an economic boom for twenty years to 2007, it really began in 1994. Economic growth averaged a very high 7.4 per cent between 1994 and 2007 (see Appendix 2). Growth rates reached as high as 10 to 12 per cent some years. While Gross Domestic Product (GDP), the measure used internationally, exaggerates Irish economic performance, whatever measure is used, the figures were high and sustained for a long period.

Ireland's GDP is 150 per cent of the average in the European Union (EU) but that does not mean that Irish citizens' incomes are 50 per cent above the average. GDP exaggerates Ireland's economic performance, pushing us up second only to rich little Luxembourg. Irish GDP is inflated by the profits made and exported by multinationals and not accruing to the citizens. More accurately, Ireland has the fifth highest income in the EU (see Chapter Ten: The Hard Facts on the Irish Economic Success).

It should be noted, however, that this is *income*, not wealth. Ireland has some way to go to build up wealth to the levels of the richer European states, but it is doing so rapidly. The skylines of Ireland's cities and towns were dominated by cranes for decades with the prolonged construction boom, which finally began to tail off in 2007. The public sector has been investing strongly in the economy and the government plans to continue that with its National Development Plan (NDP) running from 2007 to 2013. In spite of high public and private investment in Ireland in recent years, the country still has a long way to go to catch up in terms of its public infrastructure, that is, schools, hospitals, roads, public transport, public buildings, etc.

Productivity growth in Ireland soared in the boom years and the level reached that of the best-performing countries in the late 1990s. Strong productivity growth, with high employment growth, virtually wiped out unemployment – down from 16.3 per cent in 1988 (see Appendix 1) to just around 4.3 per cent between 2002 and 2007; the lowest in the EU27. Average unit labour costs were reduced by 40 per cent between 1995 and 2007. However, the rate of growth in productivity has slowed in recent years, largely due to the growth in construction and the shift to services, both of which tend to have lower productivity.

Real incomes have risen substantially. Average industrial earnings rose by 36 per cent in real terms but disposable incomes rose by a massive 80 per cent in real terms. This was in spite of fairly high inflation in some years and the greater part of the increase in take-home earnings was due to large reductions in income tax. The real rise in incomes in Ireland was in stark contrast to low income growth in the USA and many European countries. However, the social wage, in terms of healthcare, childcare, eldercare, welfare, education, public transport, etc., is still way behind most European countries. While Irish public services have greatly improved, there is still a long way to go.

The huge increase in employment has had a dramatic effect on poverty reduction in Ireland. This was especially true of *household* poverty reduction as more people in households found jobs. Yet, in spite of much progress, those at risk of poverty in 2005 were a high 19.7 per cent, the second highest in the EU15, behind the UK. A major study[5] found that all shared in the economic boom and on a long list of social fundamentals, Irish people are a lot better off today than twenty years ago, with subjective wellbeing and national morale among the highest in Europe. However, the gap between those at the very top and those at the bottom widened further.

Public finance
Public finances were in extraordinarily poor shape back in 1987 due to very high public spending and tax reductions, which virtually bankrupt the country after the 1977 election. The national debt was so high all income tax was being used to pay interest on it and not on improving citizens' welfare. Today, the national debt is the second lowest in the EU, having been the highest at 118 per cent of GNP in the late 1980s (see Appendix 3). Governments managed to substantially cut day-to-day public

spending as a proportion of GDP, while simultaneously raising it in real terms! Today, current public spending is the lowest in the EU15 as a proportion of Gross National Product (GNP) or GDP. Taxes on companies and on incomes have been cut dramatically. The increased economic activity and the doubling of the numbers at work, who were now paying tax, and much lower unemployment, greatly boosted the Exchequer's coffers. The benign economic environment has meant that as well as cutting taxes, the government has also been able to put a substantial 1 per cent of GDP away in a state investment fund, the National Pension Reserve Fund. This state fund is invested in loans to other governments and in equities in major companies worldwide. It amounted to €21bn in May 2007. The level of capital public spending has also been maintained at twice the EU level.

The Irish economy grew so rapidly in this period that current public spending, as a share of a rapidly growing GDP, was radically reduced while, simultaneously, it was increased each year in absolute terms above inflation. This twenty years was a golden era for Irish public finances. When there is a prolonged economic downturn, the demand for increased public spending rises as unemployment grows, but simultaneously, governments' tax revenues decline with lower economic activity.

Economic success

The economy became one of the most globalised in the world and far more competitive. Trade and exports in particular boomed and the share of foreign direct investment (FDI) coming to Ireland greatly increased. In the period, outward investment by Irish firms boomed and in one year, 2004, exceeded inward FDI. On all economic fundamentals, Ireland did exceptionally well in this golden era, but the greatest success was not the rapid economic growth or the rise in incomes, but in the doubling of employment and the reversal of emigration.

The reasons for Ireland's economic success – the views of seven key people

The interviews in the following chapters have been structured around approximately twenty reasons for the Irish economic success. Some of the commentators ignore issues that they do not believe were particularly important and concentrate on those they think were. There follows a chapter which draws conclusions on what were the determining reasons for Ireland's economic success. It will be seen that while there is disagreement, and in some instances it is strong, the observers broadly agree on the reasons for the Irish economic success. Understanding the reasons for the emergence of this golden era of economic achievement in Ireland should help policy-makers guard the success and enhance it and lessons may be learned by other countries in policy making and importantly, in execution.

CHAPTER TWO

Peter Sutherland, International Banker[1]

While I am not as optimistic about the future as some,
nor am I apocalyptic.

Peter Sutherland is Chairman of BP and of Goldman Sachs International. He was the founding Director General of the World Trade Organisation (WTO). He had previously been Director General of the General Agreement on Tariffs and Trade (GATT). He was Chairman of Allied Irish Banks from 1989 to 1993. A barrister, he was Attorney General of Ireland and thus a member of the Irish government. He was a member of the European Commission in charge of competition policy. Peter Sutherland is on the board of the Royal Bank of Scotland Group plc. He is associated with the World Economic Forum, World Trade Organisation, the Bilderberg Group, the Trilateral Commission and the European Round Table of Industrialists. He is European Chairman of the Trilateral Commission. He has an honorary knighthood, many other international honours and he is the United Nations Special Representative for Immigration.

Ireland's membership of the European Union is undoubtedly the most important fundamental reason for our economic success in recent times. This, the removal of borders and the removal of a bilateral dependence on the United Kingdom in terms of access to markets were central to the success.

Between 1973 and 1990, Ireland made very little impact on reducing the gap between the average GDP per capita against the European Community average. It reduced a little bit, but very little, relative to what has happened since. Ireland only rose from 64 per cent of the EU average at the time of accession in 1973 to 76 per cent in 1990 and even this figure looks better than it should because Greece, Spain and Portugal had all joined in the interval. I don't think our incomes had markedly changed, notwithstanding the fact that we'd been the beneficiary of relatively significant sums of money under the Structural Funds. We had largely wasted these funds. Much of them were spent on social programmes, training programmes, which were of limited real value. In my opinion, the money could have provided the infrastructure which we still notably lack. In contrast, other countries, like Spain and Portugal, used European Union Structural Funds effectively for the development of their infrastructure.

The failure of Ireland during that period from 1973 to around 1990 is a significant factor when you look at the alleged causes for our subsequent success. Some of those alleged causes for our subsequent success existed during the period – for example, the allegedly superior educational system (although I do not accept it is superior, in the way in which many describe).

The great paradox of our economic success was our acceptance of the economic rigour which was imposed on us by our decision to join the single currency, at a time when we had huge structural deficits in the economy, massive unemployment and a violent situation in Northern Ireland. It was almost incredible that we were prepared to take the risks that went with joining a currency that demanded very strict discipline in terms of expenditure.

The fiscal consolidation of 1987
For the first time we Irish began to realise that throwing money at the issue was not going to provide an answer. We were unable to throw money at it because we did not have money during the 1990s. In the period up to 1986 the economy was very badly strapped. We had huge debt-to-GDP ratios – completely out of control – and we'd high unemployment. Keynesian approaches could not be used. Therefore we had to allow the functioning of the market to actually work. I think we did that. The fiscal consolidation in 1987 engineered by the Fianna Fáil government but with the crucial support of Fine Gael led by Alan Dukes was vital. The budget deficit fell from 11 per cent of GDP in 1986 to below 3 per cent of GDP by 1989. Economic growth picked up from –0.5 per cent in 1986 to 6 per cent in 1989.

The second point I'd make was that our GDP per capita was distorted in the period up to the 1990s, because we had a much higher dependency ratio and a much lower labour participation rate – by women in particular. When our dependency ratio dropped (because there were fewer young children, because of birth control and everything that happened in the

1990s) this increased the GDP per capita. We had more at work and it removed this distortion in our GDP per capita, because we had fewer dependants. This was a significant issue.

FDI and low corporate tax

I think that by far the two most important issues in terms of our relative growth in the intervening period have been the reduction in corporation tax and inward investment. Foreign direct investment (FDI) in turn has been the crucial element in stabilising and ultimately causing significant growth in our economy. I have no doubt that foreign direct investment would not have happened without the lower corporation tax rate. It was the vital cause of inward investment. I think the Financial Services Centre too has not been unimportant. Another important point here is that low corporate tax is a better way to attract companies than subsidies. This is because low corporate tax is useful only if you are profitable but a subsidy can make a bad investment look good.

To me, FDI has been the key and FDI in turn has been the result of the corporation tax, largely combined with three other factors. These are a) we are English speaking, b) our education system is reasonably good, and c) we were in the euro and the British were not. I also think that the IDA have sold that third point rather well. There is no threat of a currency fluctuation with the Euro. Our attitude to Europe was more positive and we were seen as not being 'semi-detached', whereas Britain is not a member of Shengen (we are not either, but it is because of them); it's not a member of the Eurozone; and it's not a constructive engagee in the European process.

The birth of the IFSC

On the development of the International Financial Services Centre (IFSC) in Dublin, I was in charge of competition policy when the Irish government, led by Haughey, applied for a derogation to allow the IFSC to exist in 1987–8. I was able to give this permission for the IFSC. The state aid regime of the European Union has always been one which only allowed tax reductions for either industry-specific areas – like financial services or sub-regional areas. It only allowed that in very limited circumstances. I was able to give the permission for the IFSC because at that time our GDP per capita was less than 75 per cent of the EU average and our unemployment rate at 16.3 per cent was significantly higher than the EU average. At that time there were limited pockets of reduced tax activity (Shannon, IFSC and so on) and it was going to be removed ultimately (because it was a time-related permission) which enabled me to grant it.

By the time the IFSC renewal came up, everything had changed – GDP per capita had risen substantially and unemployment was down. This drove the need for a rethink on company taxation. It was recognised that the only way we would satisfy the European Union was by having a general tax rate of 12.5 per cent for all companies, in all sectors. I think the decision to go to the 12.5 per cent tax rate drove it, because there was no alternative. We were either going to lose the derogation for the Financial Services Centre or Shannon. So the Rainbow government decided to change it by reductions in the rate until it reduced to 12.5 per cent. I think that is very important. The inward investors would say they never would have come here except for the low tax. And if they had not come, our indigenous industry sector development was poor. We have some, but not many. The most successful has been CRH, which is an outstanding company. Smurfit is another example. But otherwise, apart from domestically-led companies like the banks, there were very, very few for many years. We did not seem to have an innovative and entrepreneurial indigenous sector. We do have now, but it is only beginning to grow and it's a very late developer.

One reason why we did not get the lift-off when we had the zero rate of tax on profits (and then the 10 per cent rate for many years) was because the world changed in the interim. The process of globalisation moved into a much more advanced stage in the early 1990s. We had the collapse of the Iron Curtain and the creation of, in theory, a single global economic model. State socialism was destroyed as a model – it could not work, and borders were beginning to fall. The creation of the WTO led to a new environment and a new attitude to FDI by most governments and all multinational companies. Everybody was locating outside their national markets in a way that they had never envisaged before.

The importance of the Single Market

The third element and probably most important was the success of the 1992 project in the European Union. I was Commissioner for Competition from 1985 to 1989 in the first Delors Commission and what we had had up until then was a customs union. We did not have an internal market and the 300 or so proposals which were put through during the Delors Commission period to create the 1992 project generated an entirely different approach to national markets in the European Union. The first Delors Commission made as its major project the completion of the internal market. Up to then, the customs union and the lack of controls on state aids created a situation where, if a US company wanted to locate in Europe, it was going to be attracted to locate firstly by major hand-outs from countries like France; and secondly, major impediments to get into that market. For example, in France, there was the famous 'Poitiers case' where all goods had to come through Poitiers. The Italians, the French – a lot of the European countries – used every conceivable barrier to stop goods being exported into their domestic markets, even from other EU countries. It was the 1992 project that really changed this.

Between 1973 and 1985, the European Union had largely been in paralysis. The Exchange Rate Mechanism (ERM) had been created, but virtually nothing else. 'Eurosclerosis' and 'paralysis' were the descriptions for the European economy in the early 1980s. It was that Commission, between 1985 and 1989, which created the 1992 project and drove the opening up of markets. That created an entirely new dynamic for foreign direct investment into Ireland. Suddenly, Ireland became as good a location for access to the French market as was France. Indeed it was probably better because there was less company tax and it was a less regulated environment from the point of view of labour market flexibility. Plus there were a lot of young people wanting to work.

Ireland's allegedly superior education system

On education, I will first discuss our young people and families. The success of our young people is more a reflection of innate capacities and attitudes of our young people and our parents than it is of our education system. The Irish are naturally good communicators. We present well. In addition, we do not feel – as they do in Britain – the effects of a class system, the effects of which still exist. There is a basic sense, in the vast bulk of Irish society, that there is not a ceiling that stops you or inhibits you because of who your parents were. There is a very positive attitude towards education and advancement. I have seen in BP and Goldman Sachs and elsewhere how attractive Irish young people are as candidates for jobs, but I do not think that attraction and capacity is related to a superiority in education.

The OECD report into third level education in Ireland which was published in 2006 and the Royal Irish Academy report on the same subject show that we are significantly below the European average of the percentage of people who are in PhD-level study in the area of technical capacity – science, engineering and so on. Compared to the Swedes, Finns and the Nordics generally, we have less than one-third (as I recall) of the percentage of people at that level of education. Sweden, Finland and Denmark are good examples to Ireland. If we are to maintain our successful momentum, we have to have a competitive advantage somewhere. We do not have it in terms of costs any more, nor in terms of indigenous natural wealth, so we have to develop it through skills and brain power. I don't think we have achieved that. While the statistical base for the analysis of comparative advantage between universities is not perfect, in such listings as there are, for example by Shanghai University, Ireland does not feature in the top ranks of universities. For instance, there is one Irish university, Trinity, in the top 200 in the world. Ireland is not up there at the top.

Teaching of science in the schools is also a problem. Most science teachers are biology teachers rather than in other areas of science. Also, Ireland's university pupil/teacher ratios are not good. The universities do the best that they can with inadequate resources. This is not a great success and we clearly need a fee structure now where loans can be obtained by students to be repaid and assistance is given to the poorest. In relation to teaching at second level, there is also a serious problem. Only a handful of non-performing teachers have been fired in the last ten years in Ireland. Now teachers should be admired and properly paid but they should also be measured in performance and those who are seriously deficient cannot be protected for life. They are at the moment. Our education system is simply not good enough in terms of assessments of teachers' capacities and abilities. I think the trade unions are largely responsible for this. Everyone agrees that teachers should be the most honoured and, relatively speaking, a highly paid profession. Yet there are few people I know who do not have a genuinely serious complaint about some teachers' capacity in schools for their children. I think that if there was one single reform for the Irish economic system it would be to get our teaching right, because I really think it truly needs objective testing with appropriate responses then taken. Some improvement is now taking place with the new secondary school inspectorate but we have a hell of a lot further to go.

I also disagree with the whole theory that you should not permit selection on testing of intellect to enter certain schools. I do not mean elite related to money, it cannot be that – but in terms of pre-selection for the schools. In London, St Pauls, Westminster and the other top day schools have a system which produces very good students because the classes contain similar levels of ability.

Turning back to the economy per se, I think that it was the 1992 programme that had a huge impact on FDI, assisted by low taxes on companies, by globalisation and by competition and by the enforcement of competition policy.

The firm policies that addressed our chronic deficits adopted by McSharry and supported by Alan Dukes helped to transform the country. For instance, the debt/GDP ratio has been dramatically reduced from over 100 per cent – it peaked at 117.6 per cent in 1987 – to the lowest in the European Union at 25 per cent in 2007. This is a remarkable achievement.

Infrastructure and public service reform
Two other points I would make on the negative side are from the most recent World Economic Forum competitiveness report. First, in terms of government waste (measured by expenditure), Ireland ranks number fifty-five. This is an appalling statistic. Secondly, in terms of infrastructure, we are around forty-sixth which few would deny. A third big negative that I have about the Irish economy is that I do not think that our civil service have performed well in some vital areas. I do not think there has been the necessary and desirable accountability in public projects. I think our health system is an example of such poor performance and so too are our education and our transport systems. I think we ignore our deficiencies at our peril and while the politicians must take the main responsibility, public officials too have responsibilities.

On the other hand, I think that the Department of Finance has performed well on the fiscal side of things and I give a lot of credit to Charlie McCreevy. He drove a coach and four through a whole lot of paralytic, conservative thinking about how the economy should develop.

Different models
Denmark is a very successful economy and it is not a low-tax economy. It is not an economy that has been dependent on FDI because, over a long period of time, it has been able to create a large indigenous sector. While there are not very many large companies, they are Danish owned. While Denmark is small and has just a few large companies – Moller-Maersk, ISS, Danske Bank – they are major players.

Sweden is different. I have been involved in Sweden on the board of the Wallenberg companies for the last ten years. Sweden, a country of about eight million, has many important multinational companies, e.g. Ericsson, Saab, Scania, Atlas Copco, Volvo. They constitute a substantial range of monster companies, even by European standards. By Irish standards they are out of sight in terms of their size.

There are different models. I am not in the neo-liberal camp, but Ireland had to go the route of every conceivable inducement to FDI because we had proved that we seemed incapable of creating industry on our own. Yet, I do think a huge change was brought about by completing the internal market. The completion of the internal market was the vital moment for us.

The EU had never worked for us merely because of the Structural Funds. Relatively, we got far more funding in the 1970s and 1980s. As the poor man of Europe until the Greeks joined in 1981, we received relatively large amounts of funding and we wasted much of it. A lot of it was spent on temporary short-term palliatives for unemployment to take people off the streets who were not actually doing anything. I'm not saying that the training was not good, but the jobs were not there when people completed courses. It was often a waste of money and we would have been much better off investing in physical infrastructure, like telecoms systems etc.

On the internal market, we have been consistently slow in introducing competition. The Electricity Supply Board (ESB) is a classic example of such failure. State enterprises in Ireland have had to be dragged screaming and kicking to any degree of competition. The internal market was not only useful externally, but also useful internally. Otherwise we would probably still have Telecom Éireann as a state monopoly, as we have the ESB! The result of the lack of competition probably affects the cost of electricity which is too high and it has also led to some allegedly scandalous situations involving people being paid for doing little or nothing.

Social partnership

I think that social partnership is a good thing. However, if, through a lack of clear thinking by the social partners, it results in the escalation of costs that makes us uncompetitive, then there is a problem with it. I think we are facing very high costs now and this is a major issue. In principle, social partnership is a very good idea. In various periods it has had a very constructive effect on our performance.

However, I think we are on the verge of a very cataclysmic situation. I believe that there is the extreme danger that much of the foreign direct investment will depart if the Irish cost base remains too high. I think it is too high today. If that is the consequence of centralised bargaining and, above all, the failure of the government to restrain public sector spending and employment then it could lead to disinvestment. I think public sector pay is probably relatively high. I think the per capita number of civil servants that we have, relative to total population, is probably also very high and so are the costs in this area. We need real benchmarking on these issues with published information giving everyone the facts.

Our costs have very real risks for the economy. If we get a series of the information technology companies, or one big one, pulling out – then, just like there was a wave that came in – a wave will go out. I'm terribly worried because perhaps we do not have an adequate base of embedded industry which is sufficient to deal with such a situation. We need to a) keep this foreign direct investment here for a significant period of time, b) attract the research for the existing companies, and c) also entice the management of the companies to gradually become more indigenous than the headquarters in, say, Texas. My instinct is that our cost competitiveness is now a real problem. Further, in the absence of inward migration flows, the Irish cost situation would be even worse. Prices here are 17 per cent above the average in the EU15.

In my first year as Commissioner for Competition, I also had social welfare and education (Delors parked it with me for a year until the Spanish took it over). Delors and I undertook what was called the 'Val Duchesse Process', which was social partnership at EU level. It was to try to create a model at EU level, which was subsequently achieved in Ireland. Ultimately it fell apart at European level. It did not work, much to Delors' annoyance. He always saw the social partnership and social Europe as the other side of the coin of the Single European Market. In a sense, the doubling of the Structural Funds (which was achieved in 1988) was part of this project. These were part of the balance for the Single Market programme. In this context, I think that the Irish experience has been successful.

Size is very important
It seems that the small countries flow to the top of the economic pile in Europe. I think size is very important because the evidence suggests it. I'm including Norway and Switzerland – both of which are, in effect, within the EU economic area. Liechtenstein, Luxembourg, Ireland, Denmark, Norway and Switzerland are probably the six wealthiest countries in Europe today. Every one of them is small. Is it just a coincidence?

One cannot but conclude that small size has some relevance. What is its relevance? Its relevance is the fact that, with a small country, with access to a huge market and with a rule-making authority to make sure that the bigger markets that you are accessing provide a level playing field, then you should have a real advantage. This is because properly developed policies can be focused more in a small country. They cannot be focused in the same way in large countries, because the vested interests, over the ranges of industries and services, are so vast that they cannot be played off against one another. I think that that is very important.

We also have the advantage that Ireland moved, without an intervening industrial revolution, straight to a modern economy. We did not have to dismantle shipbuilding, steel, coal – all of the old industries that really crippled and paralysed the economies during the real 'Eurosclerosis' of the 1970s and 1980s. The difficult restructuring that I was involved with, as Competition Commissioner, was in areas like steel and shipbuilding. Fortunately, I did not have to focus on these declining industries in Ireland but rather in all of the main European economies such as Germany, France and Italy. The UK too, notoriously, had to deal with the phasing out of coalmining, shipbuilding and so on.

We were trying to cut back on state aid to these industries in Europe. Governments were pumping enormous amounts of state aid into supporting them because they maintained large numbers in employment. Big countries – the French, the Italians, the Germans and some small countries (Belgium and the Netherlands) all of them did their utmost to defend their old industries by dumping on others through huge state-aid investment programmes. Instead, they should have invested all that money in modern industries. We were lucky – Ireland did not have that problem.

Our competitive advantages

Where is our competitive advantage? As I have said, I do not honestly think it is in education in the way it should be. I do not think the OECD or others have shown any comparative advantage with our education system which demonstrates that it is better than those of other countries. It is worse and we spend less on it! Where is our competitive advantage except that we speak English, we are in the internal market and we have low tax? I do not see where it is other than perhaps in some distinctive qualities in our culture that make us rather good communicators.

Personally by far the most important contribution I made was the conclusion of the Uruguay round and converting the GATT to the WTO. That to me was the biggest contribution. I drove the competition laws, enforcement and drafted the merger control laws in the Commission, but by far the biggest thing in my life was being involved in the creation of the WTO. That was fundamental to globalisation. I suspect that this influenced my subsequent choice as Chairman of one of the world's largest companies, BP and of Goldman Sachs International.

On the importance of industrial policy and the Industrial Development Agency, I believe a great deal of the thinking on it and the IDA was put together by Michael Killeen and Ray McLoughlin in the early days. I think the IDA is the great success of the state agencies – a wonderful success story. The ability to attract industry has been phenomenal. It deserves a great deal of credit. The difficulty of industrial policy is to define it. Tax is part of it, but what else is? One of the important things this government is doing for the long term is this investment in pure research. International scientists and others are very impressed by our research programme, where a lot of money is being invested. I don't know much about it but this seems innovative and good.

Another great initiative that we have undertaken is to set up the National Treasury Management Agency. It has been superb and is doing a great job I believe in spite of the negativism in some quarters of the traditional civil service.

Professional competence within the civil service

We really need a sophisticated analytical capacity within the civil service in the area of economics. It cannot rely on reports from the ESRI or the Central Bank to assist in rapid and important decision-making which can have impacts for decades to come. While people have been talking of this for some time – the lack of economic expertise – very little is being done to rectify the paucity of professional skill levels within the civil service. In a complex world, it is no longer acceptable to have 'generalists' dominating all areas of the service, however competent, making poorly informed decisions on major capital and current public spending. Too often they are not evidence-based, after serious and deep analysis. Further, it sometimes appears as if the top civil servants are afraid to stand up to poor, short-term decision-making by government Ministers which may cost the taxpayer dearly.

On innovation, there are statistics now that are much better than they used to be, which apparently demonstrate that we are producing more new ideas. I think that the evidence on patent applications, as well as new business start-ups, is reasonably good. It may be indicative of the recent economic success. We used to be terrible at business start-ups. Confidence is what is coming across to me. For example, we have a very sophisticated staff selection process in Goldman Sachs and we are getting relatively more on a per-capita basis from Ireland. This is not based on a comparative analysis of exam results or what they did, but I think it is more on this self-confidence that young Irish people appear to radiate! They are prepared to go into a room and do battle and argue almost any issue. I think this is great.

I may be wrong in taking this away from the education system, but it is more the family, the thinking, the sense that Ireland is doing well, and patriotic self-confidence. I think I recall a poll that said we were the most patriotic people in Europe (patriotic in the sense of having a great belief in our people, in our country). This is a very good thing as long as it does not become irredentist and xenophobic.

Looming challenges

I don't think we are conscious of the fact that the low corporation tax advantage could be under threat. It could also be under threat in a more fundamental way. On the one side, there is the possibility of the US changing its laws; but on the other side, if the British turned on this issue and decided that they were in favour of tax harmonisation in Europe rather than being opposed to it this would increase the pressure. There is a lot of talk in the City of London of companies migrating over here, bringing a lot of investment into the Financial Services Centre. So you can't rely on this forever, but at the end of the day it's a cost situation. One is back to costs again.

The profound impact of 1992

I think the Celtic Tiger period has been truly amazing. Nobody could have foreseen it. In that sense it is miraculous. As to the turnaround beginning in 1987, I think it was a necessary precursor to the turnaround, but I think the turnaround came in the 1990s. There was slow employment growth initially, but then the employment growth became staggering. But I think it was the conclusion of the 1992 programme which had the most profound effect on all. It changed attitudes everywhere and it was combined with the creation of the WTO. This created a positive attitude towards globalisation and therefore, towards investment, across borders more generally, permeating the US industrial psyche and that of everybody else. It was all that opening up which created a new dynamic which was very important and advantageous to Ireland.

Migration will be another challenge

Migration is very important. It is also a difficult issue to handle as we can see from the experience elsewhere in Europe; it is going to create challenges. If Ireland is to have a 5 per cent growth rate over the next few years, we will require a huge number of additional migrants coming into this country. I am involved in this at the moment because I am Special Representative to the Secretary General on Migration and Development of the UN. The inward migration figures in the last eight years for Ireland and Spain are unique in Europe. Such migration can ultimately lead to issues unless carefully handled. Twenty-eight per cent of the population in London or probably more was born outside the UK, but if you look at the Netherlands, over 50 per cent of the population of Amsterdam was born outside the Netherlands. That may have helped to cause, almost overnight, a switch from extreme tolerance to extreme intolerance in the Netherlands.

We have a big issue as to how we handle this. We have only just begun to grapple with it in the sense that we still have no holistic policy approach to it. We have border control in the Department of Justice, with other departments – Social Welfare, Education – not working together in a joined-up manner. This will be a very great challenge in the future. Over 10 per cent of our workforce are non-Irish today and if the growth rates were to continue as they are, we are going to find that escalating at a very remarkable pace over the next five or six years. It is hard to see how, with strong growth, it can be stopped. Nor should it be from a moral point of view. Also we have got free movement within the European Union and it's a relevant part of what the European Union is. So we have to grapple with issues like the arguments for assimilation as opposed to multiculturalism and so on. We have not even begun to think in depth about these issues. We attract in people who are a tremendous boon to the economy. On various levels this is great but we must be careful as to how we integrate them and we must be concerned to develop positive responses rather than negative ones from the people. Just how different these can be are demonstrated by the differences in public opinion between Sweden and the UK.

Future decisions

While I am not as optimistic about the future as some, nor am I apocalyptic. I think we have very real challenges here in terms of our cost structure and our over-dependence on the construction sector. We have a number of significant hiccups in sight. I don't say we are going to revert to being what we were in the 1980s and I accept to an extent that we have reached another level, from which it is unlikely that we are going to fall off. So I'm somewhere in between, in terms of being an optimist and a pessimist. I'm worried about the present situation and I just hope we can handle it but this requires hard decisions and we have not been good historically in taking hard decisions.

Bodies like the Competitiveness Council are vital to this. We need a rational, reasonable debate with both sides of the social partners and everyone else, reaching rational decisions. If we can do that it makes our social partnership the crucial thing for the future – if we can reach consensus on reasonable policies and reasonable politics that does not lead to capitulation to any vested interests.

CHAPTER THREE

David Begg,
Trade Unionist[1]

*Ireland's great economic success could have
generated a great social success if we had done things differently.*

David Begg is General Secretary of the Irish Congress of Trade Unions. He is a director of the Central Bank, a member of the National Economic and Social Council (NESC), of the Council of the ESRI and of the Irish Times Trust. Between 1997 and 2001 he was CEO of Concern Worldwide, the international humanitarian relief and development agency. He was General Secretary of the Communications Workers' Union.

The main reasons for Ireland's economic success which I would list are a) the EU funds and how we used them successfully, b) foreign direct investment (FDI) and the particular sectors we attracted, c) social partnership and the consensual way we make and implement decisions in many areas of life, d) membership of the EU and our experience of dealing with Europe and the confidence it gave us, e) the educated workforce, and some lesser factors.

On the EU funds, I think I'd roll back to the important advantages that we had before the boom actually took off. In practical terms, I don't think the boom took off in 1987 but around 1993–4. Further, our geographical position in the middle of this Atlantic or the Atlanticist market, in terms of the Americans ramping up their trade with Europe, was significant. Ireland was in quite a good position within Europe then. We had a very strong cohort of fairly well-educated people – not too expensive to employ, English-speaking and we were on the periphery of Europe.

We were extremely well-placed to take advantage of what was happening at that time – when the European internal market was beginning to integrate Europe. There was a fairly powerful incentive for an American focus on Europe with the development of the EU internal market and I think we were just in the right place and had the right conditions including a business-friendly location. The big advantage of the social partnership process was that it gave an incredible amount of stability to that whole environment. This was a model that was going to remain stable into the future. From a business perspective, you almost had the best of all worlds. This was a catalyst for the take-off.

The Norwegian economist, Mjoset, who did an analysis in 1992 for NESC, said the absence of a Marshall Plan for Ireland after the Second World War was an inhibiting factor in our development. These EU funds might be described as a mini-Marshall Plan and they certainly helped us with the catch-up. I also think that they were well invested in training and in physical infrastructure. The disciplines that Europe required for the implementation of the projects were probably very good for the Irish public service. It did a very good job in ensuring that the funds were well employed.

The role of foreign direct investment

Foreign direct investment is important, especially for our exports, where foreign companies make up the bulk of them. Further, as a measure of their input to our GDP FDI is extremely important. However, FDI is not as important in employment terms – the foreign sector employs 150,000 people out of two million. Further, there is an indigenous spin-off in terms of the local industry serving the foreign firms, with a spin-off in managerial and other skills, technology transfer etc. There are important arguments on what kind of governance system for multinationals, for mobile investment etc. should be in place internationally. This is a question which concerns me and should concern more people. What if every country tries to negotiate a research and development (R&D) component to ensure commitment to the long term – if they all get into this, we will all be bidding each other down for FDI.

Two sectors in particular, pharma and ICT [information and communications technology], have been very good for Ireland and pharma has done wonders for our exports to the US. Pharma has been very good for exports and for boosting our total productivity etc. ICT performance has been very good, and even with the bubble, it has recovered well. MNCs [multinational companies] are good and bad – without MNCs we would not have much of manufacturing exports but this dependence is also our weakness.

On the question of whether we are too dependent on MNCs, what I would like to see is Ireland being more like the Nordic countries. They have their own domestic MNCs. There are four or five dominant domestic MNCs in each of those countries, and they appear to have a commitment to their country of origin. In contrast, we don't have a core of Irish MNCs, though arguably, we do have a few in food – Kerry Group and Glanbia. We also have CRH and Smurfits. But the fortunes of foreign MNCs like Intel or Dell causes Irish political hearts to wobble.

Indigenous firms

Even when we have successful companies like CRH, Smurfits, or the two big Irish banks, they could be taken over by private equity capitalists who have no commitment to anything except short-term profits and rapid pay-backs of leveraged debt. I read that the deal the British unions did with BA on their pension funding in late 2006 made the company more vulnerable to takeover by these new forms of 'turbo capitalists'.

We are weak in our indigenous industrial base. Yet one sees that even the biggest firms can be taken over. The Nordics have less regard to Anglo-American share-ownership structures where predators can take over even the largest firms and if not asset-strip them, then bleed them for value to repay the debts they have run up. They ran up the debts in order to buy them in the first place. We saw this in the case of Eircom after it was privatised. The only other solution may be the paradox of an indigenous MNC which has a commitment to Ireland. This may be an oxymoron. Yet we have seen Scania, the privately-owned Swedish truck company which has been resisting takeover. The Swedes have a different share-ownership system than the Anglo-American model which allows them to be more resistant to foreign or hostile takeover. The Right calls it 'protectionism' but in many ways, it is common sense. Such share-ownership governance takes a longer-term perspective and is not dominated by quarterly results, like the Anglo-American share-ownership governance system. Many Anglo-Americans are now openly criticising it because management is subject to the tyranny of quarterly results! On the other hand, the Americans block foreign ownership of their airlines and also blocked the takeover of their ports by 'aliens'. When it comes to protecting national interests or 'national champions' the US is a world-beater, in spite of its 'free market' rhetoric. A huge proportion of its industry is built around the military. Boeing gets staggering subsidies. So does Airbus, but Europeans allow it! What depresses me is how many economists and commentators fall for this 'free' market rhetoric!

Globalisation and turbo capitalism

What I would like to achieve ultimately is probably unattainable. This is because the model of capitalism we are dealing with now is 'turbo capitalism'. It has no long-term commitment to anything, no commitment to customers, no commitment to any place – be it a country or locality – and no interest in building any kind of relationship with its own workers. Today, it is turbo capitalism where private equity firms or hedge funds invest in a company mainly to strip out value as hard and as fast as they can. They have no long-term commitment to the target firm and no interest in developing any relationship with labour. It leaves us unions in a difficult situation.

It is instructive to look at the last period of globalisation, the 1870–1914 phase which collapsed with the First World War. In spite of all the valiant efforts to put it back together again over many years, nobody could. The liberalism of uncontrolled markets and poor international governance did not work, collapsing into the totalitarianism of Communism and of Fascism. Neo-liberalism is resurgent and indeed dominant, but it did not work before and it will not work this time without proper international governance. The extreme capitalism model of globalisation without the foil of strong labour power (and the threat of an alternative communist system) to keep it in check may lead it to overreach. If it does, while communism and fascism are not viable alternatives, it still could collapse again into another form of totalitarianism. While globalisation is booming, many people are highly uncomfortable with the way it is developing. There may be a collapse in globalisation because of the lack of some form of international rules. When a system is indifferent to the human condition, then it is incapable of enduring. Globalisation has been good for Ireland and the Irish people and for the world economy, but it is very uneven – some have gained much more than others, and it does give greater advantage to corporations and against labour as it is presently structured.

Technology makes it possible to move money around the world at the touch of a button. Look what it has done for the mobility of capital. Labour is not in any sense as mobile but capital is and the liberalisation of capital markets and technological change have created conditions that have changed the balance of power between labour and capital. But this has also created a new type of market into which Ireland has fitted very well. Ireland is a very globalised country. Unions are not protectionist on trade nor have we been, but we are seeking a rebalance of power on the international rules governing globalisation. And for those who think globalisation is 'free markets at international level', beyond the reach of man, they are wrong. Markets, from the stall in the mediaeval marketplace to international derivatives today are governed by man-made rules. Without rules, markets cannot operate.

At the domestic level, the skipping of a generation in telecoms technology did create a difference, but we fell behind since, mainly due to the ill-conceived privatisation of Eircom, which was done without any strategy. It is a good example of where the focus by politicians and their policy advisors in the Departments of Finance and Communications was solely on quick financial returns. It was also driven by the utterly uncritical media circus on how much citizens could make from selling their own state company to themselves. None of the policy advisors and very few of the politicians considered what was in Ireland's longer-term interest. The system of regulation is ineffective and investment in telecoms was greatly reduced by the private equity consortium which took over the dominant player, Eircom, because the regulator did not (and maybe could not, due to poor government legislation) insist on investment in broadband. As a result, we are only twenty-ninth in the world and yet we advertise Ireland as the 'knowledge economy'!

The beginnings

In 1987 the Programme for National Recovery was important in building an atmosphere of stability in the country. 1987 itself was only the beginning and only later did it begin to dawn on people that it was for real. When the results became embedded the sacrifices were accepted as worthwhile by workers and others. The government did manage to get the public finances into some kind of order, to get inflation down with the trade unions' assistance and agreement, and gradually the other economic indicators improved. Once it was bedded down in the medium term, when it was accepted, it built confidence and became self-reinforcing. It became a self-reinforcing, virtuous circle on the fiscal front – we began to get increased employment and this led to greater tax revenues etc.

This would not have happened without the unions' agreement and support. There is still argument about how it happened. It is said that Haughey called in the unions in 1987, but the popular version in union circles is that the unions thought of the idea in the first place and that they convinced Haughey. The word was that Haughey's question was 'Can agreement with the unions help us deal with the public finances? Was this possible?' The answer was that it could. He began to see that maybe it would. It is not accepted that the strategy was his idea in union circles.

The previous government, led by Garret FitzGerald, had a very different style. Garret was on TV lecturing the teachers about 'we could not afford this and we could not afford that . . .' That was a different way of dealing with economic problems. This changed in 1987. In that year, a belief grew within the parties around what was to become 'social partnership'.

I remember in 1986 there were discussions in Congress about the future of the country. They were informed by Thatcher's UK and how she was deconstructing the British trade union movement. The feeling was that things were so bad here that someone had to take it in hand and that someone would be *everyone,* working together. After the UK miners' strike, there was a growing realisation on the Irish trade union side that we had a choice. We could go the European route or we could continue on the British route. It was a pretty unpalatable choice. Also in 1985, I think, the social dialogue idea had been brought in by Delors, the EU President. Social dialogue was imported in here and, in my view, since then, it has been further refined and taken to a new level.

Firstly, the role of the structural revolution of the economy; we were shifting from agriculture with its low productivity to new, very high productivity manufacturing. Secondly, there was the 'demographic dividend' with the decline in the dependency ratio. We had lots of young people, so when the boom came they could take up the jobs. The third aspect of the structural shift in the economy was the increased participation of women in the workforce. This was very important and remains important.

Social partnership's contribution to the success
On social partnership, it has been argued by some economists (like John FitzGerald of ESRI and Jim O'Leary, formerly of a stockbrokers firm) that what happened would have happened by market forces anyway. They say, for instance, that there has been a move to fewer strikes internationally. It can be argued that the more civilised way of doing things could possibly have arisen without social partnership. There is no real answer to the assertion by these economists that social partnership is getting too much credit. Part of the motivation of a minority of free-market economists may be that they have such a belief in the workings of the market that they do not want to credit institutions and actors for social change. It may be that our move to social partnership happened to coincide with the period of most rapid expansion that the country has ever known. The essence of the argument is that this is coincidental. I don't believe that it is.

Maybe the best way to address this is to ask 'What would be the consequence of pulling the plug on social partnership now?' I think that would be a huge blow to confidence in the economy. It would be a very risky experiment and is not justifiable. Markets operate on sentiment and so it would be very risky. It would be an incredible statement from Ireland and on where it was going. It would be an unravelling of what most people believe has been a crucial part of the success for the last twenty years or so. The validity of that statement can only be judged if it was stopped. It might not need to descend into a huge number of strikes, but I think that the effect on confidence would be quite serious . . . it's an intangible. Terminating social partnership now would certainly be seen as a move in the wrong direction, particularly at a time when so much of the economic activity depends on consumption today. If confidence is undermined, there will be a lot of damage.

Public enterprises and development

Commercial public enterprises are less important now than in the past when they were proportionately bigger and more important in the economy. They generated 18 per cent of total investment in the economy at one point and made up 80–90,000 jobs out of a million jobs in total. They played a very important role in assisting the development of the Irish economy when there was little enterprise and little FDI. But now the rest of the economy has grown so much and while public enterprise has not stagnated, it is less important today. State companies will still represent a large part of the capital accumulation of the state, of employment and some are in strategic areas. This was stated in the OECD report on the corporate governance of state companies, where even that conservative body, OECD, recognised that state-owned companies will continue to exist and play important roles in all economies. This is contrary to the views of the free marketeers who are trying (with some success) to privatise everything.

Productivity

Industrial policy and the role of the IDA has been very important in developing productivity. Growing productivity is important for two reasons. The economy is in transformation with a huge construction sector and a growing services sector and the consequences of this is in reduced, measured productivity. Construction and many services have low productivity and that is why manufacturing is still very important, with very high productivity in modern manufacturing. At one level, we are trying to move against that natural change which is happening to the structure of the economy and at another level, we are trying to move as much employment up to high value as possible.

Gary McGann, former President of IBEC, made a speech at their annual dinner in 2006 and said that in relatively recent times the IDA was the biggest investor in the Irish economy. In the globalised economy, lower costs will probably continue the migration of certain types of manufacturing industry. Integration of the global economy has increased labour supply by one and a half billion people and this will put downward pressure on labour costs for the foreseeable future. Yet paradoxically, the IDA pipeline for new projects was full in 2007.

Skills and flexicurity

Nevertheless, there is a general consensus that we need to significantly improve our skill base to the point where we can achieve a critical mass of industries that will not find it attractive to abruptly depart. Under Towards 2016 and in the National Development Plan the government has committed to making the resources for upskilling available. This is the easy part. Motivating employers and workers to improve their skills will almost certainly be more difficult. We must also examine models of best practice in other countries, particularly within the EU. How have other countries responded to the almost permanent uncertainty engendered by globalisation? The Danish model of *flexicurity* is attracting some serious attention throughout the rest of Europe right now. However, people will naturally fear that the model will offer all flexibility and no security. This cannot be the case.

Our model of social welfare is based on providing a subsistence-level payment and not creating a disincentive to work. It co-exists with, but is not integrated with, certain active labour market initiatives. It was designed essentially for an era of mass unemployment. As such, it is of little value to the people thrown out of work by globalisation. The Irish model is not appropriate to the modern age and does not target resources where they are required. Resources should be focused on those who have lost their jobs with the twin priorities of finding adequate alternative employment quickly and to cushion people financially in the meantime. The Danish model does this. Danes enjoy a high level of social protection but its programmes are sophisticated and expensive, costing about 5 per cent of Danish GDP. The emphasis of *flexicurity* is on the employability of the person rather than protection of the job, per se. It is one response to globalisation, and investment in research and development is a necessary complementary strategy.

The role of education has been vital in Ireland's Tiger success and the most astounding thing is what has been achieved with far fewer resources than other countries. The issue for the future is that it is highly unlikely that we will get such output from so little input of resources in the future. Unless we invest much more in education and training, we will be left behind. The role and importance of the educated workforce is fully recognised and we need to do a lot more on upskilling of existing workers.

Many reports on the reasons for FDI cite the educated workforce and the IDA was advertising what it was calling the 'Irish mind' with Louis le Brocquy paintings in foreign magazines and newspapers. I think that it was focusing on a competitive advantage we may have in 'creative minds'. We certainly see it in Irish literature, not just Joyce, Yeats and Beckett, but even in Irish popular writing today. The confidence of the young people, combined with a certain inventiveness and creativity, means that they can be more innovative. The knowledge economy, which the EU's Lisbon Agenda aspires to, will be based largely on such educated creativity. That will be our competitive advantage in the future, not low company taxes! But we have to invest in it.

We know that by 2020 there will be shortages of highly-skilled and highly-educated people and if we continue as we are there will be, at the other end, lots of low-skilled people who are unemployed. The Future Skills Group has demonstrated that this is likely on a non-interventionist basis and it has proposed remedies for addressing it. I think we need to go further.

First, we need to invest far more in childcare, in support for mothers, who take most responsibility for rearing children. Why educate so many if they cannot participate fully in the workforce because there is such poor child support from the state and employers in Ireland? This is affecting our birth rate too and will ultimately impact adversely on aging. The anti-state intervention lobby do not want the state to invest in pre-schooling and childcare, because it distorts the market and saps people's 'initiative'. But it is only high earners who can cope with the high cost of childcare in Ireland. These costs and the lack of state support is leading many women to postpone childbirth, to the detriment of themselves, their children and to society as a whole.

We also need to invest more in primary and secondary education, to get class sizes down and do a lot more to integrate the massive influx of migrants' children. At third level, our student/lecturer ratios are very high and the only way to address this is more current spending. Third-level participation will have to increase substantially and we are not prepared for this yet. There does seem to be a lot of spending on fourth or post-graduate level which is welcome, but it should not be at the expense of excellence at third level. It is not sufficient to educate many more at third level, but poorly, as in the US, where there are super universities and very many poor colleges.

The regional technical colleges and the institutes of technology have been very important hidden contributors to our economic success and we must not neglect them. Nor should we fall for the desire by some self-promoters to upgrade every college to a university. I do think that some of the faculties in universities – those which prove they are capable of being the best – will need to get extra investment, state and private support to enable them to compete at the very top of the world of education.

Much of the EU funds went in training and while some of this was not productive when, for example, we were training the unemployed for jobs which were not there in the 1980s, such investment in people was vital to the take-off when it came. Life-long learning and upskilling of existing workers is vital for the economy, for firms and organisations and for workers' earning potential and self-fulfilment. As the business guru

Michael Porter concluded 'there is little doubt from our research that education and training are decisive in national competitive advantage'. The Wim Kok report on the Lisbon strategy stated that life-long learning must be a major priority in the area of employment for Europe. Investment in education and training increases the flexibility of the workforce and this means new products and processes are better utilised. This should lead to increased investment in new technology which reinforces gains in productivity, as Congress has pointed out in our briefing on productivity.[2]

I should point out that union members are substantially more likely to have participated in training than non-union members. Public service workers receive more training than private sector workers and employees in organisations with some form of partnership are more likely to participate in training than those with an authoritarian style of management. We must invest in those at work, particularly those with low skills, in a rapidly changing work environment if we are to maintain Ireland's competitiveness.

Ireland is a much more confident country today than in the past and this helps us in many ways. It is important for economic success; not just the confidence that business must have in undertaking investment, but at many other levels. We have learned much from the experience of dealing with Europe. We are like the Americans in that respect now and we are more open too. The younger generation are super-confident. They shift jobs easily, travel widely abroad, demand better pay, etc. and some set up their own businesses. Look at the risks they take, for example borrowing! If the building industry collapses, then many young people who have borrowed heavily will suffer . . . though I do not think it will collapse, thanks to the state intervention in that market with the National Development Plan, which is huge and of course necessary. It will underpin construction at a basic level.

Workplace partnership

On the contribution of partnership at workplace level, there is a lot more which could be done. Yet there has been a massive shift in the way trade unions do business at enterprise level. There is far less confrontation and part of this is due to more enlightened management in many, though not all, firms and organisations. The state is playing its part, having established the National Centre for Partnership which is an innovative body. NCP is promoting evidence-based research for firms which is showing the way for firms to become more productive by harnessing the collective intelligence of their workforces. Too many firms have not yet realised that in the knowledge-based economy, their real asset will be their workforces – they will have to move from rhetoric to reality!

Tax competition for FDI

On the importance of the low 12.5 per cent corporation tax carrot, we are not going to change that now on our own, but if the EU does move to tax harmonisation in time, then we should move the rate upwards. Congress' view is that governments went beyond what was needed to be successful and attractive to FDI. The policy of tax harmonisation in Europe is desirable if you want to stop the race to the bottom or to stop countries being played off one against the other, but it is essential if the Single Market is to continue to develop and to work effectively. It alarms me to hear some European Commissioners say periodically that tax competition is 'good'. It is difficult to comprehend the blindness that is operating in some high quarters on this issue.

The beneficiaries of Ireland's low corporation taxes will assert that it is the key to our economic success. The executives of foreign investing companies thank the IDA and other state bodies for their assistance by citing the low tax rate as the big attraction of Ireland. That is all very fine on the PR front, but if we are to really understand what our competitive advantage is, we have to recognise that low company taxes is a temporary, state-induced competitive advantage. I think *certainty* in taxation policy helped and I think that the low tax rate also did help in making Ireland attractive for FDI, especially US firms which are obsessed with taxation, but it is not a long-term, real competitive advantage.

Further, Ireland does gain a lot of tax revenue from these companies and on top of that, it gained much tax revenue from profits which were not made here in the first place! Transfer-pricing by multinationals who locate profits here that are made in other countries in order to avail of our low tax rate, did generate a great deal of tax revenue on 'profits' for Ireland. We gain tax revenue, but it is artificial and we cannot rely on it in the medium term. A change in US, UK or Dutch tax laws and it will be gone – like snow off a fence.

Congress believes that the corporation tax rate in Ireland was set too low; that it annoys our fellow member states in Europe, and that it is ultimately unsustainable. Estonia has a zero rate on retained profits and the other states are bidding rates downward. The European Union wants to harmonise company taxes but we and the British oppose it. I think if the Single Market is to be sustained, then we cannot continue to undermine it with such so-called 'tax competition'. The EU Single Market has been a great success, and equal and fair access to it has been very good for Ireland.

Housing and construction

One weakness is the over-reliance on construction, where 13 per cent of all employees are working and where output is around one-quarter of total output in the economy. Such a high level of domestically-generated output is not sustainable. I know we are catching up, but we were far too reliant on construction. It was fed by the low interest rates set by the European Central Bank. If we had set our own interest rates, they would have been over twice as high or perhaps even higher for several years. This would have dampened construction. Yet the present boom has been sustained since 2001, aided by the low interest rates. There has been worldwide speculation about a construction bust. We have continuing immigration to the country, so demand for housing grows and as I said before, the state, through the massive public investment in the NDP, underwrites construction at a basic level.

Our huge problem with the lack of investment in infrastructure in the past has been compounded by what has been happening in housing. The slowdown in housing construction might suit from a national point of view, if we could divert construction people into social housing and infrastructure. It's a question of managing it. The government mismanaged it for a lot of the 1990s and early part of this decade with massive tax subsidies to the sector.

It was incredible with a great economic boom, with soaring demand and a rapidly growing population, that the government poured petrol into the flames – taxpayers' euros – into an overheating construction boom with a myriad of regressive tax breaks for property. The net effect was higher house prices, more money for builders, a great cost in lost taxes, no taxes for many rich people, lots of work – but too much work for construction workers and awful housing estates all over Ireland, including in scenic areas. Congress campaigned against these tax breaks in every budget submission and eventually we were heard by Brian Cowen. The government terminated most of them in the 2006 budget. But it left a few – for which there is no need – and a long tailing-off of over seven years. Tax subsidies for so-called 'private' hospitals and clinics continue and are quite offensive from a social perspective – tax breaks for the rich investor and against the poor, who would have had better access if the tax euros were spent on public clinics.

It is fair to say that the social partnership model is probably successful because of the small size of the economy. The tight-knit kind of community helped. There are some negatives for a small country such as the failure by government to recognise that it is difficult, if not impossible, to get a competitive market going for electricity in a small market. So the government moved a blunderbuss against the ESB, which has cost us all dearly as consumers and for competitiveness.

The beginnings of the upturn
The process which led to Ireland's economic success began in 1987 when we began to get macro-economic stability into place. This led to jobless

growth, but by 1994, the capacity surplus in the economy was used up. Then economic growth translated into jobs growth. We probably got a surge in jobs as well. For example, if you have a conservative approach about hiring people and then things improve and there was a pent-up demand, then employers begin to hire in earnest.

I do not accept that the boom only began in the 1990s. The 1960s were the best time I remember, other than the present . . . there was employment, people getting cars who never had cars, building on extensions. The 1960s were a very progressive time. However, it was not sustained because of the policy disaster of tax cuts and increased public spending after the 1977 election which led to the 1980s recession. The 1980s were bad and we only recovered with the actions taken from 1987, but what did it for us was the FDI. That was what created the expansion and then there were its knock-on effects.

Trade unions are perceived as favouring spending on good public services and we do, but we are very conscious of the dangers of profligate public spending and tax cutting. Perhaps it was the lessons of the 1977 election that changed us and why we decided to make a major effort in 1987 around the Programme for National Recovery. I do see parallels today and I am worried that the tax base has been cut too much, especially when there is still much to be done. We should have cut less, spent more on health and education and simultaneously, the country should have saved more for when the recession comes.

I do not think that anyone can say that the growth levels and job creation of the 1990s to date have not been amazing. Whether it would have happened anyway without social partnership, as some economists argue, without the huge change in every main player's attitude in 1987, I do not know. It is making a claim without facts to substantiate it. It is hypothetical.

I do agree that policy was important. What many may not realise is that the 1980s crisis and the first national agreement changed the way policy was written and executed. For the unions, it was a sea change in our attitudes. Before then we were oppositional, we were confrontational, we wanted to screw the bosses and many of us did not seriously address the issues which generated economic success. It was class war in many ways. We were outside the tent.

The employers have always had ready access to government and we did not. It would not be true to say that we did not give a damn, for there was some serious thinking going on in trade union circles, like Congress' publication of *The Jobs Crisis* in late 1984 or that of the socialist economists, who had innovative ideas on competitiveness back in 1982. It has to be said that whatever his faults, and they were many, including corruption, Charlie Haughey had the vision to respond to the Congress' initiative, to *The Jobs Crisis*. He was assisted by Bertie Ahern who was Minister for Labour. Bertie Ahern was already a man who could cut a deal, be inclusive and innovative. Haughey was capable of executing several other big ideas like the IFSC with his friend Dermot Desmond and inspirational building renovations at Kilmainham, Dublin Castle and Government Buildings.

Globalisation and the future

Looking to the future, I do not think the economy will crash. If the global economy stays stable, then Ireland should too. I think the problem in Ireland is that if, over a period of time, we do not take strategic decisions and implement them, then we could find ourselves in trouble. We need to execute well considered and consensual plans to stabilise the economy for the transition to a mature democracy. That is not to say a crash could not happen.

Harvard's Jeffry Frieden[3] is quite persuasive on the dangers to globalisation – the main one being our inability to get people more accepting of it by some kind of regulation at international level. He points out that there is growing unhappiness with globalisation with as many as 70 per cent of people in France and Greece regarding it as a threat. He argues that in a truly multilateral world, global rules and institutions would ensure a level playing field for workers and producers in all countries, big and small. There must be legitimate political governance of globalisation and for domestic policies which smooth transitions and compensate those who lose in the process. Businesses are beleaguered by foreign competition, workers lose their jobs and very many people worry that footloose multinationals try to undermine labour laws, human rights, and the environment.

Frieden argues that global capitalism may fail again and the world may revert to economic nationalism unless citizens' fears about outsourcing, tax competition, deregulation, security etc. are addressed at international level. I think that business leaders have not realised that they are sailing close to the wind in the pursuit of low taxes and deregulation. The lessons of history are staring them in the face. The first era of globalisation collapsed in 1914 and in between we had the worst recession, war and fascism. It took a long time to reinstate the open global economy with freedom to travel, with the huge growth in trade with all its benefits. The WTO is trying to put some rules in place to govern trade, but for most citizens, it appears that it is balanced in favour of MNCs and against workers and citizens.

We must avoid the exaggerated reliance on market forces to solve all problems while avoiding a reversion to economic autarkism. At present, we are dominated by the pro-market economist gurus, but ironically, this could lead to economic insularity, if the backlash against unfettered market-dominated globalisation grows more severe. Governments must combine to establish international institutions which act, not just in the interest of business, but also for all citizens.

Finally, I have to say that Ireland's great *economic* success could have generated a great *social* success if we had done things differently. If the government had not cut taxes so sharply on incomes and on companies, we would have had much more to spend on health, on education, on crèches and on earlier investment. With more tax revenue we could have better hospitals, schools, public transport, networks of trams, trains, etc. Congress did agree to income tax cuts, but did not agree to taking them so far. The largest cuts in taxes, especially income taxes, came in the late 1990s, as a result of the economic success. Had government cut income and business taxes less, then Ireland would not have the healthcare and hospitals crisis; we would have a far fairer society with better social provision; we would have a better educational system which may be the key to the future; we would have had lower inflation with lower indirect taxes and charges; and a world-class public transport system in every town and city which worked, increasing mobility, equity, commute times and is better for the environment.

CHAPTER FOUR

Frances Ruane, Research Institute Director[1]

The stage of globalisation we have gone through has favoured us . . . the next stage will favour others, who were late in recognising how globalisation was changing the world. We had first-mover advantages.

Frances Ruane is Director of Ireland's leading independent research body, the Economic and Social Research Institute (ESRI). Frances Ruane was Associate Professor in the Department of Economics at Trinity College Dublin. She is a graduate of the National University of Ireland (University College Dublin) and the University of Oxford. She was Chairperson of the National Statistics Board, a member of the World Bank's data advisory panel and a member of the advisory board to the Competition Authority. She has been on a number of Irish state boards, including the National Board for Science and Technology, the Industrial Development Authority and Forfás (policy and advisory board for enterprise, trade, science, technology and innovation). Professor Ruane has published widely on foreign direct investment, industrial policy, manufacturing, trade and related areas.

The Single Market

The creation of the EU Single Market was vital for Ireland in terms of the external environment. It provided a more accessible market for our outputs and stimulated the huge inflow of American foreign direct investment. If the Single Market had not been created when it was in 1992 and if 'Fortress Europe' (as it was being described) did not exist, then American multinationals would not have wanted to invest so heavily in Europe as they did right throughout the 1990s. This all took place in the global context where the US economy experienced huge growth internally and was seeking to grow trade and investment links with Europe. When these multinationals came to make a decision about where to invest in Europe, Ireland was a preferred location. So I think the timing of the Single Market was very important to the growth opportunities Ireland faced.

The main reasons why Ireland was the preferred location (over other EU countries) for these US firms were its English-speaking population, its low company tax rate, the availability of low-cost skilled labour, and Ireland's positive attitude to foreign direct investment since the late 1950s. The English-speaking population was a historical accident, the low company tax rate was a long-standing policy, and the plentiful supply of low-cost labour resulted from significant investment in education and skills from the late 1970s, which was not matched by increased demand for the newly-skilled people as the economy was very depressed. Towards the end of the 1980s some large companies, including Microsoft, Intel and HP, which recognised the potential of the large integrated market being created in Europe, were attracted to Ireland by its long tradition of being positive towards FDI. This positive attitude was evidenced in the low tax rate and also in the business environment, which make it possible for firms to set up relatively easily.

These islands

Much of the rest of Europe was pretty sclerotic at that stage, in terms of the burdens placed on people trying to establish new businesses, and while Britain was somewhat better, it displayed much more ambivalence about FDI and about the 'European project' generally, whereas Ireland was much more positive about both. For example, Britain was already indicating that it might not join the single currency zone, whereas Ireland was totally committed.

Another set of factors assisting the Irish growth performance was the higher growth rates in the British economy. Britain has always been and is still Ireland's major trade partner, and is particularly important for Irish-owned firms. Thus the upturn in the British economy, driven to a large degree by an increasingly rational approach to economic policy, provided Ireland with both improved market conditions and an interesting role model in terms of being focused on global competitiveness.

I think that the improved political situation in Northern Ireland also helped. From what one can tell, the situation in the North did not impact negatively on decisions of multinationals considering Ireland as a location for investing in Europe, or whatever negative impact there was had been internalised by the market. Of course, had there been greater peace in Northern Ireland in the 1990s, it could have become a very significant competitor for the Republic. While the North did not have the advantages of the low corporate tax rate, it was in a position to give much more generous capital allowances than were available in the Republic.

Structural funds

The availability of the European Union Structural Funds was important for Ireland, but their scale was ultimately quite small. They have been likened to a Marshall Plan, but I would only call them a mini-mini-Marshall Plan. However small the funds were, they became available at a crucial point, allowing the severe budget constraint on capital spending to be reduced.

I think two other important effects were associated with the EU Structural Funds. Firstly, the funds gave a new confidence to planning for economic and social development, replacing the lack of confidence that developed in the early 1980s. For example, when the first ESRI medium-term review was published, pointing to the economic growth potential, they provided the funds to support moving towards that growth path and helped to generate domestic confidence, with positive knock-on effects for private investment. Secondly, the Structural Funds introduced new quality standards into public sector decision-making, since proper planning accompanied all of the funds drawn down and evaluations were undertaken throughout to establish the value of the funds being used in terms of the defined objectives. Thus, while the Irish government had previously had economic plans, such as the programmes for economic expansion in the 1950s, 1960s and 1970s, they were purely 'indicative' plans, with no long-term resources set aside to deliver on the plans, and no evaluation of the details of such plans. In effect, the planning associated with the EU Structural Funds was the first real large-scale planning exercise Ireland had ever undertaken. The much better standards in the use of public funds amounted to a quantum leap in the quality of the planning decisions.

The positive impact of the Structural Funds is evident in comparisons between Ireland and, say, the southern regions of Italy which were at a broadly similar state of development when Ireland joined the EEC in 1973. While this area of Italy has received vast quantities of EU aid, it has simply not grown as Ireland did and this is attributed, at least in part, to the poor quality of public expenditure there compared with Ireland. (I did a piece of research with an Italian economist a number of years ago, where we compared policy in these southern regions and Ireland. While not every penny of EU money was spent wisely in Ireland, the funds in Italy have been largely wasted. There were roads built in the middle of nowhere, airports built where they were not needed, and there are ports developed where there was no trade.) The structural fund mechanism of performance worked well for Ireland, in that it was mainstreamed into government economic policy and it wasn't used for *pork barrel* politics.

Policy towards foreign direct investment

As discussed before, foreign direct investment (FDI) was vitally important for Ireland and we benefited disproportionately from the huge surge in FDI worldwide that started in the late 1980s. Not only that, but the FDI into Europe as a percentage of global FDI rose, and our share in Europe rose. In effect, we got an increasing share, of an increasing share, of an increasing activity. These were highly favourable circumstances and we need to recognise that when we look at the success we achieved.

Ireland's success also reflected the fact that its policy decision to promote FDI into the electronics and pharmaceuticals sectors from the late 1960s and early 1970s was rewarded doubly, because these two sectors were to the forefront of FDI growth. In addition to being in favourable times and with favourable sectors, Ireland had the advantage of having a good reputation in terms of how FDI companies were treated. There was a huge level of competence in the Irish system, in that we had earned a reputation as being professionals when it came to dealing with major corporations.

One factor I recognised only fully in the early 1990s was that the IDA approach to FDI operated entirely at a *company level*. In effect, Irish policy involved specifically recognising the heterogeneity of FDI companies long before policy-makers in the rest of Europe were doing it. While this approach was more easily adopted in Ireland because of its small size, it moved policy beyond thinking about sectors and even niches, and moved it onto thinking about enterprises and how policy-makers should interact with them.

I would credit the IDA particularly for the development of this discretionary policy approach, which recognised that there were huge differences between companies, a point not recognised by economists, who until the 1990s tended to focus on economic restructuring at the sectoral level. Therefore as the IDA was able to modify and be flexible around incentives, it operated them very strategically at the margin. This actually had a huge influence and leverage on companies. It developed relationships with company executives that were positive and problem-solving rather than adversarial and bureaucratic.

These relationships were key to another important element of IDA strategy. This was getting multinational companies which were already located in Ireland to encourage other multinational companies to come to Ireland. For example, when Hewlett Packard began to examine the possibility of locating in Ireland, introductions were made for the executives to meet with existing FDI investors, like Intel and Microsoft. Existing companies were engaged in 'selling Ireland' along with the IDA. That type of approach was possible because of the strong relationships and perhaps it is also an Irish cultural thing, on which the IDA leveraged. (It reminds one of the old Irish phrase about the waves of plantations: 'They became more Irish than the Irish themselves'!)

The willingness of the existing group of multinationals to engage in the business of attracting other multinationals was linked to two things – firstly, that many were in the same sectors and there were some potential benefits from upstream-downstream trading; secondly, these companies were looking broadly for the same skill sets. It suited everybody to build up a stronger market of skilled labour, so the more skilled people that were there, the better. These companies were active with other state agencies, like FÁS, in attracting back to Ireland pools of skilled Irish labour that had emigrated in earlier decades. This helped to ensure that the companies weren't competing too fiercely with each other in the local labour market, and meant that new investing companies were not 'crowding out' existing companies.

As Paul Krugman pointed out many years ago, in terms of the high quality multinationals we were lucky – would Ireland be in the same place in terms of electronics if Intel and Microsoft had located elsewhere? Their choice of Ireland as a location was like an international 'quality seal of approval'. This was of major benefit to the IDA in marketing Ireland as a base for FDI. The IDA's philosophy in the 1980s was more marketing-driven than economics-driven at that stage and paid off very well. Ireland had a reputation, a brand image, for being a top-class location for FDI at a time when the rest of Europe did not. Furthermore, the IDA had been in the business of promoting FDI since the 1950s when nobody else was doing it, so its success in the late 1980s and 1990s was in no small way due to its having a strong reputation both operationally and in terms of policy consistency over forty years.

The IDA executives were there to help and not hinder the FDI companies, and the small scale of the country meant that standard bureaucratic problems could be readily overcome. Furthermore, if the company needed a minister out to open a factory or to meet with its senior personnel, these were arranged, creating the sense that the company was valued and that any problem that might arise would be given priority.

It is recognised by economists that an important factor influencing the location of FDI is barriers to entry. One of the biggest such barriers is the 'barrier to exit', that is, how difficult it is to exit an economy. By and large, Ireland has operated very low barriers to exit, so that when a company wishes to close for global profitability reasons, there is no huge pressure on it to stay open. Nor is there any attempt to shore the company up indefinitely, though there are negotiations about the pace of closure. Rather, the IDA puts its effort into finding a replacement company, recognising that in a globally competitive world there will be a lot of entry and exit into markets. This 'moving on' approach is one of the big strengths of Ireland, compared to the rest of Europe. (I did some work on competition policy and state aids in Europe some years ago and one of the things that became very apparent, from looking at the EU Commission files, was how many countries were busy trying to shore up declining firms in declining sectors.)

However, it should be said that Ireland's attitude toward private industry not only contrasts with what is common in the rest of Europe, it also contrasts with the approach taken to public enterprises in Ireland. Arguably, the tardiness in addressing efficiencies in public enterprises is one of the negative policy actions over the 1980s and 1990s. Not only did this result in higher direct costs and inefficiencies, which had to be born by the private sector and by consumers, it also meant that these companies retained skills which could have been much better used in the private sector, helping in the process to keep unit labour costs down.

Communications technology and transport costs
The revolution in communications technology and the fall in transport costs were both very beneficial to the Irish economy. Both disproportion- ately favoured island economies because they reduced the costs of integrating into the global economy – in effect, they reduced the costs of being an island. And there was a further benefit to Ireland as the IDA export growth strategy in the 1960s and 1970s led us to specialise in products which had a high value-added to volume ratio, since these were products that could be produced competitively on an island economy.

The reason why Ireland was in the electronics and pharmaceutical sectors from the late 1960s and early 1970s was that these were sectors that are characterised by low unit transportation costs. One way of thinking about this was that since Ireland adopted a pro-trade stance from the 1960s, it began a strategy of globalisation very early and this led it to develop strong sectors in electronics and pharmaceuticals, which subsequently became key sectors in the globalised world.

One point that should be recognised about our success in electronics is that there are costs to being in a dynamic sector. Ireland was in mini- computers in the 1970s and they were displaced by the desk-top computers and Ireland had to make that transformation. Think of all the companies that were here in the 1970s that are long since gone! Not just gone out of Ireland but gone off the world stage! So we are in a fast-track kind of industry, and if you are prepared to be flexible, you will survive. If you are in a fast-track industry and you start to be rigid, you will not survive – you will be dead very quickly. What is crucial to the adjustment process is having a flexible, well-trained workforce and a system which can accommodate structural change.

The role of party politics

In terms of the internal or domestic reasons for Ireland's economic success, fiscal reform and macro-economic stability were absolutely essential. I left Ireland in 1986 to spend a couple of years at a university in Canada. When I left, Ireland was a very depressing place – even in terms of the universities. Generation after generation of students were graduating to face hopeless employment options, and involuntary emigration was the norm. When I came back in 1988, just two years later, there was a palpable difference. There was a sense in which Ireland Inc. had taken stock and collectively decided that we needed to adopt a coherent set of economic and social policies. In this context, one of the factors that does not tend to get mentioned, which I think is tremendously important, is the Tallaght Strategy.[2] The most common questions about Ireland asked by foreigners, say at international conferences, are: 'How did Ireland turn around and make such a dramatic policy shift? How was it done?' It is common in Ireland to attribute this to social partnership, but social partnership could not have happened without the Tallaght Strategy.

The Tallaght Strategy is the political event that really amazes people – getting widespread agreement in a parliamentary democracy for the sake of Ireland Inc. On my return from Canada, I was struck by the absence of the sniping that had been going on politically before I left. It was this sniping that had been leading to less and less rational policy-making.

Suddenly the Tallaght Strategy allowed more rational policy. It was absolutely central and not without its costs politically. Arguably, Alan Dukes lost his seat over it. It could be seen that the voters were very unfair to him – in effect they did not realise that what he had done was essential for Ireland at that point. I think history will be much fairer to him. The Tallaght Strategy is an almost hidden event, and it is the reason social partnership gets more credit than it deserves. If you go to other countries and you talk to political economists, they will always marvel on how Ireland managed to get that cross-party agreement to allow social partnership to thrive. Otherwise social partnership would just have been a talking shop at that time. The Tallaght Strategy allowed the country to move to a more rational economic model, recognising that being competitive was crucial to our survival and our prosperity as a country.

Sectoral development – the move to traded services

The structure of the economy has been moving progressively from agriculture to high productivity manufacturing and the growth of internationally traded service sectors. In the late 1980s, the IDA extended its range of activities to include internationally traded services as well as manufacturing. There was recognition around that time that internationally traded, high-value services were appropriate activities for Ireland to seek new FDI investment and the IFSC was part of that. But it is important to remember that this policy also included computer services and other business services, which have grown very substantially in the past decade.

The creation of the IFSC was a strategic move and I would have been somewhat critical of it at the time. I thought, like a lot of other people at that time, that it placed at some risk the special privileged position we had with manufacturing by drawing attention to our favourable corporate tax regime. This became immediately apparent when the German and Belgian financial sectors got extremely upset about the transfer of activities into the IFSC, with the consequent loss of a small number of jobs but a large amount of tax revenue. Research that Philip Lane (of Trinity College) and I did a couple of years ago points to the very significant contribution of the IFSC to Irish tax revenue – its scale is such that the share of corporate income tax in total tax in Ireland is much higher – mostly by a factor of two – compared to other EU countries. There is no doubt that the IFSC has been a success and it may be the case that what is upsetting other countries is that we have done so well, developing new activities and services which their financial systems would not have permitted. It is certainly the case that the IFSC is an unusual entity. The research done by Philip Lane in this area shows that the scale of activities in Ireland is out of line with other countries for our size.

The demographic dividend

There is no doubt that the demographic dividend has been important and it is evident both in the size of the workforce and the improving skills composition. In effect, over the 1990s there was a volume effect and then a skills effect. In this process, we had the return of women to the workforce in large numbers. (I have written about the existence of the *Celtic Tigresses* – the women who returned to work in their droves in the early and mid-1990s, before the school leavers and new graduates started coming onstream.) The increased female participation rate was possible because of smaller family size compared to previous generations, and it saw a major change in the composition of the workforce and a change in the approach to accommodating female participation. This greatly increased the flexibility of the Irish workforce at a crucial point. In the late 1980s and the very early 1990s, people (and especially women) chose part-time employment because they could not get full-time employment, and this was their only route into the workforce. Today, many women choose part-time employment over either no employment or full-time employment because it matches their lifestyle. The implications of these changes on work practices are likely to continue to be important in the years ahead.

In a stronger labour market, there is also the issue of the kinds of jobs people want to have – with choice, people show distinct preferences and these preferences change over the life-cycle. For example, some financial services jobs are very 'buzzy' but they are not as intellectually challenging or rewarding as other jobs that pay much less, for example, teaching. When the 'buzz' gets familiar, or the work-stress of the job is not consistent with family life, especially where both partners are working and have children, people make job changes – something which is quite new for Ireland. I am struck by the numbers of students I have had in the past decade who have changed careers and jobs radically – the scale of this would have been almost unknown in my own generation.

Social partnership
I think the social partnership consensus was very important to the growth process but I would emphasise again that I do not think it could have happened without the Tallaght Strategy. For example, I can recall being on platforms with leading trade unionists in the early 1980s, when I would have had a totally different view of labour market issues to them – for example, in my view, they did not show any real appreciation of the needs for employers to be able to compete. It was employers versus unions – a win/lose game that in reality in the early 1980s became a lose/lose game. When I came back to Ireland in 1988, there was an atmosphere of win/win on the union and the employers' sides with government facilitating the early part of the win/win through tax reform. To me that was the big change. That language of win/win just did not exist before I left in 1986. Suddenly, there was a changed order – there was the belief that if we do this, the workers will win and employers will gain and government can play the role of facilitator. This was a huge breakthrough.

Social partnership involved the recognition by trade unions of the needs of business and it also involved the recognition of the need for economic and social policy to be integrated. This integration goes back to the establishment of the National Economic and Social Council (NESC) in the 1970s. Its role is to provide the intellectual backdrop to social partnership with evidence-based research. The discussions at NESC are a necessary framework to recognise that there could be no gains to social policy unless the economy was going in the right direction. Central to this is the notion that both needed to work in tandem.

One of my criticisms of the current NESC is that the Department of Education and Science is not one of the departments represented on it. I find this amazing because, from my perspective, education is now at the centre of both economic and social policy. What we do in terms of our education strategy is central to meeting the challenges of the coming decades. Up until the early 1990s, education was still seen as being primarily important for individual equality of opportunity reasons, which of course it is. The notion that education is vitally important for our collective standard of living through the productivity of skilled labour was only widely accepted relatively recently. In fact the ESRI's medium-term review really highlighted this and focused on the contribution of skills to economic growth. The notion that human capital is our key economic factor is now being acknowledged widely. I was on some government committees in the mid-1990s and expenditure on education was still being seen at that time as social expenditure! It was only when the skills shortages came to light some few years later that people began to link education to growth and that led to its economic importance being appreciated. And now arguably, the balance may have gone a bit further on the other side, with some suggesting that only those types of education that are 'economically relevant' should be supported.

Public enterprise and regulation

While government recognised the importance of not shoring up jobs in the private sector, I think it is fair to say it might have been better had there been less shoring up of jobs in the public sector. One of the things I thought was a great shame at the time when we began to experience the skills shortage was that some of the reservoirs of skills in the public enterprise companies were not released, proactively. When I was on the original Expert Skills Group in 1995, it was very clear that we lacked experienced people. Where were those experienced people? They were in organisations like the ESB and Telecom Éireann. I did made a suggestion a number of times that everyone would benefit if under-employed, under-utilised resources in some of the state companies would transfer into the private sector where they were much needed. The five-year career break scheme in the public service was a good scheme to release people and it would make a great study to see what has happened in the 1990s to those who took these breaks. The climate was different then, and we have moved on now in the sense that job mobility is much more common.

We are still somewhat irrational in terms of dealing with some of the companies in the public service. While their relative importance in the economy has declined, their performance has improved overall but this improvement has not been uniform. Some remain very inefficient and add to Ireland's cost base. For example, the failure to deal with CIE [Irish national public transport organisation] properly is costing Ireland a lot in terms of developing a cost-effective and efficient public transport system. I have no problem with subsidising public transport companies, but I do have a problem with ill-run, ill-organised public transport companies, which do not deliver a proper service and on which many citizens, especially women, are dependent. The failure to deal with CIE reflects the national failure to integrate public transport with land-use planning and housing policy.

In making public transport decisions, we need to know about land-use policies – if we separate land use from transport investments, we will be continually in disequilibrium in urban areas with either housing shortages or traffic congestion. For example, the LUAS [Dublin's light rail transport system] extension to Cherrywood is a case where proper economic evaluation should have been done, but was not done. For example, it is unclear what assumptions have been made about housing density on the light-rail line and whether the capacity can deliver to additional areas at peak time without crowding out the service to those who live nearer the city centre.

Regarding public enterprises, I think that there is a great need for them to modernise and become efficient. This is now possible given the terms under which they operate. I was on the board of Bord Gáis [natural gas supplier] for a number of years and all the signs are that the structures in place for internal management should ensure that the company will perform well in the future, in terms of increasing stakeholder value. It is possible for a state company to be just as efficient as a private company if the correct governance systems are in place. My experience of Bord Gáis was positive and I think that many other bodies have moved in that same direction.

To deliver all of these industries, all the utilities need to be well regulated. This is more easily said than done as we have little experience of regulation in Ireland, and consequently there has been little development of skills and almost no research done. For example, in the energy markets, with ESB and BGE [Bord Gáis Éireann] in particular, the regulation process is difficult at least partly because the EU regulation policy has been developed for large countries rather than small countries. The scale of production is such that the Irish market will not have the same kind of competition that will be found in Germany or Britain. There is a real danger that ideology is hampering us potentially, not recognising that competition does not always deliver competitiveness. Ireland could benefit from linking with other smaller European countries to determine how best to handle these complex competition and regulation issues.

While Ireland needs to regulate certain industries, such as energy and telecoms, it also needs to have policies which indicate what these sectors need to deliver. We have come late to dealing with regulated industries and we have not worked out yet the appropriate connection between public policy and regulation. There is a tendency for regulation to be the policy, which simply does not work with major infrastructure, as the market tends to under-invest, given that it has a shorter timeframe.

The capacity constraints due to skill shortages are also an impediment in the public sector. The private sector, and especially the FDI companies, are in a position to 'buy in' any skills they need, but the public sector, and especially the civil service, faces a much greater challenge in meeting its skill needs. Since the civil service has only recruited at graduate-entry level, it has incurred the high cost of training graduates only to lose some to the private sector, while being in no position to recruit from the private sector to balance this flow. Recent pronouncements augur well that this situation may change – and it needs to extend to attracting talent from outside Ireland if the civil service is to benefit from international talent mobility in a way similar to the benefits realised by the private sector and other parts of the public sector (for example, the universities, the hospitals and the state-owned companies).

Consistent and active industrial policy

On industrial policy, the consistency, the certainty and the market-sensitive approaches were the crucial factors in our success. Following up on what we discussed before, the IDA's approach was that it picked winning sectors and within those sectors it picked winning firms. The strategy was well thought through; for example, in computer assembly, the IDA did not just go for one firm, that is, did not attempt to find a single 'winner'. Rather it brought in two of what were the most successful companies globally, namely Dell and Gateway. The IDA was aware at that time that some of the PC manufacturers were not going to survive, and by attracting several competitors in the same sector, IDA took a *portfolio approach*. This was a sensible strategy in this very competitive sector, and while Gateway did not survive, Dell did and has thrived. Furthermore, the IDA also picked activities across the span of the electronics sector, since this was a way of ensuring that the profitable activities were locating in Ireland, and it minimised risks if technology changed in any one part of the broad sector. (I did some work on this with a colleague some years ago and we found that Ireland had a presence in virtually all of the twelve different types of activities relating to electronics; this was a very different approach to what had been adopted in many other areas which were promoting electronics, for example Scotland.)

Education, skills and also confidence

On the confidence of young people, about which many speak very enthusiastically, I developed some years ago a simple concept to contextualise this which I call the *CC Ratio*. This is the 'Confidence to Competence Ratio'. What you want is that young people are both confident and competent, so that this ratio is not too high. If the Confidence to Competence Ratio does get too high there will be a delivery gap that will ultimately undermine market confidence in these people. Furthermore, if young people become over-confident, they will not see any reason to increase their competency. The grade inflation at second and third levels in recent years may be giving students an exaggerated view of their abilities, and this would tend to raise the CC Ratio. So also is the universal praise we give ourselves for the quality of our education system – I think the education system has improved in certain respects but it has not uniformly improved. We have created mass education at third level, and we have not put the resources in to deliver a quality product. By definition, the quality of the educational experience must reflect the paucity of resources provided, and there is a real issue of whether we are developing a system that is right for today's students and for the country.

There has been a significant growth in the measured 'educated workforce', but I question the quality of it in terms of what we need to meet future challenges. I am a big fan of the more broad-based and multi-layered North American educational system at third level and I think that this is the direction in which we need to move. If it is recognised that people may be living well into their eighties, that they are going to be working beyond their sixties and that education is not once-off, then it is timely to ask what is the correct type of third-level education we should have.

The notion of somebody deciding in sixth year in school what career they are going to follow for a working life which may run into their seventies is just crazy. I have encountered, over the years, so many students who went into the wrong narrow educational stream and, once inside the university, they could not move around without very significant economic penalty. There are small numbers of students who know exactly what they want to do at age eighteen, but most do not and the system is geared to that minority. I think that the kind of *silo specialisation* that we increasingly tend to have here in the Irish universities is driven by attempts to increase the entry points for these courses and these silos are working further to the disadvantage of the eighteen-year-old students who simply do not know what choice to make. A more general education followed by, for example, internships for students when they graduate would help to give them better ideas of what they want to do later in life. I would argue that it is not appropriate to be making that decision so early, with the risk that some people could end up doing the wrong thing for the rest of their life. Or, if they change in mid-life, the cost of re-education is extremely expensive.

The evidence is that having a more educated workforce contributed significantly to growth and prosperity over the past two decades. In terms of the future, I am not at all convinced that we have the right type of education system now either to enable us to compete globally or create a broadly educated citizenry. Since most people now go on for some type of third-level training and education, we need to take account of that in the design of the second-level curriculum. In terms of third level, we also need to think of the first degree as an 'introduction' for the very significant numbers who now go on to fourth level (postgraduate) education. For example, on an issue that has been debated recently, I agree strongly with the introduction of postgraduate education in medicine – I do not think that medicine should be a primary degree at all and I favour the North American approach where students take an arts or science degree first.

I think that the education curriculum in the broadest sense needs to help students to build up a better understanding of how a modern economy and society works. This would help to give Irish citizens the economic and social literacy to allow them to participate in the democratic process in a more informed way.

If I were given a carte blanche to introduce some of these concepts into the education system, I would do it through the junior-cycle geography programme, which is taken by all students. For example, such a course could introduce students to the concept of economic trade-offs, to the idea of economic restructuring, and to the concepts of income distribution and re-distribution at both national and global levels. In addition, geography is the ideal vehicle for introducing students to some simple statistical concepts which are really important for them in understanding risk in their own lives and for understanding the many documents and reports produced by government today.

The low corporation tax rate

Low taxes have a huge effect and are the key driver of US FDI. However, the longstanding zero corporate tax policy[3] looks like a rather naïve policy, when one considers just how much revenue we are getting from the low rate of 12.5 per cent now. We moved from the zero tax rate and it is now very evident that we should have done so much earlier. Had we a tax rate of even 5 per cent for much of the 1970s and 1980s, we would have enjoyed considerable revenue gain. There is, of course, the argument that a zero rate has more marketing impact – that it is psychologically important to investors . . . that may have been true in the 1960s but as time went on, it was not a sensible policy. There were lots of scare stories about what would happen when the 10 per cent rate came into effect in 1981 and while there has been no formal study done to see what happened to the companies who shifted from zero to the 10 per cent rate, there is no evidence that there was any exodus of companies.

What does matter is to have a rate that is significantly lower than neighbouring countries and to make sure that there is no uncertainty about that rate over a 10-year time horizon. A low rate is not attractive to an investor if it may possibly change dramatically and without warning. I would see the low tax, given our peripheral location, as a necessary but not sufficient condition to attract FDI. There is no doubt that American companies are very driven by tax, as American corporate culture is driven to minimise payments to 'Uncle Sam'. Of course, some firms reduce their tax payments simply as good financial management. So in a way we have produced an environment that is very favourable to companies that can organise their tax payments flexibly. The Japanese are not as tax-driven in their approach and it may explain why we do not have a lot of Japanese companies in Ireland. Overall, I think that the impact of the low corporation tax is huge and we would be very foolish to ignore it in thinking about future policy, and we need to be conscious that the impact of our present low rate is being continuously eroded by the low tax rates in the new member states.

The scale of the construction sector

I think, like many economists, that we may be in trouble with the scale of construction activities in the economy. I think it is driving growth in the economy at the moment, but it may be shielding us from realising the full extent of the re-structuring at the lower end of manufacturing. Some economists argue that the construction industry growth has driven up labour costs and consequently has squeezed ('crowded out') the bottom end of manufacturing. I would describe it somewhat differently. I think that the lower end of manufacturing in Ireland is rapidly becoming globally uncompetitive and that its decline would now be showing up in unemployment if we did not have the construction industry absorbing people who have been leaving it, or not entering it as they would have done in the past. There is a major study needed there to see how vulnerable we are to what is happening in the construction sector and what its impact is on other sectors, wages, etc.

What will happen in construction, and the knock-on effects for the economy overall, is complicated by the significant presence of Eastern European workers in the sector. Assuming that construction slows down, which would be natural as part of the business cycle, who will be employed in the sector? There is plenty of anecdotal evidence, and some research evidence, to the effect that the Eastern European workers are more educated than their Irish equivalents, and consequently have higher skill and productivity levels. Thus if there is a downturn and the foreign workers stay in Ireland, then they may displace Irish workers, leading to a rapid growth in unemployment if the skill and productivity levels of the Irish workers do not increase. On the other hand, it may be possible that if there were a downturn the foreign workers would migrate to the next market which is enjoying a construction boom; at this point that market would likely be in London to build the Olympic Stadium and related infrastructure.

Interest rates, entrepreneurship and the size of Ireland
Low interest rates were definitely significant, especially in the Irish context. We had so much capital spending to do and it helped small business. One of the things we have seen as part of the Celtic Tiger is the birth of local entrepreneurship. Low interest rates were really important for them. We know that the venture capital market and the 'angel' market are not very well developed in Ireland. In this context, low interest rates have been crucial to local entrepreneurship.

The small size of the economy was of significant importance too. But small size had both positive and negative aspects. We are a networking society, which means that people have ready access to seeing whoever they need to see and consequently, it is easy to get a problem solved. Bridget Laffan of UCD did some work for the Policy Institute of Trinity College a number of years ago looking at how we operate in the European policy-making arena. Comparing our relationships and those of the Danes, she found that we were much more networking in our approach and that we network very effectively. The Danes, like the Germans, are great systems people, but do not compare with us when it comes to forging relationships that will get things done. Of course, we need to be aware that there is a downside to having a good quick-fix ability: it means you do not deal systemically with issues and that you fail to think in terms of systems solutions. It may be the case that the Irish ability to make a bad system work well impedes its efforts and incentives to develop better systems.

Sudden take-off?
Why did we take off suddenly? It was not really that sudden – more a ramp up, if you look at the numbers on a year-by-year basis. But the power of the belief around 1988 that Ireland was sorting out its economic policy

and therefore was a safe base for domestic and foreign investors was extremely important. That was a real mindset change within Ireland. We began dealing with the problems that we could solve rather than moaning about the problems over which we had no control at all. It is no coincidence that IDA won some of the key multinational projects at that stage. We also began to look forward more systematically and I think that is where the ESRI medium-term review had its influence, when combined with the EU funds and the growth of the European market.

Was it a miraculous period or was it catching up? I think it was definitely catching up, but with circumstances which were very favourable, so that the catch-up was serious and sustained over a long period. If you look at the growth rate from 1970 to 2000 you see a dip in the early 1980s. There was a lot of catching up. The average growth rate for the period was 4 to 4.5 per cent. If we had grown continually from 1970 to 2000 at that rate, Ireland would be in a totally different place. Uneven growth left us with serious infrastructural deficits and with capacity problems.

Our engineers and planners did not develop the capacity for large project management, which meant that when money came to build infrastructure, we did not have the expertise we needed. Our failure to provide good public transport led to a shift to the use of the car, which we now recognise as one of the greatest problems we face in urban areas. We were not able to invest in systems of government when we needed to, and this has left its legacy in the speed of modernisation in parts of the public service. With shortages of resources we took short cuts, such as the medical consultants contracts, which cost us dearly.

The importance of policy and policy consistency

What all this points to is that when a country or indeed a company goes through a bad period, like Ireland did in the late 1970s and early 1980s, there are some deep structural problems created. Solving them takes a long time and it is not simply a case of money – it is lost opportunities, such as the experience that good planning would have allowed one to build up. As I see it, policy was important and so also was policy consistency. Our outward-looking view was also important and it meant that from the late 1980s, we began to benchmark ourselves against the best in Europe. This was very important psychologically. We benchmarked Dublin against Copenhagen and other modern cities; we benchmarked our education system against the best in the OECD; we benchmarked our transport system against those in Spain and Portugal. I also think that today the Lisbon Agenda has been important in establishing the practice, over a range of activities, of setting good benchmarks for us to judge ourselves against. I do not think that the larger EU countries, like Germany, France and the UK, benchmark themselves against other countries in the same way. We now do this and it is a great strength as long as we continue to choose the most appropriate and challenging benchmarks. Of course we are not alone in this strength – and we should not be unduly flattered by the fact that other countries now benchmark themselves against Ireland!

While policy works and is important, we would be wise to see it having a role but not being the sole driver of our fate. Policy can promote R&D spend, but it is up to the companies to undertake that R&D. Policy can support improved training of skilled labour, but if companies do not engage in continuously developing the skill set of the workforce, our productivity will not rise and our unit wage costs will put at risk our remaining competitive. We have the policy agencies in place to support growth and development – they need to be continuously self-critical and, to ensure that they stay focused, they need to have independent evaluations of what they are doing. Science Foundation Ireland (SFI) has a strong programme of investment in R&D, and we now have tax breaks and incentives to support R&D in companies – we need to determine how to evaluate these policies appropriately. Such evaluations require totally different metrics to evaluations of previous policy interventions. As regulation becomes increasingly more important, we need to ensure that we monitor the impact of regulations on business and consumers and on how new regulations interact with existing policies. The transparent implementation of new regulatory impact assessment methodologies is crucial to ensuring that government supports and does not inadvertently hinder economic and social well being.

Attitudes to public space

The biggest weakness in our system at this point is our attitude to space and physical planning. In the context of the economic, the social and the environmental, the Irish are enormously good at the economic and social but we don't manage the environmental, by which I mean *spatial*, very well. We have managed this aspect of our economy very badly under the Celtic Tiger, which is something all foreigners remark on when they visit Ireland. Why? There are all sorts of reasons, one of which people often link to a colonial legacy. 'I have my house and my land and I should be able to do whatever I want with them.'

When you combine this colonial legacy with low population density and the population decline of over one hundred years, you find that we effectively have built a mindset that does not handle space very well and that it is not surprising that we do not embrace planning principles. This contrasts strongly with mainland Europe, which has had higher population density and continuing urban development for centuries.

However, it is a serious problem because we are now facing potentially significant population increases. The population has grown from 3.5 million in 1991 to 4.2 million in 2006, crossing the four million mark for the first time since 1871. The range of population projections for the next fifteen years shows a further possible increase of between 11 and 20 per cent, bringing the population to at minimum 4.7 million and at maximum 5.1 million. In effect this means additional population of between 500,000 and 900,000 people in just a decade and a half. Given this recent increase and the projected increase, it is somewhat ironic that An Foras Forbartha, a national institute which dealt with spatial planning, was abolished as a cost-cutting measure in 1987! Given that development since then has been market driven, there are some who may be glad that we do not have an independent institute covering this area!

There is more intellectual openness in Ireland today than there was twenty years ago, but we have a way to go on that. This is where I would have another difficulty with the social partnership process – I think the parameters for discussion need to be reviewed and set more widely. There is a real danger that the solutions to some of our problems lie outside the current parameters, and that the process has not found a replacement for the objective of reducing unemployment, which was so central to Irish policy-making for decades.

The future
On the future, I believe that the next stage of development will be very challenging. The stage of globalisation we have gone through has favoured us, given our approach to economic openness since the 1960s. The next stage will favour others, who were late in recognising how globalisation was changing the world. We had first-mover advantages and the challenges will come from others who are seeking to adopt a version of the 'Irish model'. In effect, other countries are seeing what we saw at the end of the 1980s – if they do not deal with the political economy challenges of structural change properly, they will persist in having low rates of economic growth and consequently there will be no resources to maintain the social and economic infrastructure they have built. Our continued prosperity will require our attracting an on-going flow of FDI in services and manufacturing, but it will also require that we develop a greater dynamic in our indigenous companies in these sectors. Whether we succeed in this will depend on the culture we have created towards innovation and risk-taking, as well as on the quality of our education system. It will also depend on our having a highly efficient public sector, so that the provision of good services is not an excessive burden on those competing on global markets.

CHAPTER FIVE

Joe Macri, Foreign Investor[1]

*Steve Ballmer (CEO of Microsoft) told me
'I'm normally the sales guy – I am normally selling to
governments. That is the first lunch I have been to where
the government was selling to me.'*

Joe Macri, formerly CEO of Microsoft Ireland, is now Microsoft's Director of Business and Marketing Operations in Western Europe. Microsoft has major operations in Dublin and Mr Macri, an Australian, is a member of the Council of IBEC, a member of the Management Board of ICT Ireland (a group for the high tech or knowledge sector within IBEC) and of the Health Service Executive. He chaired the Small Business Forum, established by government to make recommendations on the development of small business in Ireland. He is also a member of the US Chamber of Commerce in Ireland, one of the more powerful business lobbies in Ireland, because of the importance of US investment in Ireland.

Let me preface my views on the reasons for the sudden economic success of Ireland with my personal experiences. I am originally from Australia. I first visited Dublin in 1988 and I subsequently visited the city at least annually and often twice or three times a year from 1988 through to 1998. We moved here in 1999 and I have lived here ever since. So I will talk about what I have read, learned and also experienced. Visiting a country on an annual basis is almost like a *time capture* – watching how the scenery changes – and I definitely saw a change.

Three reasons – opening up, education and tax
Of all the things I saw change, I will focus on the three which were the result of conscious policy decisions that affected our economic success.

These are in order of priority; 1) opening up the economy. This manifests itself not only in joining the Common Market (the EU) but also the Anglo-Irish Free Trade Agreement, based on the fundamental policy decision made in the 1950s and 1960s. 2) The education system. There was a significant policy decision in terms of free secondary education, which led to a significant change in terms of workforce capability. The point I would make is that investment in education was a policy decision that raised the bar. 3) The third reason is obviously tax. It started off as the manufacturing tax rate. The export profit tax relief was the original version of it in the 1950s. These are the three policies that were decisive in Ireland's success.

However, these three reasons are not necessarily why we have had the economic success that we have had. These decisions were made in the 1950s and 1960s but why didn't the economic success happen at that time? It was because of the timing – we had opened up our economy when the global economy was slowing down with the oil shock of the 1970s. The analogy I would give is like that of opening up a corner store next to an industrial estate. I am Ireland and I have opened up my corner sandwich store across the road from Microsoft and all the other companies here in the Sandyford industrial estate. All of a sudden all the bigger firms close their businesses. This is exactly what happened to Ireland. This is why the economic success did not happen then.

There were a number of things which happened to us which weren't policy based but which created the environment which enabled us to take off. The most important one is cost-related. The Irish pound was devalued twice on two separate occasions and we also had deflation. We then also had the situation where Ireland was very cost competitive from a labour point of view; we had an attractive corporate tax rate, plus a relatively well-educated workforce (because of free secondary education) and we had the platform to which multinationals could come to access the EU market.

What brought Microsoft?
What brought Microsoft here? I wasn't too involved in the decision but I have subsequently met people that were. Microsoft came to Ireland in 1985. The Microsoft that came to Ireland then is not the Microsoft of today. It was only about ten years old. It had only about 1,200 employees globally and its global revenues were about $120 million (compared to $44.2bn in 2006). So it was a very small company. We were nowhere on the global scene. When we arrived, nobody noticed. This was the first Microsoft operation outside of the US, outside sales offices.

What brought us here? The first point is that we didn't really make a decision to come to Ireland; we made a decision to come to Europe. We wanted to come to Europe. Secondly, why Ireland and not a bigger country in Europe? The answer was the government was hungry for the business and it still is. I would argue that this applies to subsequent governments over the last twenty-plus years. The Irish government and its agencies made a compelling case as to why Europe equalled Ireland. Thirdly, the case they made was then around a young, educated workforce that was relatively low-cost, and they had this low corporate tax rate that made it more attractive. The fourth and final piece of the decision which has been strongly argued, not only by Microsoft but others too, is it's an English-speaking country. Language is a barrier when you are an American coming to Europe. The fact that people spoke English here was definitely important. Yet I wouldn't say it was in any business plan or in any cost justification document, but it certainly was a reason that people considered.

The IDA played an important role too. However, that environment has changed now. If you talk to the IDA or if you talk to my counterparts in other countries, there are a lot of agencies now that are very hungry. However, Ireland was just a step ahead of the rest. I think it was a combination of those factors that really contributed to creating the right environment for success. There are other factors that may have had an influence, but those cited are the primary factors.

While Britain is English-speaking, it was not the alternative option. When Bill Gates was on the road as part of the small team selling across Europe, the first sales office wasn't in Britain, but in France. They actually went to Paris first. Our regional headquarters was, and still is, in Paris. There were subsidiaries for sales in France, Germany and the UK. Then came the decision on where would we put our operational base; this was a separate decision. We decided on Ireland. We had no sales office in Ireland at the time, as it is a small market.

So Microsoft first came to Europe for the sales, going to the three most obvious markets that anybody would come to. Then we made a very explicit decision not to put the investment operation in any of those three countries but to put it into Ireland. I think this gives testament to the factors that I have highlighted but also to the work that was done by the then government, the IDA and the other state agencies.

I would be strongly of the view that if it wasn't for those conditions, the multinationals would not have come to Ireland. If the multinationals did not come to Ireland, I strongly believe we wouldn't have had the scale of the economic success that we have had. The multinationals have contributed significantly to the economy over the years and also introduced new work practices and work culture which has had an impact on other companies based in Ireland.

Anchor tenants

On the issue of a clustering effect, there are other companies that have clients here and that have been attracted by the IDA in the last, say, five years. But we are what IDA might refer to as an 'anchor tenant'. My predecessors as heads of Microsoft Ireland would have had the experience of effectively helping the Irish government to sell Ireland.

Who is selling to whom?

The other story I would share with you is for me a great story. Back around 1998–9, Steve Ballmer (CEO of Microsoft) told me this after a meeting with the Irish government. He obviously has met with every government in every country that we do business in (which is a lot) and the comment he made to me was that 'I'm normally the sales guy – I am normally selling to governments. That is the first lunch I have been to where the government was selling to me.' This is the other point. This is the sort of thing that doesn't sit in business plans nor does it get mentioned in the papers. There is this very strong attitude within the Irish government and its ministers and senior civil servants which is focused on trying to attract business. This is a factor not to be underestimated.

Institutions

The role of institutions is quite important too, in the sense of having political stability or social systems in place. It is probably a good guess that the factory or plant will be less productive than another plant in a country that has consistent policy and social partnership-type agreements. So there are these important 'softer' factors in the success. I wouldn't lead with social partnership, for example, because the point I would make is, if I went to any senior decision-maker in Microsoft, they wouldn't know what that phrase meant. However, if you then talked about the environment in which we operate, then they would see the value of it.

We call these sorts of factors more 'hygiene factors'. These are the sort of things that can make life a lot more difficult or a lot better but aren't necessary the drivers. The drivers are the factors that I mentioned above. I would use the term 'hygiene factors' carefully. People tell me not to use that term, but I use it to describe things that help the environment or hinder the environment, but they don't necessarily drive the environment.

Secondary factors

I have said that there are three primary drivers and then there are secondary factors. The secondary factors which have all been supportive over the years are the low cost of labour, a large labour pool – high levels of unemployment and more women either entering or staying in the workforce ensured that there were plenty of potential employees available in the economy. Ireland's changing demographics have also been a factor – the baby boom in Ireland helped reduce the dependency rate here, whilst in the US and Europe the baby boomers born in the 1950s will soon retire, so we will see the opposite effect there, in terms of an increased dependency rate. Social partnership, as previously mentioned, was also a supporting factor.

On the important issue of productivity, Microsoft Ireland commissioned a major report on it from leading economist Paul Tansey in 2005. Let us talk first about the motivation behind why we did the Tansey Report;[2] secondly, what it has taught us and thirdly, where we are going with the joint Microsoft/Irish Management Institute (IMI) National Productivity Centre. We are in the final stages and it was actually physically being built in 2007.

The motivation for commissioning the report was partly around Microsoft Ireland's twentieth anniversary as we wanted to contribute something to the overall economic debate that would have a long-term impact as part of our year of celebrations. Separately, I sit on a number of groups such as the National Executive Council of IBEC and government groups etc. I got to know a lot of people across industry and I noticed that all of the discussions were fixated on costs. If you look at the overall elements of the equation, however, it is clear that lack of competitiveness equals cost. Now don't get me wrong – cost is important, but I would have a different focus.

At a conference in London, Alvin Toffler, author of a book called *Future Shock*, really impacted me. He spoke about moving from the agrarian society to the industrial society and that those who had vested interests in the agrarian society were the ones who resisted change. It was those nations that really embraced change that drove the industrial society, so the power base shifted. Now we are in the information society, which is the next wave. Toffler was talking about how we measure productivity and how we measure real competitiveness in industrial society, but that is now not as relevant as productivity in the information society. The information society is driven by the services sector, where it is more difficult to measure productivity. That is what got me thinking about productivity and we decided to commission a report on it.

Productivity, not costs
I think policy needed a shift in regard to beating ourselves over the head in terms of cost issues. An issue which I think is very important is the human element. Microsoft is one of the top companies to work for, not

only in Ireland but elsewhere – it was recently selected as one of the top ten companies to work for in Europe. If we, as people, don't enjoy what we do and don't have a constructive relationship with our employees, then we are not going to be productive. Rather than getting fixated on costs, we need to focus on the people. The fact is that people in any organisation drive success – whether they are the people in the Irish Congress of Trades Unions (ICTU), the people in Microsoft, the people in any organisation. Microsoft is nothing without its people.

The report identified these issues and highlighted the importance of productivity in driving future economic success. There was a lot of extremely positive reaction to our report on productivity. The good reaction was partly because of the competitiveness discussions that were underway at the time – the suggested focus on productivity was timely and relevant. Sometimes an issue just falls flat and at other times it is picked up. As a result of the relevance of the issue and the interest that it generated, I then met with a number of civil servants and ministers on the issue of productivity. I was involved in the government's Small Business Forum and the productivity issue emerged out of that Forum as well. We met with 100 small business owner and managers around the country. All the issues they were talking about were, in many ways, around the issue of productivity. It was great to see the National Competitiveness Council (NCC) pick it up and to see it come full circle. The NCC chair, Don Thornhill, drew the conclusion that improving productivity is about improving technology, management development and capability and it is about innovation. Making that message real is critical to this economy.

Education – good but not great

My view on the role of education in Ireland's economic success is informed by an OECD report. I am not an expert on this. We have a good education system. We are above average in English, average in maths, etc. However, we sometimes believe our own PR and think that we are great. We do need to think about how we can make our education system 'great' and not just 'good'. I think more work needs to be done on that front, especially in the context of ensuring that our children are equipped with the skills to fully engage in the information society.

Skills for those at work are important. A lot of people in employment do not have the skills that we need. Therefore we need to invest now as the times are good. I would be supportive of a two-pronged strategy. Martin Cronin from Forfás articulated this around the productivity report published by Forfás in 2007.[3] We have two challenges: first, making sure our environment is the right environment for export businesses, be they indigenous or multinational. Secondly, how we improve productivity for those organisations that are non-exporting, as they have an indirect effect on the rest of the economy.

For example, we have four divisions here in Ireland in Microsoft; we have the European Operations Centre – effectively an information centre and back office for all of our business across Europe, the Middle East and Africa; that is, about 500 million people. We have a second division, the European Product Development Centre which is all about globalisation – the ninety-eight products we have out there – making them available in all languages – including 'local languages' (for instance Irish Gaelic) – we actually have about 100 languages. So that is about 500 people. Thirdly, we have people focused on the local Irish market in the Sales, Marketing and Services Group. Then we have the final and newest division in Ireland, the R&D division, which is about core development of new technologies. That is a total of 1,200 people. However, we actually have an additional 800 contractors physically working at our site. Therefore there are about 2,000 people working for us. In addition to those working directly on our site there is roughly a ratio of five jobs in the supply chain for every one job we have in Microsoft. So there is a factor of about 1:5. In addition to driving productivity within our own organisation, it is clear that if those service companies in the supply chain are not productive, then indirectly Microsoft is not productive. We have to focus on that as a country.

Microsoft and the IMI believe that the National Productivity Centre is a useful resource for senior managers from both the public and private sectors. It brings together tools and resources in a practical way that highlights how the right combination of human capital, management development, organisational learning together with technology help drive productivity.

The IDA have had a wonderful success in the high-profile investments Ireland had in 2006. But then there are the job closures and for those employees it is a desperate situation (to be left unemployed in a small town). However, if you look at it from a macro-economic point of view, the net investments are still outweighing the divestments at the moment. What is driving the divestments? Until recently, the majority of closures were driven by 'in-company' issues. The example I like to use is Gateway. Everybody says 'Gateway left Ireland' but I always say 'No, Gateway left Europe.' Their decision was to pull out of the European market and focus on the US market. The result of this was they no longer needed a manufacturing plant in Dublin. Even though it was a very visible and painful job loss, the decision was made as a result of an 'in-company' issue. People only see how it affected Ireland but it is still there in the US.

Critical mass and sustainability

The question is 'Can we sustain ourselves?' A factor which is important is 'critical mass'. I would argue that this is one of the factors that helped us get our R&D centre located here in Ireland. Head office looked and they said we already have three divisions there. We have a strong infrastructure, we have a big human resources department, we have 'critical mass'. From a business point of view, this is a 'soft factor'. The R&D could have gone to Poland or wherever, but we would have had to set up from scratch and we would not have been familiar with their culture etc. In Ireland I am part of a leadership team that works for continual growth and improvement of the site. We managed the process that way – if you come to Ireland, the attraction was you get the benefit of all the infrastructure, human resources etc. This is already prebuilt and I think Ireland has that advantage at a national level. For example, a couple of times I have met with Chinese companies on behalf of the local government agencies to see if they want to come to Ireland. A lot of Irish companies are interested in China and a lot of Chinese companies are becoming increasingly interested in Ireland. The argument I put to the Chinese organisations is 'Look at the capability Ireland has in terms of supply-chain management – it is world-class because of the US investments. It is here.' I am not suggesting they poach people from my organisation! The point is, at a national level, we have that capability and critical mass. Sometimes we underestimate this. That is where the IDA on the ground do a fantastic job of leveraging this.

Policy directions

The future for Ireland is to sustain its competitive position in attracting foreign direct investment and bolstering its indigenous sector. While there are a number of policy directions required, the common theme here is around productivity. It is about management capability and organisational learning, as much as it is about technology and information.

If I look at my organisation, my cost per head, say for a Microsoft engineer, now is high compared to the cost per head ten years ago. We have lost that cost advantage now. It is partly because of high costs in this country and partly because of the fall in the dollar. Therefore I am now having to do productivity improvements in my organisation, not only to justify further investment, but also to sustain what we are currently doing. If I benchmark the productivity in my team, we have to make improvements. I look at management development; we have just under 300 front-line managers in Ireland – we put every single one of them through a forty-day programme – complete management development. As will be highlighted through the National Productivity Centre, a focus on management capability with the provision of training is a critical way in which productivity can be enhanced. This programme is a significant investment for us but we are repaid in terms of employee commitment and loyalty and in terms of productivity gains.

One of the recommendations the Small Business Forum made last year is that you almost need this kind of investment in management skills and training at a country level, but the question is how do smaller businesses do this and what is the role of government in the process?

Small size – an advantage and a disadvantage

I think the small size of the economy is both an advantage and a disadvantage. The size of the economy is not why multinationals come here. They come here because of membership of the EU etc. The reason Microsoft has gone to China and India is not because of low costs. It is because of the huge *market* opportunities. Offshoring was a huge issue in the last US election campaign and every time the US press dealt with offshoring, they showed a Dell manufacturing plant in China. But Michael Dell would argue 'I am servicing a local market called China – therefore why wouldn't I have a manufacturing plant there?' So in my view, the size of the market is not a material issue.

Catching up?

Was Ireland's success a remarkable, almost magical period or was it just catching up? I love that question! It is both. There is absolutely an element of catch-up. If you do a trend analysis of the adoption curve of technology in Ireland and compare it to the rest of Western Europe and the use of certain technologies like PC or broadband penetration into the home (we have internal measures, for example, in the adoption rates of Windows XP/Office 2007/Windows Vista etc. where we track this stuff), what you see, time and time again, is that Ireland lags and then it does a catch-up. There is normally a lag of about eighteen months. Our growth rates now in broadband are actually really good growth rates. However, they just didn't happen two years ago – there was a catch-up factor.

A point I would make is I would be both critical and defensive of the government and previous governments in relation to cost effectiveness and managing timescales. We are getting better in terms of infrastructural time lines and in terms of budgets. But it is acknowledged that Ireland is absolutely playing catch-up. We are investing significantly in infrastructure, through Transport 21 and other programmes, in terms of road, rail, air. Then there is the e-infrastructure – broadband – we continue to be much later and slower here than our European counterparts. They were all rebuilding their infrastructures after the Second World War. We did not have the capital until ten or fifteen years ago. So I do believe there is an element of catch-up.

Separate to that is a phenomenal success story in terms of what percentage of global investments Ireland has captured through foreign direct investment. I think what has happened now is that the share of FDI investment has started to flatten out. But it started off relatively high.

The future

On Ireland's future, I am a critical optimist. I believe in Ireland's future. If I didn't I wouldn't leave my family here, quite frankly! I think the country has great potential. However, we have a lot of challenges ahead of us and we have to address some issues around competitiveness, around infrastructure, health services and the education system. I believe we have capacity to do this. I do not subscribe to complacency. I would always try to balance my comments to be somewhat critical in a constructive way.

My issue isn't with the Irish government on the issue of improving efficiency in the public service. My issue is with measurement. We measure inputs. We measure how many nurses we have put in the health system; how many gardaí we have put on the street; how much money we have put into the education system (which is a lot, coming back to that catch-up story). However, it is not about the inputs. We must now turn greater attention to output, that is, to start measuring verifiable outcomes. Once you get consistency and agreement on what is a verifiable outcome, then you can really start to look at public sector productivity.

My objective, with the IMI, through the National Productivity Centre which was up and running in 2007, is that not only will we have private sector managers going through but we will also invite the public sector to participate. This is the objective for the NPC with the target of increasing productivity in all organisations throughout Ireland at the heart of this joint venture.

There is no doubt that Ireland has been very successful in the recent past and that both professionally and personally the majority of people are benefiting from this success. The key factor now is to ensure that the vision, and the policies, are in place to protect that success for the future. I firmly believe that a focused approach on achieving productivity gains in order to protect and maintain our competitiveness will help to secure a strong future for all in Ireland.

CHAPTER SIX

Gary McGann, CEO of the Irish Multinational[1]

So three critical features came together: the state backing of winners, a skilled and educated workforce and a favourable tax structure.

Gary McGann is Group Chief Executive Officer of the Smurfit Kappa Group. It is one of Ireland's first multinational companies and has 40,000 employees in thirty countries in Europe, the US and South America. A paper-packaging company, it has a turnover of €7bn. Jefferson Smurfit began the company as a small Irish boxmaker in 1934 and his son, Michael Smurfit, took over and expanded it in the 1970s and 1980s. In the 1990s it expanded into Europe. Gary McGann has previously held a number of senior positions in both the private and public sectors over the last twenty years, including Chief Executive of Gilbeys of Ireland Limited, Grand Metropolitan Finance and Aer Lingus Group plc. In 2005/06 he was President of IBEC, one of the social partners, and is on its executive board. Mr McGann is also Chairman of the Dublin Airport Authority (DAA).

I could claim to be well qualified by pure coincidence to discuss the evolution of the Celtic Tiger. My business life has relatively closely tracked the success of the Irish economy, both in terms of duration (starting in the late 1960s) and in its progression. I have worked in the civil service, the technology sector, a food and beverage company, a state-owned company and now a paper-packaging company. It is a microcosm of the Irish economy and one man's experience of some of the big themes of Irish economic growth over time. These include the importance of the state and state-owned enterprise to the economy, the movement from the land and then the movement from commodity to added-value food products, the emergence of the multinational, and packaging, one of the barometers of industrial production.

I was a civil servant from 1968 to 1976 when it was a nice time to be a civil servant as it was a fairly safe occupation in those days. When I moved into private enterprise to work in Ericsson in Athlone, the physical move itself was viewed as being akin to emigrating to Canada, let alone the step taken in moving out of the security of the civil service! My mother-in-law didn't speak to me for a year because all of her sons were either priests or civil servants and in her eyes I was taking a big risk! The civil service was and is a breeding ground for business people, but its internal strength and depth should not be underestimated. This is seen through policies implemented over time, the contribution to social partnership and its role as a guiding light for the economy.

Working for an early foreign investor

As I said, I was one of the products of the business breeding ground. When I went into Ericsson in 1976/77, you could sense the beginnings of something substantial happening in the Irish economy. Ericsson had been in Ireland since 1964 and like Rowntree Mackintosh and other foreign-owned companies it originally entered Ireland to cater for the domestic market. People today can't believe that companies came here for that reason, given the relatively small size of the market. This is especially true when you consider how large these companies are in relation to markets such as Ireland. Nevertheless we were a relatively closed and developing country, ready for competition. A parallel today is that companies enter the tiniest of the Eastern European markets because they see that there is a lot of development going on and there is the possibility of a huge market catch-up happening. It is not just your standard market growth – the size may be small but the growth rate is significant.

Thus it was in the late 1960s and the 1970s – the Irish market was catching up as a result of free trade agreements and entry into (what is now) the EU. In the late 1970s, however, it was clear that we would need to keep changing, and the openness of the economy also bred risks, in the form of competition.

The state and IDA

Amongst the uncertainty and change, the initial seeds of the growth that became evident in the 1990s were sown a long time ago. There were a number of important figures involved in the sowing. I'm a huge fan of T. K. Whitaker because I think he had great vision. There were others, like Michael Killeen, then head of the IDA, who was also a practical visionary. Killeen could see what industries could be winners in the future. At that time, IDA clearly was taking gambles. Given that we were a small economy with limited resources, we had to make choices as we couldn't back everything and clearly had to back something, and to try and match what we could provide with what foreign-owned companies needed. The common thread running through the businesses we attracted was, in my opinion, their desire to invest behind an educated workforce. In a sense we hadn't got anything else. We hadn't got oil, we hadn't got gas, we hadn't got natural minerals – the only resource we had were people and we had smart people. Crucially, they were also well educated. Despite the heartbreak of seeing so much of the investment in education leaving the country, it was a resource that the country continued to foster.

Education, the only natural resource
Killeen had the insight into the type of industry that we should back but more importantly, the Ken Whitakers and the government of the time gave him the ability to act because they saw that education was the only natural resource. This was not a new phenomenon, and our history of 'saints and scholars', missionaries and the like should have and probably did help to foster the culture. We educated many in countries abroad over many centuries when we went out as missionaries. We still do and we still seem to be good at it. The key was to do at home what we were doing abroad, but at a higher level.

The result was a well educated workforce. Many of them were and still are in the civil service. Some, like me, moved out onto a much more threatening but ultimately a more potentially rewarding path.

How Ericssons became embedded
Moving back to my personal journey, another example of a quiet low-key visionary in this country was Vincent Daly, then head of Ericsson. He is one of my real mentors.

When I joined Ericsson in 1977, as I mentioned, the company had come to Ireland to participate in a growth market and its entry justified the creation of approximately four hundred installation engineering jobs in Ireland back in 1964. But the market changed, and by 1980, projections were that the Ericsson business model would support just ten people in this country five years later. So we had to change the business model, and we achieved this so successfully that by 1985, Ericsson had over 1,000 people working in this country, instead of the ten projected. This ultimately came down to the vision of Vincent Daly, who was keen to keep the company in Ireland. Just as importantly, he recognised he had to justify this ambition. We started a software factory. We recruited three of the best engineers from Telecom, sent them off to Sweden for three years. They were sent not just to learn, because the education level here was as good as the Swedish level, but to find out everything about the Ericsson model and, most importantly, to win over the Swedes.

Another factor in the initial existence and retention of Ericsson (and no doubt many others) was the availability of state grants. We ended up in Athlone because the grant level was better in the West than in Dublin, but so also was the support structure from the town, and the importance of the business to the community.

Export sales tax relief

A further critical factor was export tax relief on manufactured product, which was a significant contributor to the decision to stay in the country, when a group-wide re-evaluation of businesses within Ericsson was taking place. Low tax was a huge factor for Ireland. If you go to any international marketplace low tax is a factor. I think the great issue about tax in Ireland was that it had certainty, no matter which party was in power. It was consistent over time. This is extremely important for companies' planning.

There is the question as to why the tax structure was insufficient for Ireland to take off earlier, when we had zero tax on exports and then the 10 per cent rate on production before the current 12.5 per cent rate. Partly I think it was a matter of momentum, which had been building up through the 1970s and 1980s. I will return to that idea later. The other factor I think was because from 1992 we had the Single Market. We had the critical mass – a decent pool of talent – we had been growing it to that point.

Three critical features – the state, skill and education, and tax

So three critical features came together, the state backing of winners, a skilled and educated workforce and a favourable tax structure. Not much difference there then between my own and the country's development. Vincent Daly knew the initial entry was just the foot in the door. The critical question was the overall development of technology and whether Ericsson in Ireland was going to develop in the same way. That's where education, engineering, electronics and so on came into play.

Of course, the big challenge was how to get the talent, the graduates, to Athlone. For many the only other option was to emigrate. Ericsson, Siemens and Phillips had the pick of the crop every year from the colleges. You had this software factory started in 1981/82 and we had fresh-faced young electronic engineers – the only reason they were there was because of the opportunity in the job – there was no other reason for them to be in Athlone. It was a unique experience to watch young people who could have been in London or Dublin or Amsterdam, there in Athlone. We only attracted them because a) we had the company in Ireland, b) the tax structure continued to support it, and c) the job was exciting and progressive.

We regularly had to defend being in Ireland to the Swedes. In a multinational, there is always somebody evaluating the reasons that they shouldn't be doing what they are doing in a particular location or country and thinking about where they should be moving to next. That is something we need to remember in this country. Every multinational has somebody making an evaluation as to why they are located where they are located, and we need an equivalent evaluation being made and an articulation as to why it is advantageous to be here. We also need the facts to support it.

O'Malley's free education back in the 1960s improved second-level education. By the 1970s that same pool was going through to third level. We were only getting the real crop of advanced capability in Ireland on the technical, the bio or pharma side by the early 1990s.

The English language
A fourth and not insignificant element in the 1970s was our culture and the English language. There is no question in my mind that Americans find it more difficult to engage in Europe with the Continental model than with the Anglo-Saxon model. Smurfit Kappa was 66 per cent owned and is currently 22 per cent owned by an American private equity firm and we are by far their largest European investment. They have looked at other countries (e.g. France) and have asked for our views. Apart from smaller investments, they almost always shy away – the enterprise culture is fundamentally different, the attitude is different, but most particularly, the Americans don't have a strong attraction to doing business other than in the English language. In my view, they experience difficulties when not being in control of communication.

So I think that being educated, English speaking and 'neutral' have been competitive advantages for Ireland. We are as close to Berlin as Boston, and critically we understand both cultures. No biases. So it is not a coincidence that the vast majority of the American FDI companies came to Ireland rather than anywhere else in Europe. All this was added to by the pool of talent that was growing and the confidence level in the capabilities of the Irish to be industrially rather than agriculturally oriented. It wasn't that long since we were predominantly an agricultural country. It was, if you like, a second stage of development – the first were the likes of Ericsson which came to Ireland for the market, the second were the US companies coming to use Ireland as a launch pad into Europe.

FDI other than American

While nobody should underestimate the importance of American investment in Ireland, there was other international investment in the country. Most foreign-owned companies eventually used Ireland as a location to serve other markets. Ericsson Ireland started to service the less attractive markets for the Swedes. The trick, of course, was to find such markets and serve them profitably and well. The Irish were always great for doing the difficult and unattractive work. So we were prepared to do the hard work. We were prepared to travel to more difficult markets – North Africa, middle Africa, Asia and so on. The Swedes were more centred on work–life balance and if they had to travel at all, it would be to the more attractive locations. So that was another factor. Of course, now foreign-owned companies are considering moving manufacturing again because of cost structures, and the size and scale of the market in Eastern Europe.

My sense is that Ireland's success was in gestation through the 1970s and 1980s. Significant growth was waiting to happen and it needed a further catalyst and I think the catalyst was the European Single Market that developed in the 1990s.

We needed more than language skills, an internationally minded workforce, a reasonable location to service Europe, along with relatively low manufacturing costs. International conditions have not been static. As stated, I think education and the tax structure were key factors not only in our fledgling growth but in the ongoing success of the country, as we continued our journey from agriculture and a relatively closed economy through manufacturing and beyond. Pure manufacturing, product manufacturing, is not going to continue to be competitive other than where it is very clearly wedded to Irish indigenous products. We are rapidly losing products that are mobile. But back in the 1990s, I think we knew this was likely to happen. After all, we had seen a wave of manufacturing lost in the 1970s and early 1980s.

We often view the Irish economic miracle as being a product of the 1990s. Statistically, of course, the growth figures bear this out. But we should acknowledge that in the 1970s and the 1980s we had a growth sector and a declining sector. We had to compensate for the continuing decline in agriculture, the loss of the uncompetitive manufacturing base that developed between the 1920s and the 1960s and the relative decline in the public service as a percentage of employment. These declines would have bottomed out by the late 1980s, and allowed the sectors that were growing to be compared with a zero rather than a declining base. We therefore underestimate the progress we made in the 1970s and 1980s by forgetting to ask the question 'Without it, where would we have been?'

The EU

I tend to glaze over when people ask are we better off being in the EU or not. It's a bit like asking are you better with two legs or one. For me there was a kind of serendipity between EU open markets, the concept of the Single Market and the Irish psyche. The Irish, by necessity originally, and by choice ultimately, have always been travellers. So there was no fear for the Irish. They never lacked self-confidence – except perhaps at home! The Irish are much more confident, more energised and more proactive abroad than they are at home. The confidence level of people going abroad was always there, but again originally by necessity and then by choice.

We set the objectives of progressing the country for the laudable objective of giving people a better standard of living. But we knew we had to move up the 'value chain'. Taking an example again from my own experience in Ericsson, we got completely-knocked-down (CKD) kits and we would assemble them. We weren't a pure manufacturing factory – we were assembling and wiring electronic boards and so on. But that progressed more and more to programming in the old-style, electrical, quasi-mechanical electrical and then that moved onto electronics. All the time, instead of just doing what the book that came with the kit said, the workforce said 'Hey, can we do more than that, with this!' and they spawned off small cottage industries. In Athlone and Dublin, there are many small companies which Ericsson and other large companies spawned.

The innovative IFSC

One of the larger service innovations was the initiative by Charlie Haughey and Dermot Desmond in setting up the IFSC, which helped in Ireland's success. Many of the first real businesses in the IFSC were spawned from existing companies where the finance staff were a bit more proactive. Ericsson, for example, opened an IFSC company, promoted by the then finance director, John Ronaghan, whose brainchild it was. I left for Gilbeys just as it was being completed, but we, in turn, set up Grand Met Finance Ireland in the IFSC. It was the first English company to set up in the IFSC, even though the Grand Met head office wanted financial services based in London, not Dublin. Then the Smurfit Group set up Smurfit Capital which exists today, originally based on the Grand Met Finance Ireland model. The tax structure again was an important part but tax savings alone are not sufficient. People weren't going to entrust huge sums of money being transferred across the globe unless they felt safe with the Irish base.

Skills and education, and most importantly in this instance, advanced telecommunications were important factors too. Grand Met Finance Ireland became the clearing house for all intercompany settlements. It put huge sums of money through Dublin. Once you get critical mass, nothing succeeds like success. We then became the financiers for people like the franchisees of Burger King (a subsidiary of Grand Met). In general, people in the IFSC started spreading their wings and then growth came in as a result of it. There were a couple of courageous pioneers, and I credit Haughey and Dermot Desmond for the IFSC. In more recent times, and on another dimension, the Dublin Docklands Development Authority has also done a great job revitalising the docklands.

The growth of the Irish multinationals

There is another aspect to the Irish economic history and that is of course Irish international companies. In business terms, Michael Smurfit, Tom Roche and others are great examples of people who established fantastic companies which set out from a small economy with very little to sell and very little basis from which to have expectations. Yet they did it. We have been talking about Ireland as a base for manufacturing and financial services. These are examples of the Irish as founders of multinational companies. We have examples of companies based in Ireland that export and other companies who have started here and spread abroad, through growth in other countries.

Baileys Irish Cream is a phenomenal example of the first type. David Dand went to the biggest alcohol distributor in the US in New York with a bottle of Baileys. The chief executive said to him 'David, you are a great guy, I have a lot of time for you but that shit will never sell.' To be fair, in later years, the distributor told the story himself. Of course, the product did sell! David had the confidence not to be put off his stride by that discouragement.

Irish traits

The Irish are very receptive to education and experience – I think we learn very rapidly. As my colleagues from Ericsson did in Sweden, you listen for a while to business concepts and you say 'I understand this – I know this. They are not speaking in a language I don't understand. I can contribute to this. Where I think they are wrong, I can argue with it.' All of a sudden, people start to listen to you because you are making sense. I've seen Irish people saying 'Oh, they are listening to me' – almost in surprise.

In general, I think we have one great trait which is humility. I think the Americans have always seen this. We can balance knowledge, intellect and capability with humility. We befriend people rather than make enemies. We work with people rather than irrationally confront them. When I was trying to attract Grand Met Finance to Ireland from London – and London is the heart of the financial services world – they were not initially impressed at all. But we just kept at it and, when the decision-makers were not convinced, rather than force a yes or no answer, we just said 'Can we come back and talk to you later?' Then we did some more research. We also found out what makes them tick. So we had the intellectual approach, but we also had the interpersonal skills to build consensus.

One of the great things Ireland has been good at was avoiding the temptation to go around with solutions looking for problems! Instead we understood the problems and sought the solutions. I think there is a big difference. There is nothing worse than somebody saying 'I have an idea for you,' when you don't want an idea and you are in fact perfectly happy with what you have.

The EU created a forum where it was necessary to be proactive and persuasive; otherwise we wouldn't get our fair share of the opportunities. That required a lot more people to become international in their mindset and to discover that they were very good and very, very capable. Look at some of them in the EU, where Irish people are incredibly well placed in many institutions.

Smurfit Kappa Group

My current employer, the Smurfit Kappa Group, in its earlier incarnation, didn't go to continental Europe that early. We began our expansion there in the early 1990s. The company had been public since 1964. It was an Irish company. Then it went to the UK at a time when Michael Smurfit would be the first to tell you that it was 'devour or be devoured'. The expansion took place as a result of the Anglo-Irish Free Trade Agreement, signed in 1965. We were going to be hammered if we didn't get out there and make it in the UK.

We stayed with the English-speaking countries (which of course, I was criticising US companies for doing, earlier). Then, in the late 1980s, the Smurfit Group got a leg into Europe when we bought a company called Container Corporation of America which was owned by Mobil Oil, which was divesting their non-core businesses. Our target was their Latin American businesses, but they also had plants in Spain, the Netherlands and Italy. So almost by default, we had plants on Continental Europe and we turned our focus to Europe. Of course, the Single Market was opening up and with Ireland a full member of the club, and the opportunities were there. We galvanised our position in Continental Europe by buying the paper packaging operations of St Gobain in 1994, and our growth has been primarily in Europe since, culminating in the merger with Kappa Packaging in late 2005. We continue to expand abroad. We are looking at opening a plant in Moscow and one in Romania and are opening a number of plants in Latin America.

Smurfit Kappa is in the most basic of manufacturing sectors that you can come across. We package products. If nothing is made, nothing is packaged. You can't package software or intellectual capital! We have to be mobile and even though we're in bricks and mortar and so on, we have to factor that into the way we think. We once did very well in printing products such as Microsoft's software manuals. However, people got used to the instruction manual being embedded into the software. Now they don't need a book and a CD – they just get it on their system. By the end of 2007 Smurfit Kappa had no printing operations in Ireland apart from newspaper printing, and we had four printing companies in Ireland not long ago.

Low interest rates
Low interest rates would also be an important contributor to our economic progress. They certainly helped property development, which in turn helped GDP. There are clear warning signals on the over-dependence of the economy on property and our dependence on consumer spending is also obviously a big issue in 2007.

The Tallaght Strategy and fiscal reform
I think the dramatic Irish economic take-off did begin in the late 1980s. Firstly, the declining sectors of the economy bottomed out. Secondly, Ray McSharry, as Minster for Finance, did important work at that time on the public finances. Thirdly, the Tallaght Strategy – namely the decision by the leader of the opposition, Alan Dukes, to support major reforms by the government – was courageous, but I think it is unlikely to ever be repeated again. I have a very high regard for Alan Dukes both intellectually and ethically. Finally, I think that social partnership was a very enlightened concept which was enormously important at that crucial time, but I believe that, while we may have improved the system over the years, we need to fundamentally rethink how to contemporise it, if it is to serve us for the next ten years (of which more later).

Critical issues for the future
Today, there are a couple of critical issues that I believe we must face in order to evaluate the success we have had and to give that success the chance to continue. We are facing some real threats in the economy. We could pay a huge price if we continue to behave as we are currently. We are in a well-off country and certainly we have to find a way of redistributing the wealth which we are creating in a more equitable manner. However, it is critical to ensure that we retain the conditions that generate that wealth. We have discussed many of the causes and the sustainers of Irish economic growth – education, EU involvement, tax regime, social partnership, flexibility. I don't know how the removal of any of these

would affect our continued growth, but I do know that a reduction in our competitiveness is a sufficient factor in itself.

Costs and productivity

I think we need to realise that there is a very delicate balance to be struck domestically with the liberalisation agenda. It is as true for a country as a company that, for us to be successful, we need to be competitive with our input costs. We talk about price competition, and anyone can drop prices. It is a high-risk strategy, because you can only win if your costs are lower than the competition. So price is not the differentiator, it is costs. We do have issues and concerns about scale because Ireland's scale and consequently our cost competitiveness will consequently be lesser, relative to international competition. The advantage of the smaller scale is the speed and flexibility to act, which can very often offset the lower overall cost of larger scale.

Commercial state companies

One important area in Ireland is the semi-state sector. I think that it is widely acknowledged that the semi-state companies that are competing in the commercial world will have to change more rapidly to keep up and be competitive as distinct from the old days of being protected. I think that there are seriously genuine attempts to move it in that direction. The Congress of Trade Unions has a huge challenge in this, particularly as the purpose of trade unions is to represent their members and to ensure they are properly treated. But they cannot hold back the tide of competitiveness and change. We have seen the example in Shannon Airport where we have achieved a change in direction that has moved the airport from its previously unsustainable and unaffordable competitive position. It did, however, take eighteen months, which was a long time by any standards. I think we progressed in flexibility, but not in speed!

State ownership is a difficult concept for commercial companies as there are inevitably conflicting factors affecting decisions. There is an extra stakeholder with an understandable political agenda. I think any person that is a senior executive of a commercial state-owned company in many instances needs to be more versatile and capable than private enterprise managers. A major drag factor is the time consumption of people like Padraig McManus, CEO of ESB; Declan Collier, CEO of DAA, and the other state-company CEOs in managing issues that are totally irrelevant to the commercial mandate of their day job. If we don't have the best executives in those companies, we are in deep trouble.

Their packages in many instances are less than they might make in private enterprise, but clearly there is more at play than that. We may say that they go in with their eyes open and with a view to making a difference. I remember Paddy Wright (former CEO of Smurfits) saying to me when I took the CEO job at Aer Lingus: 'Do you really know what you are getting yourself into?' and I said, 'Paddy, I know by your question that the answer is clearly I should be saying no, but I think yes.' I rang him about two months later and I told him he was right. I didn't really know what I was getting myself into. On the other hand, I did know what I was getting myself into with the chairmanship of the DAA/Aer Rianta. The DAA is the institution mandated, amongst other things, to deliver one of the most important pieces of strategic infrastructure, notwithstanding all the challenges and obstructions. People need to give something back to the country in which they have developed their career.

Regulation reform

The DAA brings me to the subject of regulation. The current regulation model is, in my view, flawed and not delivering. Competition is always ten times better than regulation. Regulation is used as a proxy for (and I believe a second-best alternative to) competition where, in its absence, there would be monopoly. I acknowledge that where there are natural monopolies or very dominant firms, regulation may be required. But it must be well balanced, well structured and it must change as the world changes. This is not the case today with, for example, the airport regulation system. I would question if the regulator adds any value, compared to the old days when the government department, manned by motivated civil servants, advised the minister in the event that the company was likely to engage in activity that might damage the economy or consumers. We are getting the worst of all worlds now – the political imperative, the civil servant perspective, the regulatory 'interpretation' and then the state company's mandate to execute against all the odds! This is a lot of constituents to try to satisfy in order to achieve a competitive outcome.

On regulation, I think it's time to do an audit of what is going on and to consider whether as a mechanism it is going to advance the country's agenda or is it going to hold us back. There are good models of regulation. Again, taking aviation, the United Kingdom has a well-developed, well-tested regulation structure. We would have been well advised to have adopted it. In any event, whatever model we use, we need informed regulators with unequivocal mandates and the leverage to execute them fairly and sensibly.

Modernising the civil service

I had an enormous belief in Whitaker and still have in other like-minded public servants, the managers of the Irish civil service and more importantly 'Ireland Inc.' – I hate that cliché, but we'll call it that. The executive wing of the civil service needs leadership that is strong and visionary. The country needs a strong civil service. I have great regard for the integrity of the civil service. I don't think anybody has any idea of how hard the senior civil servants work. People talk about the challenge and commitment of private enterprise but the civil servants work unbelievable hours balancing all sorts of political agendas, and the good ones are so committed. The key question is whether we are able to attract the cream of the crop as we were able to do in the past. It is an enormous challenge given the alternatives created by the economic miracle. Whatever model we have in our civil service, we do not need layers of bureaucracy in which decisiveness is seriously lacking, leading to endless prevarication. If you need a decision, in a small open economy (where agility and flexibility is paramount) it needs to be expeditious.

Revisiting social partnership
When I was President of IBEC in 2005/6, we already recognised the need to revise the strategy on social partnership to re-establish coherence. The social partnership 'club' feels as if it has become almost like a bad marriage with everybody taking everyone else for granted. You can almost predict the ebbs and flows – somebody sulks, walks out, the partners despair, the Taoiseach intervenes and it is a real piece of theatre. Theatre is critical in bringing people with you over the line, but if it is perceived as artificial theatre, then it loses credibility. I think we are borderline on that in terms of social partnership. My sense is that there is a common agreement amongst the key partners that the model needs to be revisited. I believe that the existing model is now fractured. It has served an enormous purpose over the years but a social partnership framework and structure for the next ten years now needs some fundamental and original thought.

We have honed and changed social partnership but have we stood back and questioned its capacity to deal with the new challenges we are trying to address? After the latest agreement, Towards 2016, had been negotiated and the public service benchmarking decisions were being made, there was a mess on the nursing front. The SIPTU [Services, Industrial, Professional and Technical Union] side of nursing were staying with benchmarking as part of the agreement, but the other two nursing unions were out on the street. No matter how you portrayed it, this did not feel like a successful social partnership. Yet the fundamental concept is good. Surely negotiation and agreement-building is far better than any confrontation? Of course it is! Agreement is eventually arrived at – in an orderly fashion with social partnership, and in a disorderly fashion without it.

Company tax harmonisation

On the tax side, there is real pressure for tax harmonisation from the EU. I recognise that once the other EU member states bring down their company tax rates, then our competitive tax advantage will reduce, so therefore we have to work on other competitive strengths. But we must not give up on tax harmonisation. Our low tax environment has served us well. Remember we are an island off the west coast of Europe, with a five million population and limited natural resources other than our people. Therefore our future has to be international and we must be more attractive in our offerings, given our peripheral geography. We need some advantages. It is not consistent to say that the Frankfurt region, with a population of five million, should be treated exactly the same as Ireland, and let the best man win! Business is about finding advantage and I don't think Ireland should give up on the tax advantage – it has been hard fought for and is well tried and tested.

Alongside the building blocks of the success of the economy there are, in my view, a few concerns. These are all essentially linked to competitiveness – our cost environment, the semi-state sector, the regulatory environment as a substitute for competition, the health of our civil service, the state of social partnership and the move towards tax harmonisation.

Intellectual capabilities and courage

I think the scale of the Irish economic success has been miraculous. I think the building blocks had been put in place long ago and progressively contributed to our success, even though there was not a lot of underlying statistical measurement. It was the result of the intellectual capabilities of the people who had the courage and the foresight in the past, but the scale of it certainly caught me by surprise. Policy has been important, though we have made some mistakes too on public institutional reform. But I take my hat off to the IDA. People like Kieran McGowan and lately Sean Dorgan and their likes, as well as their teams, have been a critical, professional and timely part of our success story.

Ireland took off suddenly for several reasons, and as mentioned, the reasons had an impact on my own career and were part of my experience. In summary, the take-off was part of the convergence with Europe and the opening of the Single Market. Secondly, the skills learned in multinational subsidiaries and through the educational process were vital. Both the academic and the vocational, or on-the-job training, delivered a very advanced and skilled workforce of sufficient numbers in a timely way. Thirdly, the Americans had an affinity to this English-speaking island, where there were no adverse political concerns and a healthy tax environment. Fourthly, I think the ability of the Irish to operate internationally was important. It is interesting that most of the multinational companies appointed their own CEOs to start with but these managers went home very quickly. The Irish showed they could competently do the job. It is a lesson we learned in Smurfit Kappa and transplanted – for example our Latin American managers are all Latin Americans.

The future
I'm somewhat worried about the future because it is not clear to me what, industrially, the backbone of the Irish economy will be. I'm very clear at least that the intellectual capital is there and that, as with the past, this is where the future will be. I personally think in manufacturing terms, and I would worry that we might give up trying to have a strong manufacturing base, at least for the next generation. There is a generation who are unlikely to migrate to the more advanced intellectual capital-type industrial or service environment because they are not trained nor skilled in that area, and quite frankly, may be too entrenched to become so. We might again have high unemployment if the sectors which we consider new but are becoming 'traditional' were to decline too quickly. We need to work hard to stay as competitive as we can.

Competitiveness
I think competitiveness, no matter what we are involved in, is going to be critical. The cost of labour is less important when the added value is huge, but it is never unimportant. People get around to cost-efficiency, competitiveness and benchmarking, no matter how good the product is. When I was in Baileys, we had reasonably strong margins but we were aware that we had to get costs under control, because once the rapid growth phase of the product was over and we were to settle into a pattern, then the international group headquarters would start examining how are we comparing to other group companies and potential locations.

Conclusion
I think we have done a better job on the social side than people will actually admit to, but we must do much more. We haven't tackled social disadvantage as a vital component of the success, as distinct from a by-product of it. You must create wealth to distribute it and I think you have to make sure the risk-takers are properly rewarded. There is money to deal with social inclusion, to make a better society for all. But why do I see more people sleeping rough than I did twenty years ago? Why are there more drug addicts? Clearly part of it is the modernising of the country, the opening of borders and so on. Why are we not able to do more? The only

way we can make a real impact is to focus on the children coming up in the next generation. I did work with Joyce O'Connor in the National College of Ireland because I believe in inclusion – in opening the door for all to Education, Education, Education. This has been our passport to success and will continue to be. There are many success stories surrounding the more inclusive education environment and I don't think the successes are being exposed enough. More importantly, social progress has got to be a core part of the game plan of our economic success and not a by-product of it. At the end of the day, self-respect comes from education. Confidence comes from self-respect and ambition from confidence. If you don't aim, you don't achieve.

One final concern I have is a more psychological one. Without wishing to sound regressive, or like an ageing 'crank', I am concerned that our younger people, the product of the previous generations' successes, are taking it for granted. I am hugely impressed by our young people – many of them have taken the concept of success to the next level. But my concern is that they might consider the trappings of success and wealth to be their right rather than something that needs to be worked at and sustained. I hope and trust that we will not develop a soft mentality. There is a saying that 'you need to have bad days to really appreciate what the good days look like.'

CHAPTER SEVEN

Bertie Ahern, Taoiseach[1]

*Sound, evidence-based policy-making is clearly
critical to our economic success, but other factors like
workforce adaptability and business innovation have huge
roles to play. What we are seeing in this country is that all
of the factors which should allow us to continue to
succeed and to develop are here. So I think
the future is bright.*

Bertie Ahern has been elected Taoiseach (Prime Minister) of Ireland for three terms and had been in the position for ten years in 2007. Bertie Ahern was first elected Taoiseach in June 1997, re-elected in June 2002 and for a third term in June 2007. He had been Tánaiste (Deputy Prime Minister) from November to December 1994 and was Minister for Finance in 1991–4. He was Minister for Labour between 1987–91 and served as Minister in other departments too. He had been Minister of State and Government Chief Whip in 1982 and opposition whip before. First elected to the Dáil in 1977 for the constituency of Dublin-Finglas, he has been closely involved in the Northern Ireland peace process and was President of the European Union in 2004.

I don't think that the emergence of the so-called 'Celtic Tiger' was all that sudden. It had been in gestation for quite some time prior to its emergence. The economy had already moved into a relatively strong growth curve from 1987 to 1993, when I was Minister for Finance. In that first period, 1987–93, we had a GNP growth rate of 3.4 per cent per annum for a six-year period and one of the American magazines described it as 'the Celtic Tiger'. So that was a strong position and that provided a very strong basis and stimulus for the stronger growth levels that followed on later.

Four or five reasons for the economic transformation

Most of the analyses of our recent economic history agree that there were multiple reasons for the rapid, indeed radical, transformation of the Irish economy. There might be around twenty broad reasons, but I will narrow it to four or five. There are the cumulative increases, over time, of education provision and participation – there was just a huge change in education. There was our membership of the world's second biggest market, our relatively low rates of corporation tax, the capacity for rapid expansion of the labour force and the fact that we speak English. I think that these were the main factors – not that they were the only ones but they were the main factors. And these factors combined to make us attractive for foreign direct investment (FDI), especially from the United States, but not only from the United States. FDI thereby boosted employment levels, boosted the tax take and the wealth base of the economy.

Furthermore, I think that we did benefit from the EU transfers, which we used well. We used the regional fund well, we used the social fund very well and the agricultural money, which we are still using. We used these funds to build up physical infrastructure, to train our workforce and to improve the marketing capacity of our industries.

The key catalyst for growth and stability

While you could say a lot more about external factors, I strongly believe that the social partnership provided the essential context for stability and it was the key catalyst for growth, especially at the time of the severe fiscal crisis from the mid- to late 1980s. Would I agree that the turnaround began in 1987? My answer to that is a very simple 'yes'. I believe that the social partnership agreement, the Programme for National Recovery (PNR), born out of the Congress' document, *The Jobs Crisis*, and in Autumn 1986, I convinced the Party to go down and talk at Raglan Road (then the head office of the Irish Congress of Trade Unions) – that played a vital role in the whole turnout.

I should acknowledge that we were somewhat lucky in that the launch of social partnership agreements coincided with a bit of an upturn in the international economy. However, that would not have made any difference if we did not get our house in order. The series of agreements came into being in response to what were just appallingly difficult economic circumstances in the mid-1980s. The Irish economy was truly in crisis then. I was looking back at the figures the other day and they were terrible!

If you look at the main economic indicators, they were all terrible!

Unemployment – 17.5 per cent in the beginning of 1987; inflation was running at an average of 12 per cent in the ten years to 1987; real take-home pay had *decreased* by 7 per cent in the seven years from 1980 to 1987; emigration was at its highest level in 1986/87 since the late 1950s. On top of this, our public finances were in crisis in 1987. Our current budget deficit at that stage, in euro, was one and a half billion. That was a National Debt/GDP ratio of 125 per cent in 1987 when today we are at 25 per cent!

The Programme for National Recovery
I used that quote, at the time, from the London *Times,* which had a famous headline that the international moneylenders were going to 'Pull the Shutters Down on Ireland'. This was real devastation. But the government and the social partners sought to address the crisis together through the many ways outlined in the agreement, the Programme for National Recovery.

Our theory at the time was based on two big things. Moderate wage growth should give us competitiveness on which to build; employment would stabilise. With significant reductions in public spending, some control over public finances would be achieved. Secondly, the trade union members would gain in the longer term from these corrections and, in the interim, the government accepted union arguments that the value of social welfare payments would be maintained. This was a big thing at that time, because welfare payments were falling in real terms each year. Also the income tax regime would be reformed for the benefit of PAYE [Pay As You Earn] workers. These worked in parallel.

The shared understanding of autumn 1987 was critical to securing agreement on the PNR and it also set the tone for much of the subsequent incomes determination policy. Net income gains would be achieved through a combination of, on the one hand, moderate pay increases and on the other, adjustments in the personal tax regime.

Why did we take off then?
Why did we suddenly take off? Why did we not take off in the 1960s? The 1960s were good. I say the way it was in Ireland of the 1920s – we had a civil war; in the 1930s we had an economic war; in the 1940s we were getting over the Second World War; and in the 1950s we had an economic recession. From 1962 to 1968 we had a good period; in the 1970s we had the oil crisis; and in the 1980s we had our own financial crisis. It took us a long time to get ourselves going!

I think the Celtic Tiger phenomenon is now generally regarded as taking off in 1993, but its origins go back to the first social partnership agreement in 1987. I can say, at this remove, that my big concern in 1992/93 was that we were getting very good economic growth, at 3 or 4 per cent GNP growth on average (for a few of those years it was 5 per cent), but it was 'jobless growth'. The debate – when we were negotiating the PESP [Programme for Economic and Social Progress, the second national agreement in 1991] – was how do we get job growth? It was all *jobless* growth. In the first period, 1987 to 1993, the annual average GNP expanded by a very respectable 3.4 per cent and over the period from 1993 to 2000, the equivalent rate was an unparalleled and unprecedented 8.3 per cent!

So 1993 was the year; having had six years of trying to do everything right and doing it right, it was 1993 that triggered it off. The average rate, after the boom period, for 2000 to 2005 was 4.3 per cent. So if you look back, it followed from 1993. The reason growth jumped in 1993 was, even though it was painful at the time, it was the successful handling – not just by me as Minister for Finance, but the successful handling, by us all – of the currency crisis. It started in June of 1992, after the Maastricht Referendum collapsed in Denmark. If we had, as Spain, Portugal and other countries did, devalued then, as a lot of people argued we should (in the autumn or at Christmas 1992), then we would have ended up devaluing twice or three times.

The fact that we devalued once – did it at the right time, got a 10 per cent devaluation (in January 1993) – led to sixteen reductions in interest rates in the matter of about twenty weeks. That's when the economy took off! Attitudes changed, business started investing, things started moving forward.

Social partnership, while not the sole factor, was hugely helpful in the stability of managing ourselves through the currency crisis. Even though there was an election in that period, 1992, the social partners, and the trade unions in particular, held their nerve, did not take a short-term view, and we devalued quickly to ease the pressure to eliminate high interest rates (overnight rates were 17 per cent to 19 per cent). There was a massive reduction from 13.75 per cent at its lowest in the beginning of 1993, to coming out the other side with an interest rate of about 5 per cent. This allowed people to move on.

I think all the social partnership agreements to date placed a particular importance on structural reform, including what was a pro-employment emphasis, in taxation and social welfare policies. Secondly, the agreements have provided certainty and stability on a multi-annual basis. These were particularly important factors at that time. These were clearly conducive to investment and to planning. I think it yielded significant dividends in terms of industrial peace (which it did; the figures show the number of days lost due to strike action fell very significantly over that period against the pre-partnership years). I think, from the government's point of view, the social partners accepted the need for consistency between different aspects of public policy – whether it was fiscal policy, whether it was labour policy, whether it was competition policy on the one hand. On the other, there was an incomes policy which was fair. I think that was a very important factor in 1993 from a number of perspectives.

Creating the virtuous circle
Once interest rates came down, investment growth improved, net income gains improved and wealth creation improved. We have come to accept the inter-dependencies between economic and social goals in this country, but this is a distinguishing characteristic of social partnership. Just as a strong economy enables social exclusion to be effectively tackled, so does a cohesive and consistent society lead to a positive investment climate.

I think one of the things we learned in the 1990s was that social policies, aimed at promoting equality and tackling problems such as poverty and educational disadvantage, were key to a healthy society and were eminently desirable in their own terms. We put them into the second agreement, the PESP, and we kept them in thereafter. That had a very strong stabilising effect on the economy.

If you take all these factors together, the transformation from economic crisis, which happened first from 1987 to 1993, but particularly from 1993, was significantly enabled by the characteristics of social partnership, working in balance with all the other developments. That's why we stabilised the economy; started growing the economy. I think the country's social partnership model engendered a degree of economic stability – business certainty – which has proved capable of transcending political change in tackling all the asymmetrical shocks that we've had over the period.

1987 to 1993 was a slow period. Then what happened from 1993 on was rapid employment growth. In 2006 there were 85,000 new jobs. I remember when I was Chairman of the Cabinet Committee on Employment, I used to say we needed to create 30,000 jobs a year to break even. We used to ask ourselves: *would we ever create 30,000 jobs a year?*

An extraordinary increase in employment in just fifteen years
An interesting figure is that in 1990 we had one million working and by 2006 we went through the two million mark. From the foundation of the state in 1922 to 1990 we remained at around one million jobs, but it only took us fifteen years to get to two million. In any country's terms, a 100-percent increase in employment in a fifteen-year period is extraordinary! The huge increase in people at work has allowed us, in recent years, to give the

resources now (as we have been able to do) to boosting welfare, to give dignity to those who cannot work. I was very committed to the concept of a minimum wage, but we also needed to help those who hadn't got a job by giving them the increases we gave in the last three budgets. Now, not alone can you get a job, but we've been able to give greater dignity to those without jobs.

The rapid economic growth has been remarkable, but has it been a 'miraculous' period? Or has it just been a catching-up period, as some argue? What's the secret of our success? Foreign visitors are in here every week of the year asking that question! Chinese, Japanese – sometimes it's a bit over-flattering – because I think these are great countries in their own right. I think that the growth and persistence of Ireland's growth, over a long sustained period, is unprecedented. The OECD reports show it is unprecedented, not only in our own history, but you'll find few, if any, parallels elsewhere in the world. The only exception would be Japan after the Second World War, and that was reconstruction.

I acknowledge that economic growth since the 1987 period has some features of 'catch-up'. There is no argument about that! Provided we did the right thing, we were going to catch up . . . if we did the wrong things, we weren't going to! That is particularly evident in regard to infrastructural investment. The tackling of accumulated deficits has been telescoped into a few short years. We've probably built more roads since 2000 than we built in the previous forty years! It is catch-up and it certainly is the case in regard to certain areas of social provision, such as childcare, we never did anything about it before. Work/life balance, lone parents – these are areas where we hadn't a great track record.

Miracles or informed consensus-based decisions?
However, I think the remarkable change in our economic position has not been the product of miracles, but it has been due to decisions that were informed by analysis and were reached and underpinned by consensus by governments, the unions, employers and farmers.

I think those decisions, particularly in 1987 and in the years following, were often difficult and painful. I think, on the analysis front, the Programme for National Recovery was informed to a significant extent by the Strategy Report produced by the National Economic and Social Council (NESC). And that it was influenced by *The Jobs Crisis*, prepared by ICTU. The NESC comprises representatives of government and the social partners. I think it was analysis done by NESC, *A Strategy for Development, 1986 to 1990*, on which we all agreed and it underpinned the Programme for National Recovery. That, in turn, allowed us to take off. I think it is a key document, but nobody talks about it now!

A Strategy for Development set out the principles to govern the regeneration of the economy and to improve social equity. That document set the framework for the Programme for National Recovery. It was the document which I was reading during all those negotiations. It gave us the basis, along with the ICTU's *Jobs Crisis*, of producing an overall economic and social analysis which has informed every agreement since.

Consistent economic policies

We haven't changed any fundamental principle in our economic framework for progress since 1987. And there's not too many countries that can say that now! That for twenty years we have had the same analysis of how to do things. We get all our views into the NESC – get it out in a document where the parameters have broad agreement and then implement that for a period. I think it has been a great twenty-year philosophy. Whether it lasts another twenty or not is another question. But it has lasted twenty years.

I think some would argue that it took a fiscal crisis to bring us back from an economic abyss. That is true. Social partnership has engendered a long-range perspective in national economic and social policy. This is particularly evident in the current agreement, Towards 2016.

I would not subscribe to the view, however, that our economic success would have inevitably happened. I do not agree with that view. Many of the factors which contributed to our success were perhaps being thought about before 1987, but on their own, they were clearly not enough to bring about the strong economic performance that we have seen since then.

It's difficult for any fair analysis of anyone looking back at the last twenty years in this country, to resist the conclusion that social partnership agreements were the 'X Factor' which made the difference. As someone who was involved in negotiation of all agreements, except one (I was involved in implementing that one), I would say that! Yet, I think an analysis going back twenty years would show that social partnership was *the* factor that allowed us to be able to make the brave decisions and allowed us to have a sense that we could be successful. Social partnership had a huge part in that. That is my honest view – from a person who has been sitting at the cabinet table for seventeen and a half of that twenty-year period and involved as Leader of the Opposition of the other two-and-a-half-year period.

Consensus on policy formation

Has policy been extremely important? My view on that is yes, it has. And since 1987 (which is now twenty years, it's hard to believe isn't it?), policy formulation has been informed by a shared understanding at the National

Economic and Social Council and it has been supported by consensus in successive partnership agreements. This has helped us to spearhead much of the economic and social progress in the past twenty years. That's a statement of fact.

Looking a bit deeper, social partnership has had a unique influence on policy development and implementation. In particular, in my view, the requirement for extensive and often, intensive, stakeholder consultation has frequently resulted in policy being evaluated out of a self-contained slot onto a broader plain. I think that has been hugely helpful. This, in turn, has led to the pursuit of appropriate balances between different aspects of public policy, especially between fiscal, between labour, between competition policies on the one hand, and real incomes policies on the other.

Openness works

We have an open economy. Our economic policies could not have been achieved without the lift in economic growth from foreign investment. In our experience, openness works. It does work in a country which suffered as a consequence of protectionism for long enough. We've secured unprecedented gains from opening up to Europe; opening up to the wider world; but of course, openness on its own is not enough. We've had a pro-business, a pro-employment environment, underpinned with a mix of mutually consistent policies – on taxation, incomes, investment, education and skills. All of these were consistently employed and continue to be of critical importance in this era of globalisation.

We have been greatly helped as well by demographic factors. Ireland has one of the youngest populations in Europe, with 40 per cent under twenty-five. Demographic trends mean that we continue to have a capacity for growth far ahead of our EU partners. Demographic factors and our infrastructural investment are coming together in the sense now that, providing we keep ourselves well focused, the future is good. That is, as long as we don't get arrogant and think that we can walk on water – as some people do in this country – who think that you just press the auto-pilot button and it all goes. I think that if we are sensible, if we make adjustments when you have to make adjustments; if politicians of the future have the political courage to do that, then the future outlook is good.

I had to make adjustments in 1984 and everyone howled at me then. They said that adjustments will lead to ruination. They called the adjustments 'cutbacks' – because public expenditure was only going up by 8 per cent instead of 12 per cent! They said it was a 'cutback' even though spending was going up! It was nonsensical stuff! I said we'll do this for a short time and then we'll get back into growth again. And we did! Everyone forgets what you said then.

Looking to the future

I hope politicians of the future have more guts than politicians in the past. In my view, politicians in the 1970s and 1980s didn't have much courage. Most made mistakes in many analyses they did in the 1970s and 1980s, and that includes some of my own party as well.

Looking to the future, we how have almost 40 per cent of our twenty-five- to thirty-four-year-olds being educated to third level. We are still getting in really good foreign direct investment; we're educating people now to a high standard, and we are spending lots of money on Science Foundation Ireland and the R&D programmes.

One week in 2007, it went without notice in the country that we had about twenty-five major companies bringing their European R&D, and some world sectors, into this country. We used to always say these foreign multinationals would run out of the country because they don't have their research here. In 2006, twenty-five of them decided to come in here and open up their research here. It should be a huge story in itself.

Sound, evidence-based policy-making is critical

Most importantly, our people have a reputation for a positive attitude, for hard work, flexibility and above of all, for innovation. Looking to the future, our people are coming up with new ideas, processes, new methods of operating. Research and development is happening in this country, so new products, new processes will be invented in this country, which will lead to greater innovation. That innovation will lead to more investment coming here; that will give more quality employment. Sound, evidence-based policy-making is clearly critical to our economic success, but other factors like workforce adaptability and business innovation have huge roles to play. What we are seeing in this country is that all of the factors which should allow us to continue to succeed and to develop are here. So I think the future is bright.

We just have to keep developing the sectors we are good at. We are really doing well in financial services, the broad range of chemicals, in the broad term of pharmaceuticals, medical appliances, medical innovation, bio-medical engineering, bio-pharma and in the food area, in quality food. We might not be able to compete in the mass production of foods, but I think we really can do well in quality foods and food ingredients.

With the benefit of hindsight

What would I have done differently, with the benefit of hindsight? If I, for one, if I had realised, when I went into the Department of Finance (at that time the National Debt to GDP ratio was about 110), if I ever had thought that by 2006/7, we would have a debt/GDP ratio of *under* 25 per cent, then I should have done more of the infrastructural work. If you were to net off (as Cadbury accounting rules would allow) the pension reserve, the debt/GDP ratio would probably be about fifteen per cent. At that time, to get into EMU, you were required to have a debt/GDP ratio of 60 per cent or lower, by the EU. I remember wondering how are we ever going to get below 60 per cent for this country?

When we had the high unemployment of 230,000, I would have built the Metro to Dublin airport, and probably the eastern bypass tunnel (and at more attractive prices than we will be able to do it in the future). So if there was one change that I would have made, it would be far greater investment in infrastructure.

Another disappointment that I see was that the private sector did not proceed with a second Dublin tunnel. Back in 1992, the government had decided between two routes. One route was to go west (underneath the Liffey, underneath Heuston Station and on out to the Chapelizod bypass), the other route was the one we did build – the Port Tunnel. I had hoped that the private sector would build the other one. Tom Roche Snr had done the feasibility study for it and their work was far advanced. The analysis was that their one was up through town and so should be much more viable than the Port Tunnel. The state would do the harder one, the port/airport one. They looked at it for another year and decided not to proceed.

With a huge workforce at that time and a lot of skilled and trained people, we paid them dole or left them to emigrate, rather than take the risk of further investment. If I had ever known that the debt/GDP ratio would be 25 per cent today, I tell you, I would have got all the infrastructure built years ago! If you had asked me if that would have been the right thing to do, it would have been.

Nobody saw it! If I had stood up in one of my budgets (of 1992 to 1994) and had said, listen, I am deciding to put the debt/GDP ratio up another 5 or 6 per cent next year, not on current spending, but on investment through the Capital Programme for infrastructure. If I'd said 'I am doing this, because I believe this investment will reduce the national debt dramatically in the years ahead,' everyone would have said 'What kind of an eejit is that?' Well that's how it goes! That's the only thing I would dramatically change.

And we would have had the benefit of the infrastructure which would have left us in a stronger position now to develop the economy into the future.

The IDA and foreign direct investment
On the role of foreign direct investment (FDI), the four sectors chosen by the Industrial Development Authority (IDA) were crucial. First, financial

services have created thousands of jobs, high-quality jobs. It never ceases to amaze me how broad financial services are. Financial services are a huge employer and a quality employer.

Secondly, there is the whole chemicals area. It is complicated but there is very good employment, very good capital investment in the chemicals sector. It is only when you go down into Cork, Ringaskiddy, that you see the quality of the employment, top-class engineers and scientists etc.

Pharmaceuticals is the third sector. Pharmaceuticals are terrific! A lot of those companies came in here probably to manufacture and then maybe move on. You take six of the top ten drugs in the world today – six of the top ten life drugs in the world today are made in this country. They are now researched – advanced research – in this country. It is incredible that a small island has 60 per cent of the top ten drugs used throughout the whole world and their advanced research is being done here. So the knock-on of that for the future is very good. Their R&D bases are coming in here and their scientists are coming in here and the work is being done here, the investment is here. Wyeths is a €2bn investment.

We have now located three or four more factories around the country for future companies that we are targeting for the end of this decade. I've done a lot of work with the IDA in trying to cajole these companies to invest here. I have gone to places like Davos to talk to the chief executives of these companies, with the IDA, to try and tell the story of Ireland and of why they should come here and nowhere else.

All the executives of these companies who come in and sit here [the Taoiseach's office], particularly in pharmaceuticals and chemicals, tell me they make their investments based on thirty-year investment plans. They do not work on a five-year, ten-year plan. So if you get these companies in here between now and 2010, then they will be here till 2040! These are the real things that make the difference for Ireland. So, we are not fluttering around on things that might change fundamentally in a year or two and then they'd be gone.

The final sector is the whole medical appliances and medical supplies industry – a huge industry. There is multi-trillion investment in these industries. We now have a base of these companies here. We have nearly 1,000 companies in this country in those four categories – financial services, pharmaceuticals, chemicals, and medical appliances and supplies. That is the basis for a strong Ireland into the future!

We have the right sectors, but we could do with a few more. We have to try and make sure we get spin-offs such as bio-pharma and keep our sciences up to the top of the scale. It is hugely important to keep our young people up to the fore. We have to make sure that we are constantly upskilling the people. I think it's great that so many leaving school are going into third-level education. You need to get them into the third-level education because, the longer you keep them in the educational system, the better. It almost doesn't matter what faculty they are studying in.

We have been looking at what areas are most short of people. It's in the whole tourism-related area. You don't have to be a rocket scientist to be in a job in the future. There is a huge number of good quality jobs in the services area. You have to be quite an expert being a plain, simple barman now, with the range of people now in Ireland and the range of drinks. It is no longer a fella coming in for a pint of Guinness and a pint of Bass. Your regular barman has now to be able to do cocktails for the French and Swiss who are coming. There are umpteen opportunities. The same with our tradespeople as our construction sites become more complex. One job might be gone in one area, but there are a whole lot of new jobs emerging in other sectors.

Working together at firm level
In regard to the importance of new forms of work and of partnership at firm level in our economic success, I've put a lot of effort and money into the National Centre for Partnership. We have to try to bring partnership down to the shop floor. It works well where people do it well . . . where people work out what are the objectives which they are trying to achieve; how is the company doing; giving employees the facts about the company; making people feel that they are part of the company. Where you get businesses that share information and genuinely work together; where they don't have rigid hierarchies – giving homilies down to the workforce – it works far better. We need far more workplace partnerships. I have put a lot of effort into this and tried to put a lot of resources into it.

CHAPTER EIGHT

Olivia O'Leary, Broadcaster[1]

Civil society should create the sort of space where we could have real debate about the sort of country we wanted to have, or the sort of values we regard as central to our society. We still have not had that debate.

Olivia O'Leary is a political analyst and broadcaster whose astute observations are well known in Ireland and the UK. A former *Irish Times* journalist, she was the key presenter of the BBC's *Newsnight*, RTE's *Prime Time*, BBC Radio 4's *Between Ourselves* and other programmes. While known for her political insights, she has been a perceptive observer of the rapid economic progress in Ireland and also of how it has impacted on Irish society.

There were many reasons for the sudden emergence of the Celtic Tiger. There was a large dollop of luck and there was a certain amount of national will involved as well. The obvious factors were a) our position in the EU, b) the decision in 1987 to try to get the country's finances together, c) the decision to provide the industrial relations stability which we have since had, and d) the already existing carrot which was the low corporate tax rate. There was also e) the foreign investment process, particularly the US route which had been established by the Industrial Development Authority (IDA) since the 1960s. Central to the success of that process was f) the fact that we spoke English, g) that we had never had a proper industrial revolution, which meant that we did not have heavy old-fashioned industry that needed to be reformed and so we were able to progress in a leap, h) the educated workforce and the investment in education. All of these things contributed to the take-off.

Reasons beyond the economic for success

However, I think that there were other reasons going on outside the economic. Things had been moving in the undergrowth for the previous two to three decades, and they exploded into the open in the late 1980s. Suddenly we saw the fast erosion of the old 'authorities' and the old vested interests. Socially, things were changing. This is not to say that the 1980s wasn't a disastrous period politically and economically. It was. I think we could have achieved the prosperity we now have back in the 1980s had there not been a government so at odds within itself that it could not decide to take the right economic direction. There was constant tension between Fine Gael's attempts at fiscal rectitude and Labour's syndicalism and statism.

Challenging the power of the church

But socially things did change in the 1980s. Garret FitzGerald challenged the power of the Church. There was a real attempt to establish a state where church and state were indeed separate. I think that that is actually very, very important as it frees up energies and freedoms that are otherwise repressed. I think an enterprising society needs those freedoms and that sense of individuality and freedom. I think it is no coincidence, for instance, that other post-Catholic countries such as Portugal and Spain, which have also separated church and state, have begun to experience the same sort of economic boom as ours. I do think there is a lot of truth in the old adage that the Protestant work ethic enabled industrial development and wealth creation. The notion of *individual responsibility* would seem to be central to entrepreneurial spirit.

Those great and, at times, enormously time-wasting, campaigns in the 1980s, over issues like contraception, divorce and abortion, took place on territory where the Catholic Church had traditionally had an absolute stranglehold on public debate. Not any more.

Class change through education

I think that there was something else going on in the undergrowth – class change. The investment in free secondary education in the late 1960s and then in the very early 1970s, student grants for third level – all this educational investment created a different sort of social mobility. I think the class system in Ireland really began to loosen up from the 1970s onwards with the fact that there was no longer just a very small elite which had a monopoly over educational wealth. I think education was that movement in the undergrowth which generated greater mobility.

The other thing that started to happen in the 1980s – here the dreaded name *Thatcher* comes in – was the breaking down of the old state monoliths. I think that was extraordinarily important. Up until then there was the great authority called the 'state', which the Church totally approved of, as the Church totally approved of the class system – one authority backed up the other. The authority of the state began, little by little, to be taken apart. The state was no longer involved in job creation in the way that it used to be. It was no longer providing telephone or airline services, or indeed running hotels or fertiliser factories. We didn't look any more to the state as a job provider. Instead we began to look to the private sector and to ourselves. The vested interests were being challenged.

A hunger for change

The economic misery of the 1980s – the economic stagnation, the unemployment, the dreadful emigration – left people hungry for change. Therefore, instead of the normal resistance that one might have found in 1987 to what that incoming government was trying to do, people welcomed any movement forward. Take the economic interests of the employers and unions. They had been so battered by recession that the employers were desperate for any progress towards growth and the unions were desperate for jobs. Their membership was decimated by unemployment and they were terrified that what had happened in Britain with Thatcher might happen here. Charlie Haughey offered them a different way out. For all they knew, if they had not agreed to the partnership process, Haughey would quite have easily gone down the Thatcher route. They knew that only too well.

So the awful economic depression of the 1980s created a readiness for radical change. The usual resistance that might have been expected was gone. Indeed, the cuts in spending in education and health in the late 1980s would usually have led to massive protests. There were protests from the teachers' unions and from the health unions, but not what one might have expected. Basically everybody decided that we had no choice.

Because change was vital if we were to stop the erosion of our sense of self as a nation. I recall parents talking to me in the middle of the 1980s saying 'We do not regard this as our country if our children cannot live here.' I remember a woman saying to me 'I spend Christmas day talking to Philadelphia, Sydney and New York because that is where my family are. Don't talk to me about being a citizen of this country. If this country can't keep my children here, if it cannot provide jobs and livelihoods for my children, well then, that puts a major question mark over my sense of citizenship and my sense of belonging.'

People who made a difference

I think that the economic devastation of the 1980s challenged our very sense of identity. We knew we needed to do something. For his decisiveness at the end of the 1980s – if not in his previous incarnation as Taoiseach in the early 1980s – one has to give credit to Charles Haughey. But there are other politicians whom I believe were very important. One was Alan Dukes, Leader of the Opposition who offered support for economic reform to Haughey's minority government through his Tallaght Strategy. What if it had been the other way around? What if it was Alan who was Taoiseach and Charlie Haughey who was opposition leader – would this have happened? I don't know. We were lucky that it did happen that way because Alan Dukes made reform possible.

The other thing that happened at the same time (and remember we are living on an island) was that there was another party leader who took a decision in the common good and who was willing to take a stand, even though it would hurt his party. That was John Hume. It was very much an individual decision on his part. He knew the risks he was taking by contacting the Provos but nothing else had worked. Nothing else had stopped the violence. He met the Provos and they needed him. Hume was the vital link; his was the hand that went out to bring them in.

So what did you have on screens of America from Northern Ireland for the first time in decades? You had Ireland as a *good news* story just at the time when the IDA was trying to get American investment into Ireland. These things matter. America is a *good news country*. I think that the sense that the Irish were trying to get things together – not only economically, but politically as well – all that helped put us on the US investment map. This probably helped the IDA enormously at a time when the Irish political and business class in the US was maturing and a whole generation of Irish-American business people were beginning to surface in senior positions in corporate America.

One last politician I will mention is Garret FitzGerald. While there were an awful lot of things Garret FitzGerald got wrong – the economy in the 1980s being one – there were some things he got right. One of them was that he established stable foundations for an ongoing relationship between Dublin and London. He set up a real relationship of co-operation. This was vital as it meant the two governments established close channels of communication which could not be blocked by the extremists on both their sides. This was the foundation on which the peace process was built and the political stability that it helped create was central to attracting foreign investment.

Cultural, social, political and institutional factors also drove change
So I don't think that what happened in 1987 was just an economic phenomenon. It was cultural, social, political and institutional. It was necessary institutionally to throw off the oppressive power of the Catholic Church and to separate it from the state. It was necessary too to throw off the weight of state control of the economy. Until those oppressive authorities (church and state) were undermined, I don't know if we would have felt free enough to develop the entrepreneurial spirit.

Consensus and compromise
There was a national will for economic change and the readiness for consensus and compromise and this was reflected in the social partnership process. Charles Haughey helped to create both the consensus and the compromise. Bertie Ahern was probably a far greater exponent of the whole consensual approach. Haughey just took it and ran with it. Union leaders will tell you that Haughey made it clear they had little choice, that he put his cards on the table and said 'This is how it is. Take it or leave it.' Not only that – when the employers' representative bodies were dragging their feet about coming to an agreement, he went over their heads to business leaders that he knew personally and involved them in the talks, forcing the representative bodies to come in behind them. He was absolutely hands-on in the whole process.

The type of society we have today is different. We have successfully freed ourselves from the stranglehold of the old vested interests. This has helped us to build an economy. However, it doesn't help us to build a society. This is one of the things we haven't put in place – the sort of civil society that's needed to take the place of the authoritarian institutions – particularly the Church.

Debate about the sort of country we want
Civil society should create the sort of space where we could have real debate about the sort of country we wanted to have, or the sort of values we regard as central to our society. We still have not had that debate, partly because there is the slight shadow of the Church there still, but also because we have never had the tradition of speaking out openly. There was always an authority figure somewhere watching us, pulling us down if we said the wrong thing. And you could pay dear for speaking out. It could cost you your job or your ability to get a phone or a house or a job or even a loan for a house!

So we've got rid of the authority figures but we haven't yet filled the spaces they left behind. We need an adult and open debate about the sort of society we want, a society we can shape ourselves, with values that we choose.

Whose values?
There are a whole series of issues we've never had a proper debate about. Do we want the sort of health or education service we have inherited? For instance, do we want the Roman Catholic Church to control almost all the primary schools? Why is it that in a system where everything is paid for totally by you and me, yet the people who make almost all the decisions are parish priests? That creates a situation, for instance, where we have the Archbishop of Dublin saying, on one hand, that he wants this to be an inclusive society that welcomes immigrants and their families. That is what he is saying in public. But at parish level, like out in Diswellstown and areas like that in west Dublin, the local priests are deciding that people have to produce baptismal certificates now to be allowed to get their children into school. It may be that this is a way of rationing spare places, but it means that children of immigrants from places such as the Baltic states (which are not all Catholic) are excluded. Nobody is being 'racist' – all they want is your baptismal certificate.

Who controls Irish education?
There we are allowing an unelected authority to make a decision on how our educational system is run and it is determining the values in such a system. We have to be brave enough to address this. Former TD [Dáil Deputy] Liz O'Donnell did address this in the Dáil [parliament] and there were ructions. The Taoiseach said the Church was doing a great job in the educational system and all the rest of it! I don't deny that. I had wonderful Mercy nuns at school and they schooled me for scholarships and without them, I would never had got through to university.

But still, those who pay the piper should call the tune. We have got the church out of our beds and our sexual lives, but we still have not challenged it in many very important areas – such as schools and hospitals.

Space for debate – free of fear
We have a society that still has not created enough space to talk to itself and to decide what its values are. That, we desperately need to do. More than anything else, we need to create space for debate and discussion, free of fear. We still haven't managed to do that.

There are all sorts of other areas which we need to address. For instance, we have welcomed in immigrants (and without them we would not have a lot of the prosperity which we now have) but we have not sat down and decided what the core values of being Irish are. Are there basic human rights that we will not allow to be compromised, no matter what the religious belief or cultural traditions of the incoming group? I think there are such basic rights and they must include full freedom for women economically and socially. Can we agree to having a situation in this country where – behind the smokescreen of cultural or religious tradition – women are oppressed? We used to allow the Roman Catholic Church to do that. We shouldn't ever let it happen again.

Therefore, if we welcome people into this country, they should have the benefit of whatever human rights that we think should apply to every Irish citizen and to everybody resident in this country. This is a debate we need to start having very, very quickly. We don't want to follow Britain's form of multiculturalism, where the authorities turned a blind eye to what was happening to some of its citizens. Take, for example, those young women who were taken off to the Yemen and Pakistan and married off to people whom they had never met, at the age of fourteen or fifteen. They were all British citizens who were not protected by their own country. I do not want to see that happening here.

We have to look too at how we protect children and how we support parents. Are we ready to develop and pay for proper childcare systems for parents who work? Do we help those who stay at home to look after their families and ensure that they are not punished by inadequate pension provision in later years?

So there are a lot of debates on values that we actually need to have. We got used to being told, for years and years, what our values should be as a nation. We haven't learned to develop our own. We are still an 'adolescent society'. We are reacting against things rather than deciding what it is we want. So I think that this is the big issue for the future. We need to find arenas in which that debate can take place.

I think the national broadcasting service is one arena where those debates need to take place in a braver and wider way than they have taken place so far. These debates also need to take place at a community level.

One of the things that strikes me is that there is reluctance on our part to actually take hold of our country. You can see that in the abusive way that public spaces are treated, that national monuments are treated. People still aren't ready to believe that 'this is ours'. It is a post-colonial attitude. It is still there and it is long past its time.

Some of the great cultural institutions have tried very hard to make that connection between the people and their inheritance. For example the National Museum is doing a fantastic work of evangelising. It got playwright Frank McGuinness – the man who wrote *Observe the Sons of Ulster Marching Towards the Somme* – to come on radio and talk about its recent military uniform exhibition. Its guitar exhibition brought in the sort of people who would never usually put a foot inside a museum. Its collections and the exhibitions have been expanded. Its costume section shows how people dressed and how different cloths like linen or worsted are made. That ordinary stuff is terrific because, unlike museums like the British Museum which shows the imperial booty from other people's countries, which are meant to impress, or even to intimidate, this is an attempt to show you the type of lives ordinary people have lived. I think that sort of cultural proselytising is very important. I think that the National Gallery and the National Library have done the same. The Joyce and the Yeats exhibitions were both terrific.

I think we need more reaching out to ordinary people from public institutions like these, to show them what is theirs, in order to develop their sense of self and their respect for public space. We also need a lot more travelling exhibitions so that people in Kerry can see the exhibitions, without having to pay the price of a six-hour train journey to come to Dublin to see them.

Let's behave like a Republic. I think that that is probably where we need to go. This is a Republic. That means something. It means there is a *real* commitment to the universality of what is provided in terms of public service; in terms of equality of opportunity; of inclusiveness.

A sense of community

The notion that this is '*our* land' and '*our* landscape' has not quite yet come into operation. The idea that you can build what you want on your father's land is more predominant than the idea that you are the keeper of the landscape for the nation. We still don't have the attitude that we are only a temporary holder of the land. Look at the Irish countryside and there are gaping gashes in it – unlike the English countryside where the planning authorities are stricter. See the rape of Donegal!

The Irish planning process does not work and the whole local authority system is utterly unresponsive to its own local residents. There is no functioning local democracy and local councillors have no real powers compared to those of unelected officials. We really need to have a proper relationship between the local authorities and the people. There is no place that we meet. The local authority does not bring us together. In France, the local community is involved in the process with the *Mairie* in each local village.

Some places in Ireland have that sense of community naturally . . . we have a house in my father's home town, Graignamanagh. There is a strong sense of community there. There is a local band (said to be the oldest in the British Isles) and it plays at every local festival. It plays on Christmas and Easter mornings. During August it plays during the regatta, the swimming races, the boat races, etc. The whole community came together to restore the thirteenth-century Duiske Abbey. There is a good local citizen's advice bureau, manned voluntarily, by the local community. People write books regularly about Graignamanagh. It just has a spirit of its own and that comes from the sense of pride people have about the place.

A sense of hope that is contagious
I am not one of those who bemoan all that has been lost along Ireland's road to prosperity. I have no wish to go back to the economic and intellectual poverty of the fifties. There is a sense of hope in Ireland now that is contagious. But we still behave as though all the good times might disappear tomorrow. So we go on a mad spending spree instead of investing our wealth in the things that will make life better for the long term – better education and health services, better public infrastructure, better planning, and a country which is shaped as we wish it to be, not as others have decreed we must have it. We've worked for this country. Now we must make sure it works for us.

CHAPTER NINE

Analysis of the Reasons
for the Irish Economic Success

From the comment and analysis in the previous chapters, it is clear that there are many reasons for the emergence of the Celtic Tiger and the Irish economic success. Back in 1997, the author set out fifteen reasons.[1] A number of other reasons which may have impacted are added below, as well as others added by the interviewees, giving around twenty reasons for the economic success. These are not ordered in priority because there is not agreement on what were the most important, as has been seen.

Policy had an impact on those reasons which have an asterisk *. The reasons for the Irish economic success are divided into those which were external to Ireland and those which were internal, and policy-makers had influence over many of the latter.

External reasons

The external economic environment
This factor is almost a given. The contribution of the external economic environment is of vital importance to any economy in this era of globalisation but it is especially so to a small open economy like Ireland. A benign external environment is of help. An international shock can have a big impact on a small, globally integrated economy as Ireland has become. For some of the earlier years of the take-off, economic growth in EU15 countries was low and was even negative overall in one year, 1993, but it rose from 1994. It was also low in the UK in the early 1990s, but was strong in the 1990s in the US.

The EU funds and membership of the European Union
One of the great success stories of the EU over decades has been the international social solidarity of wealth redistribution, through the transfer

of billions between and within countries, to narrow the gap between them. This has been of great benefit to states like Ireland, Greece, Spain and Portugal. Germany was the main benefactor, but the cost of subsidising the reunited Germany over fifteen years left it a poorer country and Germans are no longer willing to subsidise the Poles or Bulgarians to the same extent. Today, in a Europe up from 300 million to over 500 million, the inequalities are greater than ever. For example, central London is three times wealthier than the EU average, while north-eastern Romania is barely at one quarter.[2] The rich regions want to pay less. The subsidies to Polish and new accession farmers today are a fraction of those paid to Irish farmers. Ireland was fortunate to join Europe when it had a more social democratic leadership.

The EU structural and cohesion funds amounted to a mini-mini-Marshall Plan, according to Professor Frances Ruane, but were of help to the Irish economy, especially when the government was cutting capital investment. Membership of the European Union, especially with the access to the huge Single Market from 1992 and the enforcement of competition law, conferred one of the major benefits to Ireland.

Bertie Ahern believed the EU funds were very important and were used well. 'I think that we did benefit from the EU transfers, which we used well. We used the regional fund well, we used the social fund very well and the agricultural money, which we are still using. We used these funds to build up physical infrastructure, to train our workforce and to improve the marketing capacity of our industries.' David Begg listed them as important and also made the point that Ireland spent them well. 'The disciplines that Europe required for the implementation of the projects were probably very good for the Irish public service. It did a very good job in ensuring that the funds were well employed,' and 'helped mitigate a disastrous period.' But Begg was critical of the use of some of the funds spent on training, which was not productive 'when, for example, we were training the unemployed for jobs which were not there in the 1980s', though the 'investment in people was vital to the take-off, when it came.'

Professor Frances Ruane called the Structural Funds 'a mini-mini-Marshall Plan' but said, 'however small the funds were, they became available at a crucial point' when capital spending was being cut, and they brought new standards into public-sector decision-making. She found that these funds were well spent in Ireland compared to southern Italy. In contrast, Peter Sutherland argued that 'other countries, like Spain and Portugal, used European Union Structural Funds effectively for the development of their infrastructure.' He did not mince his words on the use of these funds. He argued that we 'largely wasted these funds'. He said that 'much of them were spent on social programmes, training programmes, which were of limited real value. In my opinion, the money could have provided the infrastructure which we still notably lack.'

The Single Market

The other businessmen interviewed did not focus on the EU funds, but rather on access to the market. But Sutherland placed a great emphasis on, not just membership of the EU, and on the establishment of the Single Market in 1992, a project with which he was centrally involved, but on its success as a functioning Single Market. He said that 'the 300 or so proposals which were put through during the Delors Commission period to create the 1992 project generated an entirely different approach to national markets in the European Union.' Until 1992, there were myriads of state aids, little control over them, and grants and subsidies which were given out by governments which generally favoured their own national companies. They also created artificial barriers to market entry, such as the 'Poitiers case', where all goods exported to France had to come through Poitiers, and could be stuck there for months! This unified market meant US firms operating out of Ireland (or Irish or Belgian firms) now had an equal chance of selling into any corner of the European market of 300 million. While it was seen that Microsoft set up in Ireland to come to Europe before the Single Market, its formation was of undoubted importance to the company. Virtually all of those interviewed stated that the Single Market was central to the economic success. In conclusion, perhaps one of the most important factors in Ireland's economic success and perhaps the major determinant of the *timing* of the success was the creation of the European Single Market in 1992. The EU funds helped too, but their timing and the rules around them were important.

Foreign direct investment*

While the flow of foreign direct investment (FDI) is ultimately determined in the boardrooms of multinational companies (MNCs), it is strongly influenced by a government's industrial and other policies. Thus governments' domestic policies can greatly influence the distant boardrooms and it is strongly argued by several of our interviewees that this was so.

On the role of foreign direct investment (FDI), the Taoiseach, Mr Ahern, said that we made ourselves attractive for the investors with investment in education, our openness, our membership of the world's biggest market, 'the capacity for rapid expansion of the labour force and the fact that we speak English', low company taxes and 'a pro-business environment'. He also said the 'the four sectors chosen by the Industrial Development Authority (IDA) were crucial.' These were financial services, chemicals, pharmaceuticals and 'the whole medical appliances and medical supplies industry – a huge industry'.

The Taoiseach concluded that 'our economic policies could not have been achieved without the lift in economic growth from foreign investment. In our experience, openness works.' And he admitted that ours was 'a country which suffered as a consequence of protectionism for long enough'.

Peter Sutherland believed 'that by far the two most important issues in terms of our relative growth in the intervening period have been the reduction in corporation tax and inward investment. Foreign direct investment (FDI) in turn has been the crucial element in stabilising and ultimately causing significant growth in our economy.' He believed that the development of the International Financial Services Centre (IFSC) in Dublin was important too as part of FDI and he gave an interesting insight into how it was achieved within EU rules. He believed that FDI was very important because the performance of indigenous industry was poor with only a few companies of international calibre at that time. 'We did not seem to have an innovative and entrepreneurial indigenous sector. We do have now, but it is only beginning to grow and it's a very late developer.'

Why they chose Ireland

Peter Sutherland gave a valuable insight into why FDI firms chose Ireland at the time they did and so boosted the Celtic Tiger boom. Until the Single Market was enacted in 1992, the lack of controls on state aids meant that a US company wanting to locate in Europe would be 'attracted to locate firstly by major hand-outs by countries like France; and secondly major impediments to get into that market.' He said that many of 'the European countries used every conceivable barrier to stop goods being exported into their domestic markets, even from other EU countries. It was the 1992 project that really changed this.' He held that policy in Europe was also important and particularly helped Ireland at that time. 'It was that Commission, between 1985 and 1989, which created the 1992 project and drove the opening up of markets. That created an entirely new dynamic for foreign direct investment into Ireland. Suddenly, Ireland became as good a location for access to the French market as was France.'

On the impact of Irish policy on FDI firms, Sutherland was unstinting in his praise for certain individuals, as were other interviewees. He said of industrial policy and the IDA, 'I believe a great deal of the thinking on it and the IDA was put together by Michael Killeen and Ray McLoughlin in the early days.' He continued, 'I think the IDA is the great success of the state agencies – a wonderful success story. The ability to attract industry has been phenomenal. It deserves a great deal of credit.'

David Begg of ICTU said while 'FDI is not as important in employment terms – the foreign sector employs 150,000 people out of two million,' it is very important for exports and output, dominating both and also boosting indigenous spin-offs. Begg raised other issues around FDI including governance of multinational firms and the process of globalisation.

Sutherland said that there were over 300 rules agreed by the then fifteen member states to establish the Single Market. These rules were then enforced, and the huge Single Market began to work very well. In a discussion of globalisation, which he strongly supports, David Begg called for similar rules to be established to give greater security to workers and citizens. 'In a truly multilateral world, global rules and institutions would ensure a level playing field for workers and producers in all countries, big and small. There must be legitimate political governance of globalisation and for domestic policies which smooth transitions and compensate those who lose in the process.' He concluded by saying 'business leaders have not realised that they are sailing close to the wind in the pursuit of low taxes and deregulation. The lessons of history are staring them in the face. The first era of globalisation collapsed in 1914 and in between, we had the worst recession, war and fascism.'

Begg also raised the question of whether we are too dependent on MNCs, and said Ireland is 'weak in our indigenous industrial base'. What 'I would like to see is Ireland being more like the Nordic countries' which have 'four or five dominant domestic MNCs in each of those countries, and they appear to have a commitment to their country of origin.' He was worried that the successful Irish MNCs 'could be taken over by private equity capitalists who have no commitment to anything, except short-term profits and rapid pay-backs of leveraged debt.' He warned that 'it is turbo capitalism where private equity firms or hedge funds invest in a company mainly to strip out value as hard and as fast as they can. They have no long-term commitment to the firm and no interest in developing any relationship with labour. It leaves us unions in a difficult situation.'

Hungry for business

The reasons why one of the world's leading companies came to Ireland was elaborated by Joe Macri of Microsoft. He pointed out that it was not a leading company when it set up in Ireland, and he gave superb insight into why it chose this country. He asked 'What brought us here? The first point is that we didn't really make a decision to come to Ireland; we made a decision to come to Europe. ... Secondly, why Ireland and not a bigger country in Europe? The answer was the government was hungry for the business and it still is' and it 'made a compelling case as to why Europe equalled Ireland. Thirdly, the case they made was then around a young, educated workforce that was relatively low cost, and they had this low corporate tax rate that made it more attractive.' The fourth reason was that it's an English-speaking country and 'language is a barrier when you are an American coming to Europe'. And he pointed out while language was not 'in any business plan or in any cost justification document, it certainly was a reason that people considered.' He also said that 'the IDA played an important role too'.

Macri gave a wonderful insight into the commitment of that government, the state and its agencies, in selling Ireland to foreign multinationals. The CEO of Microsoft, Steve Ballmer, told him that after a meeting with the Irish government, he was mightily impressed. He said 'I'm normally the sales guy – I am normally selling to governments. That is the first lunch I have been to where the government was selling to me.' Macri made the point that this kind of thing does not make it into corporations' business plans!

He said the FDI greatly contributed to the scale of the economic success that Ireland had. 'The multinationals have contributed significantly to the economy over the years and also introduced new work practices and work culture which has had an impact on other companies based in Ireland.' There was also 'a clustering effect' and he said that Microsoft Ireland, as an 'anchor tenant', effectively helped the Irish government to sell Ireland to other companies.

Gary McGann, head of Ireland's first foreign multinational, Smurfit Kappa, told an interesting story of how Irish executives persuaded a foreign MNC to establish roots and remain here. The Swedish telecoms company, Ericsson, had only set up a plant here to build a modern telecoms infrastructure for the state and then leave when the job was done. He said that when the work was finishing by 1980, the 'projections were that the Ericsson business model would support just ten people in this country five years later. So we had to change the business model.' He said that 'by 1985, Ericsson had over 1,000 people working in this country, instead of the ten projected. This ultimately came down to the vision of Vincent Daly [the Irish CEO of Ericssons] who was keen to keep the company in Ireland.' He showed how the Irish managers set out 'to find out everything about the Ericsson model and, most importantly, to win over the Swedes', which was done successfully.

McGann pointed out that 'while nobody should underestimate the importance of American investment in Ireland, there was other international investment in the country', such as Ericsson's. He also said the IFSC was important in attracting firms here and told a story of how one firm was won over to invest here. Again English-speaking comes out as much more important to US firms than one would have thought. McGann told how the US private equity firm (which owns part of Smurfit Kappa) is a very reluctant investor in Europe due to culture – because 'the enterprise culture is fundamentally different, the attitude is different, but most particularly, the Americans don't have a strong attraction to doing business other than in the English language. In my view, they experience difficulties when not being in control of communication.'

A good news country

Olivia O'Leary gave a different perspective to the others on FDI and one which is very important. She said John Hume played an important part in the Northern Ireland peace process at a crucial time. 'So what did you have on screens of America from Northern Ireland for the first time in decades? You had Ireland as a *good news* story just at the time when the IDA was trying to get American investment into Ireland. These things matter. America is a *good news country*' and this 'helped the IDA enormously at a time when the Irish political and business class in the US was maturing and a whole generation of Irish-American business people were beginning to surface in senior positions in corporate America', she suggested, also bringing out the importance of the new Irish-Americans now heading large US corporations. Ms O'Leary said that the role of the IDA since the 1960s in establishing the whole foreign investment process, particularly the US route, was important, as were membership of the EU, along with low taxes, English-speaking and other factors.

Globalisation

To conclude, Ireland stands out as a real success of the process of globalisation. But had Ireland opened up to globalisation, to foreign direct investment, ten years earlier, it might have avoided many years of forced emigration and relative poverty. It might have taken off sooner. Yet Ireland must be one of the world's greatest showcases for the benefits of FDI and of successful globalisation. This little island with its relatively low costs, burgeoning population of relatively well educated young people, with its low company taxes, grants, active state agencies and membership of the EU, and latterly the Single Market, was a huge beneficiary of FDI and of the process of globalisation. The firms that invested here have done very well too, with particularly high profits cited by the US Bureau of Commerce.

There is some unease around the area of globalisation internationally, not least in the US. There is, however, growing recognition, even by institutions like the OECD and World Bank, of the necessity to compensate the losers in globalisation. This is an area where rules are being made, but it is clear that growing numbers of citizens need reassurance and the development of rules for the international market, such as are being drawn up by the WTO under the Doha Round, will be a helpful start on international governance.

The revolution in communications*
Ireland's economic failure was for so long blamed on its peripheral location as 'an island, off an island, off Europe'. The revolution in communications and reduction in transport costs were a factor in the boom. These were not dealt with by the interviewees except for Frances Ruane who made the point that both disproportionately favoured a small island economy as they reduced the costs of integrating into the global economy – they 'reduced the costs of being an island'. There was a further benefit to Ireland as the IDA's export growth strategy had led to the specialisation in products which had a high value-to-volume ratio, that is, ICT, pharma and latterly, financial services.

Internal reasons

The internal reasons for Ireland's economic success were as follows and it will be seen that most of them were subject to domestic policy influence.

Fiscal reform and a stable economic environment*
A reform programme was begun by the coalition government in the 1980s, but it was not implemented until 1987 by the Fianna Fáil government, when a reduction in public spending was made by Ray McSharry. This was greatly facilitated by the Tallaght Strategy, and was agreed with the unions in the new social partnership agreement. The importance of social partnership in getting consensus for what could have been a very painful process was emphasised in the interviews, but several contributors made the important point that without the Tallaght Strategy of Alan Dukes, Leader of the Opposition, where he undertook that the main opposition party, Fine Gael, would not oppose changes and fiscal reform, it probably would not have been successful.

The interviewees held that fiscal reform was very important. Bertie Ahern said that there were 'significant reductions in public spending', which meant some control over public finances would be achieved. It was believed that trade union members would gain in the longer term from the fiscal improvements and Mr Ahern said that the government accepted union arguments that the value of social welfare payments would be retained. He also said that 'social partnership, while not the sole factor, was hugely helpful in the stability of managing ourselves through the currency crisis', which included the devaluation of 1993. The devaluation of the Irish pound in February 1993 had a strong positive impact on the economy (and the devaluation of 1986 also helped.)

At that time there were cuts in public spending including a freeze in recruitment, an early retirement scheme, deferral of special pay increases and cutbacks in public capital investment including public housing. Fortunately, the external environment improved, with interest rates falling and a boom in the UK which reduced unemployment in Ireland as emigration grew. Rising sterling and wage moderation improved Ireland's cost competitiveness, pushing up exports to the UK. The EU Structural Funds were doubled and helped investment, which had been cut.

The structural revolution in the economy
A shift in employment from agriculture to services, and the continuing but much greater impact of high productivity manufacturing, was to be of crucial importance in boosting productivity to very high levels and thus economic growth. This, in turn, generated employment, tax revenue and so on. This factor was not focused upon by the respondents, but was nonetheless important. The third phase of the boom, with the shift from manufacturing to domestically driven growth from 2001, may not be as enduring because it is not based on the high productivity of manufacturing. There are high productivity services, but Ireland does not have sufficient scale in the area, as yet.[3]

The demographic dividend
The fall in the dependency ratio and growth in labour force participation were very significant. Ireland had had a very high dependency ratio with a large number of young dependants. The shape of Ireland's population pyramid was not the normal one for most of its history, but was 'waisted'. Ireland's population was thinner in the middle due to mass emigration and there were consequently fewer people of working age in the population. Thus it had a 'waist' which also reflected a waste of talent, with many unable to find work in Ireland. This was to change dramatically after 1980. There was the additional bonus of many of the young people leaving education looking for work just as the jobs boom began in the early 1990s.

Again, this factor was not focused upon by the respondents as a major determinant, probably as it was not policy driven, but it was extremely important. They did mention the large numbers of new labour market entrants as Ireland's baby boomers left education, with better qualifications than their parents, just as the ICT boom came to Ireland.

Social partnership*
It has been seen that a crucial ingredient to the success has been the social consensus, which began in 1987 with the first of the new comprehensive

national social partnership agreements. As this is more complex than the other factors, and as the Irish version is unique, it is worthy of considered examination, including the views of other observers and commentators.

The Taoiseach, Bertie Ahern, said 'I strongly believe that the social partnership provided the essential context for stability and it was the key catalyst for growth . . .' In his interview, he placed strong emphasis on it, calling it the 'X factor' in Ireland's economic success. He said that in 1987, 'our theory at the time was based on two big things. Moderate wage growth should give us competitiveness on which to build; employment would stabilise. With significant reductions in public spending, some control over public finances would be achieved. Secondly, the trade union members would gain in the longer term from these corrections and that, in the interim, the government accepted union arguments that the value of social welfare payments would be maintained.'

He continued with a strong emphasis on the social – 'Just as a strong economy enables social exclusion to be effectively tackled, so does a cohesive and consistent society lead to a positive investment climate.' Looking to the future, the Taoiseach concluded, 'I think the country's social partnership model engendered a degree of economic stability – business certainty – which has proved capable of transcending political change in tackling all the asymmetrical shocks that we've had over the period.'

Mr Ahern gave a considered analysis of social partnership at the Irish Management Institute conference in May 2004, during the second of his three terms in office. 'This government believes in the social partnership process. We believe that the series of agreements we have had since 1987 have been good for employers, good for employees and good for the country as a whole.' It is a model that 'puts men and women at the heart of economic development.'[4]

Mr Ahern said that the Irish model of social partnership was being studied by many around the world and with our development of this social partnership model 'we have engaged in an important piece of social innovation, which has facilitated and encouraged the economic innovation that has served us so well'.

He was critical of those who thought it was a 'cosy consensus'. 'Sadly for its practitioners, it isn't! The social partnership process requires a major investment of time and effort; hard choices have to be faced and strong leadership is required on all sides. It is, of course, easy to knock social partnership – although opponents often seem a little shy about disclosing their alternative! The fact is, however, that social partnership has a track record of delivering – not perfection, which was never claimed by its proponents – but tangible results all the same. And it remains more likely to deliver positive results than any free-for-all alternative.'

Reflecting back and looking to the future in the interview for this book, Taoiseach Mr Ahern said 'social partnership agreements were the "X Factor" which made the difference. . . an analysis going back twenty years would show that social partnership was *the* factor that allowed us to be able to make the brave decisions and allowed us to have a sense that we could be successful. Social partnership had a huge part in that.'

Constructive criticism

All three businessmen were supportive of Ireland's social partnership and believed that it contributed to the economic success. However, each had constructive criticism of aspects of it. Sutherland said 'I think that social partnership is a good thing. However, if, through a lack of clear thinking by the social partners, it results in the escalation of costs that makes us uncompetitive, then there is a problem with it.' And he thought costs were now a serious problem. He was part of the Delors cabinet in Europe – as Welfare Commissioner for a time – and social partnership, along with the Structural Funds, were 'part of the balance for the Single Market programme. In this context, I think that the Irish experience has been successful.' He concluded, 'We need a rational, reasonable debate with both sides of the social partners and everyone else, reaching rational decisions. If we can do that it makes our social partnership the crucial thing for the future.'

Macri said he would not 'lead with social partnership' though he sees it as one of 'the important "softer" factors in the success.' He would not lead on it because 'if I went to any senior decision-maker in Microsoft, they wouldn't know what that phrase meant. However, if you then talked about the environment in which we operate, then they would see the value of it.'

McGann said that social partnership was a very enlightened concept which was enormously important at a crucial time. McGann's views are especially important as he led the employers' body, IBEC, in negotiations during the Towards 2016 agreement (which is the current one and is the first to span ten years). Social partnership has 'served an enormous purpose over the years' but 'the model needs to be revisited'. He held that 'the fundamental concept is good. Surely negotiation and agreement-building is far better than any confrontation? Of course it is!' But he concluded, saying 'but I believe that, while we may have improved the system over the years, we need to fundamentally rethink how to contemporise it, if it is to serve us for the next ten years.'

Olivia O'Leary made the point that things were so bad back in the late 1980s that 'there was a national will for economic change and the readiness for consensus and compromise and this was reflected in the social partnership process.' She believed, however, that on the issue of consensus 'there are a lot of debates on values that we actually need to have.' The Irish 'got used to being told, for years and years, what our values should be as a nation. We haven't learned to develop our own.' She seemed to be saying that Ireland is still an 'adolescent society'.

She appeared to be calling for a *civil* social partnership model to be discussed and agreed when she said 'This is a Republic. That means something. It means there is a *real* commitment to the universality of what is provided in terms of public service; in terms of equality of opportunity; of inclusiveness.' She believed public institutions need to be better at communication with citizens 'to show them what is theirs, in order to develop their sense of self and their respect for public space'. She argued that we need more support for childcare and for parents and while we welcome immigrants we need to decide 'what the core values of being Irish are. Are there basic human rights that we will not allow to be compromised, no matter what the religious belief or cultural traditions of the incoming group?' There has to be a better 'relationship between the local authorities and the people. There is no place that we meet,' she believed. 'We've worked for this country. Now we must make sure it works for us.'

Integrated policy-making

Professor Frances Ruane argues that while social partnership was very important to the success, 'it could not have happened without the Tallaght Strategy'. In the 1980s, things were very bad and a win/lose game was becoming a lose/lose game, but after the first deal, it became a 'win/win on the union and the employers' sides with government facilitating the early part of the win/win through tax reform. ...Social partnership involved the recognition by trade unions of the needs of business and it also involved the recognition of the need for economic and social policy to be integrated,' she said. NESC is important in providing 'the intellectual backdrop to social partnership, with evidence-based research'.

Professor Ruane placed a lot of emphasis on how decision-making has shifted to a more rational level in Ireland and social partnership is part of this process, with more evidence-based policy making. 'There is more intellectual openness in Ireland today than there was twenty years ago, but we have a way to go on that.' A 'difficulty with the social partnership process' is that 'the parameters for discussion need to be reviewed and set more widely'.

Trade union leader David Begg said that 'the big advantage of the social partnership process was that it gave an incredible amount of stability to that whole environment . . . From a business perspective, you almost had the best of all worlds. This was a catalyst for the take-off.' Back in the late

1980s with Margaret Thatcher and the UK miners' strike, 'there was a growing realisation on the Irish trade union side that we had a choice. We could go the European route or we could continue on the British route.' Also the idea of social dialogue had been introduced by Delors, the EU President, as part of a social counterbalance to the Single Market. 'Social dialogue was imported in here and, in my view, since then, it has been further refined and taken to a new level,' Begg said.

Begg argued that some economists assert that the economic success would have happened anyway through market forces and that social partnership got too much credit. He believed that a minority of free-market economists have such a belief in the workings of the market that they do not want to credit institutions and actors for social change. It may have been 'that our move to social partnership happened to coincide with the period of most rapid expansion that the country has ever known'. We do not know, he said, but the answer might be to ask, ' "What would be the consequence of pulling the plug on social partnership now?" I think that would be a huge blow to confidence in the economy. It would be a very risky experiment.'

Begg believed that social partnership meant that governments did share some power with the partners, with employers, with unions, with farmers and social groups, but governments ultimately held the reigns of power. 'Finally, I have to say that Ireland's great *economic* success could have generated a great *social* success if we had done things differently. If the government had not cut taxes so sharply on incomes and on companies, we would have had much more to spend on health, on education and on earlier investment. . . . Congress did agree to income tax cuts, but did not agree to taking them so far,' he concluded.

Union backing

Social partnership is strongly supported by most people and all institutions in Ireland, but it is not without its critics. Within the trade union movement, a sizeable proportion of the membership opposes it, around one-third, with some unions and members against it on principle. A number of the larger unions are traditionally against all such agreements and the very small far-left parties are totally opposed to them. However, crucially, in the late 1980s, when the first partnership agreement was being considered,[5] the broad left in the then influential Workers Party, the Communist Party and the Labour Party backed it, with personalities like Des Geraghty and Pat Rabbitte of the Irish Transport and General Workers Union (ITGWU) backing the union leadership, which included John Carroll, and there was a similar response in the Federated Workers Union of Ireland (FWUI), led by Paddy Cardiff and Billy Attley.

The Celtic Tiger boom could have come years sooner, according to Billy Attley. Billy Attley is a former president of SIPTU and a former leader of a predecessor union, FWUI. He said that a form of social partnership was being discussed in the 1981/82 pay talks, several years earlier than the PNR talks in 1987, which would have addressed the huge national debt, fiscal crisis and kept welfare benefits above inflation.[6] He said that things were so bad then that some commentators were saying that we could not afford welfare at the then current levels and it would have to be cut! He says that the Irish employers looked to Thatcher's attacks on the British unions and believed that this approach might work to their advantage. It took tens of thousands of job losses, falling wages, falling profits and several years before they came back to the table. Their organisation was still reluctant to do so, even then. He said that the then Taoiseach, Haughey, had to go over the employers' body to key individual employers, before the main body joined in serious discussions.

Peter Cassells, former General Secretary of Congress and long-time negotiator for most of the agreements said that the 1980s were very bad for workers – with pay cuts of around 8 per cent, mass emigration and unemployment. The unions felt that it 'was inevitable that something was going to happen – the issue was whether you would influence what happened or not. We decided that we would.'[7] The background thinking to the first agreement was contained in the NESC strategy, which took a different line on the economy than it had in the past and which accommodated both employers and unions. 'We were aware that the employers had looked at Britain and some wanted to adopt a hard HR strategy', with no national or even sectoral negotiations. While the unions agreed to moderate pay increases, 'the selling point for them with the members was a reduction in the working week by one hour to 39 hours'. Public sector increases were phased in later (that is, delayed) and there was agreement that welfare would not be reduced, Cassells says. The unions were consulted on the currency crisis and reluctantly accepted the devaluation in 1993.

Catalyst
Peter Cassells believes that social partnership was the catalyst which brought together many factors which were already there, such as FDI, favourable taxes, the educated workforce; and helped create a virtuous circle. He believes that what is not clearly understood is that social partnership is a process – not a single negotiation and agreement, but a process which continues, reviewing, refining, and reforming many areas of the economy and society. He does not think that the Irish system of partnership is comparable to others like the Swedish or German, but is

unique to our institutions and mores. He does not hold that it is perfect; for example, it has not delivered on childcare or on the important issue of healthcare reform. Thus he believes that it needs to be changed to enable these areas to be addressed by all the partners.

Today, Jack O'Connor, President of SIPTU,[8] is somewhat critical of social partnership. He says, 'Social partnership, as it is called, has been the catalyst for twenty years of economic growth and prosperity. It is the critical component of underpinning "confidence" in our economy. However, it is a decidedly unequal relationship, at best only mitigating the dominance of capital and the strong neo-liberal outlook of our governments.' He holds that, 'on balance, it still probably remains the best way forward'. He concludes by saying that 'its future is threatened by the growing income disparity and the failure to curb the arrogance of the more rapacious elements competing for dominance among the employers'.

Many supporters of partnership within the union movement are critical of the government which they believe lauds social partnership at every opportunity here and internationally, but does little to assist in the relative decline of the trade unions. Unlike unions in many other countries, the Irish trade unions have had strong membership growth for many years, but because employment has exploded, the proportion of the workforce they represent has declined from 45 per cent in 1997 to 37 per cent in 2007.[9] In the 1970s, when there was no social partnership, the state development body, the IDA, under Michael Killeen, encouraged all foreign investing firms to recognise trade unions. Today, neither the government nor the IDA encourages firms to recognise unions, in spite of the official strong support for partnership at national level by government! However, the IDA does not discourage firms from unionisation either.

Trust
Social partnership in Ireland is not legally binding, but the agreements are based on trust. This means that they are more flexible for both sides, but particularly for employers, who do not like labour regulation. The 2006 agreement negotiations took a staggering 126 days to complete because this trust was undermined by a small number of employers, including Irish Ferries, which had previously been a reasonably good employer. Congress refused to complete the negotiation of a deal that did not include a considerable improvement in labour standards, particularly after the Irish Ferries debacle. The Irish employer organisations, which had been undermined by a few firms, reluctantly had to agree to improvements for workers in labour standards which were contained in a special section in Towards 2016.

Other critics on the far left argue that trade unions have been undermined by being incorporated into the system which, they believe, subordinates their concerns to those of employers and the state (for example Allen 2000, 2007; O'Hearn 2003). Allen argues that 'in Ireland, pressure for flexibility and work intensity comes directly through social partnership agreements'.[10] He believes that 'whereas in the past workers were granted pay increases in response to rising rates of inflation, today they must first show verifiable improvements in productivity to get a pay rise. The remarkable fact about social partnership is that there is little sharing between the partners.' In fact, workers did not simply get pay increases for inflation in the past, but have always sought to share in economic growth on top of inflation, through rises in productivity. That average earnings rose by 80 per cent above inflation over the twenty years of social partnership demonstrates conclusively that the process and Congress has been remarkably successful in generating very real improvements in workers' living standards.

This twenty years was a wonderful era for workers. Employment doubled, emigration ceased and take-home earnings rose very, very handsomely. It was in stark contrast to the so-called 'free-for-all' of the early 1980s, when average earnings fell by 8 per cent. Allen asserts that the emergence of a neo-liberal state was actually 'facilitated by social partnership'.[11] He bases this belief on the changes in labour law which imposed greater procedures on trade unions before taking industrial action. In Ireland, unions have been usually quite careful on procedures before going on strike, the last port of call in the process of negotiation. This was seen in the 2006 negotiation for Towards 2016; considerable improvements in labour laws were won and the new National Employment Rights Authority (NERA) was established.

Income distribution
Kirby[12] appears to be critical of social partnership because it does not overcome the weaker position of trade union and social groupings in relation to power and he is correct in this (a point made above by Jack O'Connor). His critical analysis of the inequalities thrown up by the Celtic Tiger is an excellent counterblast to complacency around the economic success. He cites increases in earnings as positive, but points to the shift in national income from labour to capital, from wages to profits, over the years in Ireland. This worldwide trend in income distribution was highlighted by the usually conservative OECD in June 2007 in a report[13] which pointed out that there are losers with globalisation, and argued that they should be protected by nation states and international bodies. It conceded that it needed to reassess the impact of freer trade on workers because a 'wedge' had appeared between the rosy analysis put forward by

economists and 'the much more sceptical view of the general public'. That scepticism was particularly strong in the US and France. The OECD also said 'wages had been shrinking as a proportion of national income in the US, Japan and Europe, perhaps reflecting the weakened pay bargaining position of workers'.

Paul Teague,[14] a constructive critic of social partnership, argues that the EU and governments are quick to make decisions which assist market-orientated policies, but are much slower to adopt EU directives to regulate and supervise firms or to create EU-wide forms of economic and social governance, which makes the *Social Europe* much more difficult to achieve. Rory O'Donnell, a former academic, as Director of the National Economic and Social Council, is both a strong supporter of social partnership and argues regularly and cogently in its favour in many writings and presentations.

A criticism of social partnership is that it does not include the Houses of the Dáil [Parliament] or Oireachtas and particularly excludes the opposition parties. Agreements have grown to cover very wide areas which many parliamentarians believe should be debated in the houses and not 'behind closed doors in closed rooms by unelected groups'. There is some validity in this view, but difficult and complex negotiations are usually thrashed out outside the glare of publicity and as it is the role of the opposition to oppose, it is unlikely that negotiations could be concluded effectively if they were part of the process, in their natural role. The Oireachtas generally votes on the result. The leaders of most of the participating groups – government, unions, most employers and farmers' groups, are elected.

Critics

Critics of social partnership include a very small number of vocal journalists who fundamentally do not believe that 'the representatives of callous-handed workers' should be allowed near, never mind, into, Government Buildings. From the far right, these journalists, mainly in Sunday papers, are opposed to trade unions having any influence and particularly access to any form of power.

More serious critics include Jim O'Leary, a former stockbroker economist, now lecturing in NUIM. He said 'the most significant economic claim made for partnership is that it resulted in wage moderation, thus improving competitiveness' and boosting output and employment across the economy.[15] The virtuous circle was initiated when the government agreed to cut taxes and, in return, trade unions agreed to trim their wage demands, which is the view of most commentators.

O'Leary asks was there something in the social partnership process that allowed the government to come to the table with bigger tax cuts than would otherwise have been possible? He claims that the wage bargaining process under social partnership, 'far from producing lower public sector pay increases, may have generated bigger increases in public sector pay rates than would otherwise have eventuated. By extension, what this suggests is that the wage bargaining process under social partnership may have reduced rather than increased the scope for tax cuts.' However, income tax in Ireland has been reduced to the lowest level in the advanced economies,[16] far more than was sought by the unions and in fact, they did not seek the shift from income to indirect taxes, which is regressive. However, he argues that the government simply announced tax cuts (which might have taken place anyway) during the wage talks, thus providing the negotiating parties with information that would influence the outcome in a positive way. He has been a very strong critic of public service benchmarking, the parallel process of a new system of pay determination in the public service, which emerged more recently under social partnership.

Professor John Fitzgerald of the ESRI[17] has argued that social partnership may have brought about a more orderly labour market, with fewer industrial disputes than in the 1970s, but it 'served more to validate the results which market forces had made inevitable', a point contested by David Begg of Congress.

Other informed commentators such as Niamh Hardiman[18] say 'the broadening of the range of issues that social partnership deals with can be seen as a positive development, as it brings a broader range of expertise into policy deliberations. In line with similar developments in other European countries, this may facilitate a rapid process of "policy learning". It has even been suggested that the engagement of unions, employers, and other civil society actors in wide-ranging policy deliberations encourages these actors not only to understand others' perspectives more fully but also to rethink their own interests and identities.'[19] Social partnership has become intricately involved with processes of consultation, target-setting, and reporting, prompted in part by obligations incurred at EU level. But the core deal on pay and disposable income continues to be the pivot of social partnership.

Hardiman believes that 'rather than seeing social partnership as displacing the proper role of government, we have seen that the policy process still depends centrally on ministerial initiative and is ultimately subordinate to the electoral priorities of government'. Social partnership can help address 'the well-known deficiencies of the system of public administration – particularly in tackling issues that cut across departments' jurisdictions' but it is no substitute for public service reform, she argues.

'Social partnership is now deeply imbricated in the political system, and its contribution to shaping the policy agenda, while less visible, is widely acknowledged.' Governments have a major challenge in continuous public service reform in all countries and this will be a major political challenge for the future, for all governments of whatever hue. The Irish public service is small by international standards and is efficient according to one major report with international comparisons.[20]

From most perspectives, the best way to achieve continuous improvement is to engage and motivate all employees, who often know the best way to achieve efficiency, combined with external reviews introducing best international practice. In short, partnership should work, but it has not delivered great results as yet in health or indeed in several other areas. Critics of partnership, not necessarily advocates of authoritarian management, can validly argue that embedding partnership structures can lead to tardiness and even immobility. The form of public service partnership being attempted needs a continuous review.

Conclusion

Social partnership, as Bertie Ahern said, is not easy. It is also time-consuming and there is more conflict than is apparent to outsiders who believe it is 'cosy'. For unions and employers, the biggest accomplishment has been in getting into the heads of each other, to understand, unambiguously, what are the deep concerns of the other side. For employers, it is the need to plan and to increase productivity in the globalised economy and the unions' role in this is to ensure that it does not displace workers or reduce their incomes. It means strong lines of communication with each other through bodies like the NESC, National Competitiveness Council, the Company Law Review Group, and also once-off groups like the High Level Group on Manufacturing, the Review Group on Industrial Policy, etc.

Deep, empirical and theoretical debates inform the resultant policies which should mean that it can be evidence-based, more speedily executed, without too much conflict and with fewer mistakes being made. As Frances Ruane said there is more rational policy formation today in Ireland and while we still have a long way to go, much progress has been made. Social partnership has put in place processes which resolve major conflict, often long before the public is even aware it is looming. It is part of a more participative and inclusive society where social partners express their views and, importantly, are heard.

Perhaps the most important contribution of social partnership is its role in policy execution. Many countries can devise and adopt the very best of economic policies, but putting them into practice is more difficult.

Partnership has another important contribution. Following each agreement, a monitoring group is established which meets at the highest levels, ensures that progress is being made according to the agreement and publishes progress reports. Further, where there are disagreements, its main body, the National Implementation Body (NIB), meets if objectives are not being achieved or very serious difficulties arise.

Social partnership has been dealt with in some detail. There is broad consensus among our interviewees, albeit of degree, on its importance in the economic success of Ireland. It is an interesting and somewhat controversial area and one which is still developing. There are strong and differing opinions on its role in the future but as Peter Cassells said, it is a *process*, and one that is developing.

Low corporation taxes

There is no doubt that the low company tax regime made Ireland an additionally attractive place for FDI, especially US investment. The Taoiseach put it as one of his four or five key reasons for the success. As Professor Ruane said, US firms are particularly sensitive to tax, seeing it as a business cost (which it is not, being a payment from profit).

An intriguing question is how, when Ireland was offering anything it could to attract FDI for the three earlier decades – at zero tax until 1981 – the multinationals did not flow in? Why did US firms, which regard tax as a 'burden', not flock into Ireland when taxes on exports were zero?

Peter Sutherland supplied a compelling answer. Ireland did have low company taxes, yet firms did not flock here until the 1990s. Therefore, it appeared that low taxes, while an incentive to firms, did not have the power of attraction. The reason they came in the 1990s was the Single Market, established in 1992. US firms had been planning to invest substantially in Europe prior to the Single Market's establishment. With the new Single Market's competition laws and enforcement, it meant that they would not be discriminated against if they operated from anywhere in the Union. Most interviewees agreed that the low taxes were very important for Ireland. While additional factors included the tens of thousands of educated workers looking for jobs, for US tax-sensitive firms, the low tax on companies decided it and once the Single Market was working, Ireland was the place to invest for access to Europe. As Gary McGann said, US firms in particular like to control communication, and Ireland or the UK were the only two countries where English was spoken.

Sutherland said 'I have no doubt that foreign direct investment would not have happened without the lower corporation tax rate. It was the vital cause of inward investment.' Begg said 'I think *certainty* in taxation policy helped and I think that the low tax rate also did help in making Ireland attractive for FDI, especially US firms which are obsessed with taxation, but it is not a long-term real competitive advantage.' He also agreed that Ireland does gain a lot of tax revenue from these companies and on top of that, it gained much tax revenue from profits from transfer-pricing by multinationals.

Joe Macri saw the low tax as being one of the three main factors in Ireland's success and Gary McGann said, 'Low tax was a huge factor for Ireland. If you go to any international marketplace low tax is a factor.' He also believes that 'certainty, no matter which party was in power' was important around tax. 'It was consistent over time. This is extremely important for companies' planning,' he said. McGann also said that the other EU member states are reducing their company tax rates, and our competitive tax advantage will be reduced, 'so therefore we have to work on other competitive strengths. But we must not give up on tax harmonisation. Our low tax environment has served us well.' And as 'an island, off the west coast of Europe, with a five million population' we must be more attractive.[21] Olivia O'Leary also saw the low tax rate as a major attraction.

Tax harmonisation

Frances Ruane believed that the low tax rate is important in the success. 'The impact of the low corporation tax is huge. . . I would see the low tax, given our peripheral location, as a necessary but not sufficient condition to attract FDI.' She made the interesting point that US firms 'are very driven by tax, as American corporate culture is driven to minimise payments to "Uncle Sam"' – in short, they see tax as an avoidable cost. But she is critical of the previous zero rate – we moved from the zero tax rate and it is now very evident that we should have done so much earlier. 'Had we a tax rate of even 5 per cent for much of the 1970s and 1980s, we would have enjoyed considerable revenue gain.' She thinks Ireland should defend its company tax regime but 'we need to be conscious that the impact of our present low rate is being continuously eroded by the low tax rates in the new member states.'

The move by the European Commission in 2006/7 to introduce what it calls a 'common consolidated tax base' for assessing the profits of companies is strongly opposed by business and the government in Ireland. It is seen as a way to introduce tax harmonisation and it would pave the way to change or increase Ireland's low rate of company tax.

Sutherland said that low corporation tax advantage could be under threat from Europe or 'there is the possibility of the US changing its laws – but on the other side, if the British turned on this issue and decided that they were in favour of tax harmonisation in Europe rather than being opposed to it this would increase the pressure.'

It is clear that Ireland cannot rely so heavily on low company taxes for competitive advantage if a change in the US law could wipe this advantage out overnight. The low tax regime has been to Ireland's advantage. We have gained many investments from it and a great deal of tax revenue. It is obvious that the Irish government or its agencies cannot change the tax regime as it would cause uncertainty, but the day may come when a law change elsewhere could wipe the advantage out overnight. This is a major uncertainty.

In the meantime, every day brings further tax competition with reductions in company taxes which diminishes the Irish tax advantage. There is also a dilemma for citizens of Europe. Do they wish to see companies paying little or no taxes in the future? This is where we appear to be going as governments fight each other with increasing incentives and corporate tax reductions (just as they did before the competition rules were established under the 1992 Single Market) to gain FDI.

The increased mobility of capital of FDI 'implies a lower corporate tax rate' according to an empirical analysis of nineteen OECD countries by Garretsen and Peeters.[22] In that sense there is 'a race to the bottom', but they found that the core countries, with greater agglomeration, tend to maintain higher corporate tax rates. However, peripheral countries (like Ireland) tend to have lower rates. There is, however, downward pressure on the rates in the peripheral countries.

A clear understanding of competitiveness

The recognition of the importance of competitiveness and a clear and commonly held definition of the term was an important component of the success, which assisted policy and social partnership. Unlike in many other countries, it is not seen crudely as movements in wage earnings, but includes the banking system, infrastructure, education, etc. For employers, getting Irish unions engaged in the issue of competitiveness was important. There does, however, appear to be a confusion between competitiveness and competition in some quarters.

This manifested itself around energy and electricity. In a small island economy, with only an interconnector with a smaller Northern Ireland, competition is difficult, as most experts understand, but several policy-makers do not. This led to high prices for electricity in Ireland in a vain effort to encourage competition. Competition is the best economic solution, if achievable, but sometimes there are natural monopolies or contestable markets do not work effectively. These are best dealt with by effective and evolving regulation. In the meantime, competitiveness is being sacrificed at what has become an ideological altar to 'competition'.

Peter Sutherland said that 'bodies like the Competitiveness Council are vital' for helping us take hard decisions, which would be based on evidence and a shared analysis. The future for Ireland with its high cost of living, high house prices and rising labour costs is in competitiveness which is not focused on costs alone, but the pursuit of efficiency through productivity, as Macri said. Ireland's level of productivity is high, assisted by high-end manufacturing, especially around ICT-production, pharma and chemical manufacturers. The future will require a greater emphasis on productivity through ICT use. ICT is being used everywhere, but not as efficiently as it could be and a big emphasis in education and training around its use will generate benefits in the services sector, including the public services.

Public enterprise and civil service reform*

Commercial public enterprise contributed much to Ireland's economy and society since the first companies were established in 1927.[23] The sector was much more important in Ireland in terms of employment, output and investment for many decades until twenty years ago, when the private sector was relatively small. Further, its efficiency impacted many other sectors and the overall economic performance of Ireland. However, subsidies were given to public and private firms up until the late 1980s in Ireland (and in Europe too) to shore up employment. That was the way economies were run for many decades. In many countries it was the sunset industries: shipbuilding, coal, steel and public transport which had become inefficient, which received public subsidies or were nationalised.

In the late 1980s, the Taoiseach, Mr Haughey, in a well-meaning instruction, ordered the commercial [sic] state companies to increase employment by tens of thousands in an effort to reduce unemployment. They also were not allowed to shed jobs easily for many years. Frances Ruane argued Ireland was slow to address the inefficiencies in public enterprises. 'Not only did this result in higher direct costs and inefficiencies, which had to be borne by the private sector and by consumers, it also meant that these companies retained skills which could have been much better used in the private sector.' She was also particularly critical of CIE and the proposed LUAS extension – 'a case where proper economic evaluation should have been done, but was not done'. She also held that the system of regulation introduced by government, particularly around energy, is inappropriate to a small island economy and it has pushed costs up, not down.

Professor Ruane said the civil service 'needs to extend to attracting talent from outside Ireland if the civil service is to benefit from international talent mobility' similar to the benefits realised by the private sector and parts of the public sector. Peter Sutherland said Ireland needs 'a sophisticated analytical capacity within the civil service in the area of economics. It cannot rely on reports from the ESRI or the Central Bank to assist in rapid and important decision-making which can have impacts for decades to come. While people have been talking of this for some time – the lack of economic expertise – very little is being done to rectify the paucity of professional skill levels within the civil service.' He is opposed to the 'generalists' 'making poorly informed decisions on major capital and current public spending. Too often they are not evidence-based after serious and deep analysis.'

There appears to have been a dumbing-down of professional expertise in the central civil service, in an increasingly complex world where 'generalists' rule and where specialists, where they exist, are regarded with suspicion. The evidence of the need for some specialists is overwhelming, but little is being done. There is a clear case for establishing a new division of specialists – economists, accountants, lawyers, engineers, negotiators, IT specialists – to oversee major capital and indeed large-scale current spending by all departments and the public sector in general from inception to completion. Such a division of expertise is required to a) save huge sums of public money, b) match and oversee professionally the private contractors' expertise, c) build a corporate memory of professional expertise in major capital (and major current) projects, and d) represent the public interest effectively. The decision in late 2007 to establish a Central Expenditure Evaluation Unit (CEEU) in the Department of Finance to examine spending in the public sector is a tentative step in the right direction. It remains to be seen if will be adequately staffed and by real professionals with the expertise required and with a more visionary leadership, which can take a wider perspective on the value of public spending than the usual accounting or cost minimisation approach of Finance.

In the future, public service reform and efficiency will be the challenge for governments of all political persuasions. This was evident in the 2007 general election in Ireland, and it is a major issue internationally. There was no criticism of the public service impeding the economic success; rather there was strong praise for it – for the IDA and for other bodies. However, several of our respondents felt there are deficiencies in areas of expertise in the public administration, especially in the central civil service, which need addressing.

Every government has to ensure that public services are efficient and give value for money. There has been some strong criticism of the Irish public service. The policing system has been seen to be corrupt in some pockets in Ireland and the quality of local administration is deficient in areas. The major issue here is the disconnect between financing and service delivery, since the abolition of local taxes on domestic houses in 1977.

The health service is excellent when one gains access, but getting access has been a major problem for years and access is far easier for those who can pay privately. It is very much a two-tier system.

The number of government employees per 1,000 inhabitants is low in Greece, Italy and Ireland but high in Belgium, Denmark and France, according to the major study of public service performance undertaken by the Dutch government in late 2004.[24] The study finds little connection between public sector performance and the level of government spending, with the Nordics and Austria with high spending and high efficiency and the US and UK with low public spending and poor performance at the other end.

This study found that Ireland and Finland score well above the average in the area of 'quality of public services' with scores for education, healthcare, law and order and, surprisingly, Ireland is in top position in the last category. 'Ireland achieves its top position thanks to its very low crime rate, good score for education and an average score for health.' Finland was beaten by Ireland because of its poor score on law and order. 'Ireland and Finland combine relatively limited expenditures (albeit of GDP) with high levels of performance', the report concluded. However, when the three conventional functions of government – distribution, stabilisation and allocation – are examined, Ireland drops down a few places because of a weak score on allocation of welfare. Thus, if it were a more equal society, Ireland would score higher. Finland wins on the overall performance of countries followed by Luxembourg, Denmark, Sweden, Austria, Holland and then Ireland, according to this study. The Irish Government commissioned the OECD to undertake a major review of the public sector in January 2007.

On the public sector, Joe Macri argued 'it is not about the inputs. We must now turn greater attention to output', and we need 'consistency and agreement on what is a verifiable outcome' to ascertain what is public sector productivity.

Industrial policy*
All our contributors agreed strongly that Ireland's active industrial policy has contributed substantially to economic success. Industrial policy has been consistent since the early 1960s and offered certainty to foreign investors. The IDA appeared to 'pick winners' – not individual firms, but expanding industrial sectors. As well as high productivity manufacturing, it has sought out and attracted financial services. Policy-makers have successfully sought out the fastest-growing industries and sectors. Several of the contributors singled out the IDA for singular praise and indeed Sutherland and McGann named particular early senior executives,

especially the late Michael Killeen, one of its CEOs, for special mention on strategy. The representative of FDI, Joe Macri, said the IDA was always a step ahead of other countries and it widely used companies like Microsoft to sell Ireland. McGann praised Michael Killeen for seeing what kind of industry should be encouraged and both industrialists also praised consistent government policy and the role of government itself and ministers in backing the industrial policy and its execution.

Frances Ruane, whose background is in industrial policy, said that consistent industrial policy by governments and IDA and market-sensitive approaches were the crucial factors in our success and 'IDA's approach was that it picked winning sectors and within those sectors it picked winning firms'. She made the important point that the decision to go for electronics and pharmaceuticals sectors from the late 1960s to early 1970s was rewarded doubly, because these two sectors were to the forefront of FDI growth. The IDA approach to FDI operated at a company level on one hand and moved it onto thinking about enterprises and how policy-makers should interact with them.

She also pointed out that willingness of the existing group of multinationals to attract other multinationals was linked to the fact that many were in the same sectors and there were benefits from upstream-downstream trading, and also these companies were looking for the same broad skill sets. She said we were also lucky in terms of high quality multinationals, asking 'would Ireland be in the same place in terms of electronics if Intel and Microsoft had located elsewhere?' Ireland also operates very low barriers to exit, so that when a company wishes to close for global profitability reasons, there is no huge pressure on it to stay open, Ruane said, and the IDA puts its effort into finding a replacement company.

Institutional change*

The contributions of institutional change to economic growth and well-being have been neglected by economists until relatively recently. This was probably for the good reason that it is a difficult area to measure. It was seen that institutions are remarkably important and good institutions and the culture which they instil are vital to economic success. They vary from enabling institutions like a good banking and finance sector, to disabling ones such as the Catholic Church which stifled any questioning of authority or enterprise. Ireland did have many good institutions at Independence but the protectionist era of the 1930s Depression internationally meant that it did not open up to new influences. This of course suited the philosophy of self-sufficiency which was prevalent, especially with Eamon de Valera.

The non-economist, non-business observer, Olivia O'Leary, was particularly strong on the issue of institutions which are enabling. She said 'it was necessary institutionally to throw off the oppressive power of the Catholic Church and to separate it from the state'. She also said it was 'necessary too to throw off the weight of state control of the economy. Until those oppressive authorities (church and state) were undermined, I don't know if we would have felt free enough to develop the entrepreneurial spirit.' But we have not finished on institutional reform with the Roman Catholic Church still controlling almost all the primary schools which are fully funded by the secular state, 'yet the people who make almost all the decisions are parish priests'. She also believes that the whole local authority system is unresponsive to its own local residents.

O'Leary mentioned Alan Dukes and the Tallaght Strategy and Garret FitzGerald's establishment of 'stable foundations for an ongoing relationship between Dublin and London' and this 'was the foundation on which the peace process was built and the political stability that it helped create was central to attracting foreign investment.'

Cultural confidence-building

Confidence is more a sociological than an economic reason, but its impact can be as large. Changes include a greater respect for a professional approach, more openness, greater participation, accountability and more democratic institutions, equality for women and greater inclusiveness. Again this was an aspect of the success which Peter Sutherland ascribed almost more importance to than education.

David Begg said that the first agreement built confidence and 'became self-reinforcing . . . a self-reinforcing virtuous circle on the fiscal front.' He believed that 'Ireland is a much more confident country' on a business level and at many other levels and is more open too. Frances Ruane held that some young people may not be as competent as they are confident and Gary McGann saw confidence as being important in building success too. Olivia O'Leary focused on the lack of confidence we still have to discuss important values openly with each other and we are still 'reacting against things, rather than deciding what it is we want'.

The educated workforce*

Perhaps the key ingredient in the prolonged Irish economic boom has been the young, educated workforce. The ESRI describes the changes in education as 'revolutionary'. It found that the rising level of educational attainment contributed around 1 per cent per annum to the growth of the Irish economy in the 1990s. There was a massive expansion of capacity in the 1970s and 1980s in schools, colleges and teachers.

For Taoiseach Bertie Ahern, education was the first reason for the economic success which he mentioned in his interview: 'there was just a huge change in education'. He was ambitious to continue investment in the area saying 'you need to get them into the third level education because the longer you keep them in the educational system, the better. It almost doesn't matter what faculty they are studying in.' Education was one of three major factors for the success given by Joe Macri of Microsoft. Olivia O'Leary believed that the 'educational investment created a different sort of social mobility. I think the class system in Ireland really began to loosen up from the 1970s' and 'education was that movement in the undergrowth which generated greater mobility'.

However, Peter Sutherland was very critical of what he described as the 'allegedly superior educational system'. He simply did not accept that it is superior, but he did accept that 'our education system is reasonably good'. He said that the success of our young people is 'more a reflection of innate capacities and attitudes of our young people and our parents than it is of our education system. The Irish are naturally good communicators.' He said that unlike Britain, Ireland has an advantage as there are not 'the effects of a class system. There is a basic sense, in the vast bulk of Irish society, that there is not a ceiling that stops you or inhibits you because of who your parents were. There is a very positive attitude towards education and advancement.'

Sutherland said that there is a problem with science teaching in schools. He was particularly critical of teaching at second level, and he said there is a serious problem when 'only a handful of non-performing teachers have been fired in the last ten years in Ireland'. He said that if there was only one single reform for the Irish economic system, 'it would be to get our teaching right, because I really think it truly needs objective testing, with appropriate responses then taken'.

For the future, Sutherland argued that 'if we are to maintain our successful momentum, we have to have a competitive advantage somewhere' and it should be in education. He said 'we can no longer compete on costs' and so we will have to develop 'through skills and brain power' but he argued that 'I don't think we have achieved that'. The proportion of students participating at third level is still too low and he said Ireland does not feature in the top ranks of universities in the world. He concluded his criticism of the Irish educational system by saying that we simply do not have a competitive advantage in education. The OECD or other reports have not 'shown any comparative advantage with our education system which demonstrates that it is better than those of other countries. It is worse and we spend less on it!'

While Professor Ruane said that 'the evidence is that having a more educated workforce contributed significantly to growth and prosperity over the past two decades', she also questioned the quality of Irish education 'in terms of what we need to meet future challenges'. She concluded by saying that 'I am not at all convinced that we have the right type of education system now either to enable us to compete globally or create a broadly educated citizenry.' Joe Macri also thought we need to think of how we can make our education system 'great' and not just 'good'.

David Begg believed that while education and training were vital for economic success, 'the most astounding thing is what has been achieved with far fewer resources than other countries. The issue for the future is that it is highly unlikely that we will get such output from so little input of resources in the future. Unless we invest much more in education and training, we will be left behind.'

Olivia O'Leary warns that for the future, we should consider if we want to continue to 'allow an unelected authority to make a decision on how our educational system is run and is determining the values in such a system'. She said 'we have to be brave enough to address this'. Gary McGann believed 'in opening the door for all to Education, Education, Education. This has been our passport to success and will continue to be.' Frances Ruane argued that 'education is now at the centre of both economic and social policy. What we do in terms of our education strategy is central to meeting the challenges of the coming decades.' Peter Sutherland is correct to be somewhat sceptical of the Irish educational system and to focus on the overall atmosphere or thirst for education, which is motivational.

A brief examination of Ireland's educational performance
As education is so important, a brief examination of Ireland's educational system is in order. Spending on education per student in Ireland is low compared to other European countries and it was under half of that in the US in 2003.[25]

If we briefly examine each of the seven levels of education – pre-primary, primary, secondary, further, third, fourth and life-long learning – we can see where progress needs to be made.

Pre-primary only exists for the children of the better-off in Ireland, in spite of widespread recognition that investment at this level pays disproportionate dividends. Under the new NDP only a few publicly funded places will be made available. The EU average of three-year-olds in pre-primary education is over 67 per cent whereas Ireland was at 2.4 per cent in 2004.[26] State support at this level is negligible in Ireland, though there has been small positive movement. The importance of the area cannot be emphasised enough. A University of London study in 2007 has found that in the UK, by the age of three, children from disadvantaged families were lagging almost a year behind those of the three-year-old children of graduate parents in vocabulary tests, and were further behind on the understanding of colours, letters, numbers, shapes and sizes.[27]

Primary: There is universal participation and resources into primary have doubled in recent years, but class sizes are still too high compared to other countries and the pupil/teacher ratio is the sixth highest in the EU27. The number of teaching hours is above the OECD average, but spending per student is below that average. Policy has focused on social inclusion with some success. There is also the issue of resources for immigrant children whose first language is not English.

Secondary: Ireland has now achieved the participation rate of 85 per cent set by the Lisbon Agenda. Ireland's performance is a little above the EU27 average for early school leavers. However, ideally there should be 100 per cent participation and completion of this level. This has to be the immediate target. Teacher motivation is also an area which needs addressing, along with the termination of public subsidies to 'private' schools. Olivia O'Leary's point about religious control of schools in a multi-cultural society has to be addressed too, because the beneficiaries of state funding for private schools still hide behind an outdated argument on the need to support minority religions. 'Private' schools should be private, i.e. fully privately funded – with no taxpayer subsidies. The €100 million subsidy given to private schools should be spent on schools in disadvantaged areas. Ireland performs above the OECD average in reading and scientific literacy for fifteen-year-olds, but they are below on maths.

Further education: The establishment of FETAC and other initiatives has been quite successful in this area. But half a million Irish adults are functionally illiterate and this is a very serious problem. It emphasises the importance of the change, the urgency, required in adult education.

Third-level: There has been a great increase in numbers at this level, but as this is not happening universally, more needs to be done. Forty per cent of those aged twenty-five to thirty-four have a third-level qualification (with women at 47 per cent and men at only 36 per cent), substantially above the EU27 average of only 29 per cent. While the ranking of universities is fraught with potential bias, Ireland has only one university, Trinity, in one of these leagues. There is no major *academically elite* university in Ireland. This may be necessary for economic success in the future as countries compete for modern high technology sectors, though this is a subject for debate.

Fourth-level: Ireland's number of PhDs is below the EU15 average of 1.6 per 1,000 population of twenty-five- to thirty-four-year-olds.

Life-long learning: performance is low with only 8 per cent of those of working age being in the category. Further, those with more education are more likely to avail of life-long learning than those with low educational attainment, possibly because of the cost for those who need it most. There is no paid educational leave in Ireland. A high 35 per cent of adults of age 25–64 do not have a Leaving Certificate.

There are some other areas for improvement in Irish education. Ireland does not perform well in what is called PISA ranking in maths. There is a need to encourage greater participation in sciences and engineering and around ICT training and use. Twenty-five per cent of adults have problems with literacy. The educational system is also failing many young, deprived people, as shown by the numbers still leaving school early with literacy problems. Furthermore, boys are still lagging well behind girls in many public exams.

While we have had a huge increase in the throughput of students in schools and universities in recent decades, we now need to shift from lower educational attainment to much higher, from quantity to quality. On OECD data, Ireland is lagging behind the best performers.[28] Only 62 per cent of the population of working age have attained upper secondary compared to the average of 66 per cent and it is well behind the leaders (and even taking a younger cohort, we are still below the leaders). Third-level qualifications are a little better, with 26 per cent of the working-age population[29] with some kind of third-level qualification compared to a mean of 24 in the OECD, and the figure is higher for the lower age cohort, but it is behind the leading countries of Finland, Norway, Sweden, Canada, US and UK.

In conclusion, the educational system in Ireland has been a key reason for the Irish economic success. There has been significant improvement in this area, but much more needs to be done if it is to continue to contribute to economic success in the 'knowledge economy'. Ireland, along with the other EU states, has signed up for what is called the 'Lisbon Agenda' and the knowledge economy at the heart of this is education. Most states now recognise the value of education and so we will be chasing a moving target, one that is getting faster, especially as education internationalises.

The contribution of investment in education and skills

The vital contribution to the economy of the investment in education and skills was powerfully summarised in the Future Skills Group Report 2007[30] as follows:

- The increases in Ireland's labour quality are estimated to contribute almost one-fifth of the total growth in output during the boom due to higher levels of educational attainment and upskilling in the 1980s and 1990s.
- 'Labour quality' in Ireland increased by 13.2 per cent between 1994 and 2003.
- The improvements in labour quality contributed 1.0 per cent per annum to average annual GNP growth (which averaged 6.4 per cent per annum, 1994 to 2003) and annual average GNP growth per adult (4.7 per cent per annum).
- Further, labour quality improvements had a positive impact on the employment rate; as much as two-thirds of the increase in employment over the period 1994 to 2003 reflected the increase in educational attainment. The consequential increase in aggregate hours worked, combined with improved labour quality, suggest that increased educational attainment contributed up to 2.1 per cent per annum to GNP growth per adult.
- Investment in education increases growth and boosts national prosperity; for example, a one-year increase in average education has been found to raise the output per capita by between 3 and 6 per cent.
- Increasing either primary or secondary school enrolment rates by one percentage point leads to an increase in per capita GDP growth of between 1 and 3 percentage points.
- The impact of increases at different levels of education appears to depend on the level of a country's development. In particular, while primary and secondary skills appear to be related to growth in the poorest and in intermediate developing countries respectively, it is *tertiary* skills that are important for growth in OECD countries.
- Both the initial level and the subsequent growth of tertiary education are found to be positively and significantly related to per capita income growth in OECD countries. It has been found that a one percentage point increase in the annual growth of human capital increases growth by 5.9 percentage points.
- Pre-primary development is a key determinant of performance at all levels of education. There is strong evidence that pre-primary interventions could help to address educational disadvantage in Ireland and in particular help to lower the subsequent drop-out rate from secondary level. Investment at this stage is comparatively more successful at addressing educational disadvantage than later interventions. According to some research, early interventions can make returns of up to 700 per cent. Common characteristics of successful pre-primary programmes include: the promotion of speaking and listening

skills, the cultivation of the foundations of numeracy, and interaction with other children and adults over day-long time periods.

- There is clear evidence that human capital plays a key role in fostering technological change and diffusion, although the extent of this is not always captured in empirical studies.
- There is evidence that the rate of technology transfer is enhanced by human capital.
- In addition to the monetary and economic benefits accruing from education and training outlined in the previous section, there are additional externalities which positively impact on society as a result of improved educational attainment. These positive externalities offer further validation for sustained and enhanced investment in education and training.
- The Future Skills Group argues that greater educational attainment is linked to superior health status, lower risks of unemployment and poverty, and increases in some aspects of social cohesion such as reduced crime potential and greater political participation.

The Future Skills Group set out a vision for skills for the expanded workforce of 2.4 million in 2020 and the 'knowledge economy' and found that there will be a shortage of highly skilled people and too many with low skills in that year and so there will be unemployment among those with low skills, unless we invest more and re-orientate our educational system. Of the 2020 workforce, 1.4 million is already at work today and half a million of these need further training and to move up at least one level of the educational ladder. Its ambition is that the retention rate at Leaving Cert will have to move to 90 per cent and the numbers at third level will have to shift from 55 per cent to 72 per cent.

Abolishing university fees

The abolition of fees was a very popular move, but it has had no impact on social mobility. On the contrary, it has allowed better-off parents to use the money to pay for private fee-paying schools.[31] These schools have seen a huge increase in numbers of pupils as better-off parents spend the money that they would have spent on university fees at these schools and on grind courses to improve the points of their children, seeking educational advantage in the highly competitive Leaving Cert years. It was seen that 'private' schools, of course, are not private, as in other countries, but receive huge public subsidies in Ireland. This has had an adverse impact on the state educational system and on social equity. The abolition of fees took a major source of money away from our universities, just as international competition between universities increased. This has increased the dependency of universities on the state. When the economic downturn comes, the state may decide this is an area it will cut and if it does, fees will be required for colleges to maintain standards.

The reintroduction of fees, accompanied with increases in financial assistance to low income families and students, must be a key policy option for those concerned with a more equitable educational system. It would also boost universities' much needed revenues if they are to progress. While most experts agree that abolition of fees was a regressive move, and many politicians will agree privately, it will be a courageous politician who reverses this inequity.

Conclusion

Ireland's educational system has been the major driver of our economic success. It is good but not great. But in many respects, it has been successful despite itself. It has delivered much with relatively low inputs of resources. The consensus of our contributors is that education at every level, from pre-school to life-long learning, has to be the priority. This requires the investment of much greater resources, that is, money and people, if Ireland is to continue to be economically, socially and culturally successful and to fully endow all of the people for the future.

Other factors in the boom

There were a number of other factors which were mentioned by different interviewees, including low interest rates, the small size of the economy, and the large size of the construction sector.

The role of construction

The large size of the construction industry in Ireland has boosted domestic demand, which has been the main driver demand in the economy since 2001, as exports did not grow as fast as in the past. Construction accounted for a disproportionate share of the economy in 2007, with over 12 per cent of the workforce and a quarter of all output. However, the sector has low productivity and is funded by borrowings. It has generated a 'wealth effect' for those with high house prices, many of whom borrowed and spent and so have boosted domestic demand. A great deal of the domestic boom is funded by borrowing against property. This is not sustainable in the long run but it has allowed the economic boom to continue for several years. If there were a crash in construction, the economy would be severely hit and unemployment would rise rapidly. A soft landing would be in everyone's interests.

Economist Professor Ruane was concerned with construction, but from a different perspective to most. She said some economists believed it had impacted adversely on manufacturing – driven up labour costs and consequently crowded out the bottom end of manufacturing. However, she held that lower-end manufacturing was becoming uncompetitive and would be shedding jobs, but construction had picked these up. Other interviewees were also concerned about the size of the sector and what will happen to the workers when the downturn comes. The view that the foreign workers will go home as the downturn impacts may be sanguine.

Low interest rates

Interest rates have been historically low for many years in real terms. These certainly helped, but the other Eurozone countries have enjoyed them too, though with less impact. Did they drive the Tiger?

With the huge capital spending programmes in Ireland in construction of property and infrastructure, low interest rates did help. Professor Ruane made the point that small businesses in particular did benefit from them and this helped local entrepreneurship – 'low interest rates were really important for them'. Begg thought this helped the boom too and the Taoiseach pointed out that the fiscal stability achieved at the beginning of the boom, in the late 1980s, helped reduce interest rates which stimulated investment and the pick-up in the economy. The low rates enabled the consumption-driven boom, though the level of personal debt in Ireland is now very high.

Pro-business environment

The pro-business environment was emphasised by several interviewees including the Taoiseach and interestingly, union leader David Begg, who referred to Ireland as a 'business-friendly location'. Others praised the way government and its agencies were incredibly active in persuading international firms that Ireland was the place for them to set up, with the story of Microsoft's President Ballmer being knocked out by the sales pitch from the Irish authorities.

It should be clear that in Ireland the term 'pro-business' does not mean 'anti-union' or anti-citizen or pro-corporation in the way it is understood in other countries. It means that governments understand that business is important for employment, for economic growth and for tax revenue and also as a small country, FDI is vital. Thus, consistent policies which enable business to operate smoothly within the law are important and the many state promotional agencies are geared up to both winning new FDI and assisting indigenous industry to grow and develop. Ireland still has a large number of state-funded bodies devoted to helping business, manu-facturing, services, farming, tourism and even fishing. There has not yet been a debate on transferring the cost of these bodies to the beneficiaries in the private sector, now that the economy is mature. The thinking is, perhaps, that there are external benefits beyond private business to others in the economy and importantly that the costs of these many agencies are subsidies to businesses which are still below the EU competition radar.

There have been critics of aspects of Irish government policy which say it attracted the chemical/pharma industry here with poor environmental enforcement. This does not appear to be correct because the majority of such plants were established in Cork and the local authority there was quick to establish an effective environmental unit and EU laws were already in place. Additionally Ireland has had an Environmental Protection Agency since 1994. The value of these firms to the economy is beyond dispute in high-paying unionised jobs, in value added, taxes and some spill-over in skills and innovation.

Ireland has a very low tax wedge – the difference between the cost of employing a person and what that person takes home in net pay. The cost of employing someone is low in Ireland, especially compared to France or the Nordic countries. This is due to low income taxes on workers themselves and low social security payments for both employers and for employees. It has been seen that the unions agreed to tax reductions initially to assist employers in employment, but as the boom continued and employment grew annually for over fifteen years, governments were enabled to continue to cut income taxes to the lowest levels in the developed world or improve public services substantially. They chose the former option and cut income taxes. Further, as the social security fund was growing with the doubling of employment and unemployment was low, employers' social security contribution, never high in Ireland, was further reduced, to give the very low tax wedge. The greatest reductions in income taxes (and in company tax rates for non-trading companies) came in the second decade of the twenty year era.

The dilemma here is that the social security fund could be depleted rapidly when unemployment grows again. This is another example of the virtuous cycle, where a booming economy reinforces employment and it boosts tax revenue etc. It is when the downturn comes that mutually destructive forces move into action! Reducing the tax wedge has been pro-business and pro-employment. Yet countries with high tax wedges still have high employment.

It is not all good news for business, however. Major infrastructural projects are slow to be executed in Ireland (roads, waste, public transport systems, tramlines, electrical grids, tunnels, etc.) due to indecisiveness, to some micro-management by government, to delays by local authorities, and strong public opposition. The laws in these areas would not be described as pro-business. Nor are they pro-consumer. Getting rid of waste in Ireland is expensive for business (and consumers too) because governments have been both unable and unwilling to make decisions in the face of both NIMBYism[32] and some genuinely concerned opposition. The balance has yet to be struck. This has lost Ireland FDI and will continue to do so for some time. In contrast, as mentioned by Olivia O'Leary, too many believe they can build a house wherever they like in Ireland and the urban and rural planning is appalling. Irish peoples' attitude to *space* is unusual.

The small size of the economy/society

Some commentators have argued that the small size of the economy allows for a greater degree of co-ordination and problem-solving – where everyone knows everyone else and efficient networks can operate. It was seen that this is an advantage but it can be a disadvantage, where hard decisions are difficult to make.

Other questions

The following questions were also discussed with interviewees.
- Would you agree that the turnaround began in 1987?
- Why did Ireland suddenly take off at this time?
- Do you think it has been a remarkable, almost miraculous, period or was it just catching up, as some argue?
- Do you think policy has been extremely important?
- What is your view of the future?

The responses to these questions are given in the interviews. The future outlook and some other issues will be dealt with further in Chapter Eleven.

Conclusion – what drove the Tiger?

As this book has clearly demonstrated, many factors drove the Irish economic success. It was seen that there was substantial agreement around five of the factors, which all interviewees agreed had a major impact on the economic success of Ireland. One was membership of the European Union; another was foreign direct investment, particularly by US companies seeking access to the EU. All agreed that social partnership played a vital role and a fourth major factor was the plentiful, educated workforce (perhaps with two or maybe three sub-factors, for instance that labour is relatively cheap). Low corporation tax was a major factor cited by most of the interviewees.

In addition, there was widespread agreement that industrial policy, as pursued by successive governments and state agencies, was important. It was consistent and the IDA picked winning sectors which were growing rapidly – ICT, pharma, and international financial services, and recently medical devices. A further point, which was not really made, was that those indigenous firms which survived the lean 1980s were now stronger and several became major players internationally. There is now a small number of major indigenous firms emerging on to the international economy as serious multinationals, supported by the sister state body of IDA, Enterprise Ireland and guided by the policies of Forfás. It has been seen that outward FDI from Ireland is now high.

These five or so reasons were the main factors in the economic success of Ireland. Some of the others were also very important and some could be merged, for example cultural confidence-building and institutional change. It can also be seen that most of them are interdependent – education having a pull factor on FDI and vice versa. The demographic dividend, with many young workers, was another major factor, but they are now augmented by immigrants.

As the man who presided over ten of the most successful years in Irish economic history, the Taoiseach's view is important. Very economically literate, Bertie Ahern's view was that the most important factors were the cumulative increases, over time, of education provision and participation, our membership of the world's second biggest market, our relatively low rates of corporation tax, the capacity for rapid expansion of the labour force and the fact that we speak English. These factors made Ireland attractive for foreign direct investment. He said social partnership 'was the key catalyst for growth' – the 'X Factor' of our success, and also that Ireland benefited from the EU transfers.

Peter Sutherland, with the perspective of an international businessman and a political background as first Competition Commissioner in the EU, a former cabinet member in Ireland and first leader of the World Trade Organisation, said foreign direct investment was vitally important. He was strongly of the view that the Tiger took off when it did precisely because the Single Market was set up in 1992 and its rules on competition, which gave a small economy access, were enforced. This gave Ireland's exports unfettered access to every corner of the vast 300 million consumers and hundreds of thousands of firms in the fifteen member states. Sutherland also cited social partnership as a major factor, but he was not uncritical of the way it works. He was highly critical of the quality of the Irish educational system at all levels but interestingly, he believed that many Irish have a positive attitude to education which, he believed, gives them an edge internationally.

This gives them confidence but as Frances Ruane, Director of the ESRI, said, confidence without competence is a disadvantage. This new Irish beast is haunting the land in increasing numbers! Professor Ruane made the point that Ireland benefited disproportionately from FDI – the share to Europe rose and our share of it rose too and the sectors IDA chose to pursue were to boom. Consistency in policies was important, as was the low tax regime and the demographic dividend. She argued that while social partnership was important, it could not have happened without the Tallaght Strategy.

David Begg of the Congress of Trade Unions believed that FDI was vital and, unsurprisingly, believed that social partnership was a major factor, ensuring stability for firms in planning and, with the income tax reductions, giving workers rises in real incomes. Membership of the EU and the educated workforce were key factors in the success. He believed that the jobs boom, long a major aspiration of trade unionists, was an undreamed-of success. It also meant a tight labour market, which in turn helped unions in wage bargaining.

Joe Macri spoke of three factors which were the result of conscious policy decisions that generated Ireland's economic success – in his order of priority; 1) opening up the economy, 2) the education system and 3) the low company tax regime. He said that the IDA played an important role too and that two factors that do not appear in business manuals or corporate strategies were important, namely being English-speaking and the 'softer' factor of social partnership.

Gary McGann mentioned some key people in the background of Ireland's success, a point perhaps overlooked by economists. He cited low company taxes, the educated, English-speaking workforce, the role of the IDA and grants, membership of the EU and social partnership, which he thought needed revisiting.

What reasons do other economists give?
Frank Barry and other leading economists,[33] in a very useful book on the Irish economic miracle, cite fiscal stabilisation in the late 1980s, the EU Structural Funds, the improving educational attainment of workers, increasing FDI flows, wage moderation and peaceful industrial relations. He points out that there was disagreement between the contributors of 'the factors which precipitated some of these beneficial developments and the precise mechanisms through which the beneficial effects came into being.'

Barry[34] gives his reasons for the success as:
1. Ireland was the first country to target MNCs and the IDA was well ahead of its competitors;
2. Very low rates of corporation tax and generous grants;
3. English speaking;
4. Low labour costs compared to other advanced countries and favourable access to large export markets compared to lower-cost economies.

Zdenìk Cech and John Macdonald*[35] argued that there were many factors, both long- and short-term, which 'prepared the Irish economy for this impressive economic turnaround at a time of international buoyancy'. It was mostly due to rapid inward investment, and the extraordinary performance of the second half of the 1990s was mainly due, they argue, to the favourable external environment and the sizeable pool of available labour at that time. They also state that 'an appropriate and stable economic policy environment can be seen as a precondition for successful convergence'. Secondly, the timing of the economic turnaround, including a long period of unbroken growth in the world economy in the 1990s, and some of the specific features of the Irish economy were also crucial.

Cech and Macdonald give six broad reasons and include some subsidiary ones – all of which are largely in agreement with the reasons set out by our interviewees.

1. **Macroeconomic stability and institutional quality.** The fiscal correction of the late 1980s was a necessary precondition for an economic turnaround. In addition, the falling interest rates up to the launch of the euro gave Ireland an additional monetary stimulus. Ireland also scored high on most of the subjective indicators of political stability and institutional quality.
2. **EU internal market and membership of the euro.** Ireland benefited from increased openness, as the country's attractiveness for foreign direct investment inflows was boosted by the launch of the EU internal market. During the 1990s, the requirements for joining the euro area acted as an external anchor to help establish macroeconomic stability. Since then, Economic and Monetary Union (EMU) has continued to provide an external incentive for macroeconomic policy discipline.
3. **Social partnership and wage competitiveness.** They cite the series of national agreements from the late 1980s onwards that ensured a high degree of support from all stakeholders in the economy. These resulted in industrial peace and wage moderation. Progress in fiscal consolidation also allowed the authorities to trade off tax reductions for moderate pay increases.
4. **EU funds.** Transfers from EU funds, also in the light of fiscal consolidation, helped to finance a resumption of public capital spending and helped to improve public sector efficiency.
5. **Educated and abundant workforce.** Ireland's population had been growing strongly since the early 1990s and the country had been investing heavily in education since as far back as the 1960s, producing a supply of skilled labour ready to meet the needs of the incoming FDI.
6. **Industrial policies.** Industrial policies played a key role in Ireland's success, they believe.

Cech and Macdonald conclude that there is 'no single recipe for a successful turnaround in economic fortunes'.

Patrick Honahan and Brendan Walsh[36] reject the view of Ireland's take-off as 'a productivity miracle or the outcome of ingenious fiscal policy'. They see it as 'a belated convergence not in productivity but in the share of the population at work outside low income agriculture'. They argue that the preconditions 'for such convergence were already present in 1973, but a sequence of fiscal policy errors in the 1970s derailed the convergence for more than a decade'. There is much truth in this view of a delay which some of our commentators have also subscribed to, yet the speed of the success when it came was stunning. Again one can argue that if it had occurred earlier, say in the 1980s, many would not have had to emigrate and most citizens would have enjoyed a higher standard of living for longer.

When these fiscal policy errors were eventually corrected, Honahan and Walsh say that 'employment growth was facilitated by a collective pro-employment approach to wage bargaining resulting in improved wage competitiveness,' thus placing emphasis on wage determination. They argue that the steady convergence with Europe was delayed by fifteen years by the first oil crisis and the government's policy response to it. 'In particular, lacking were a stable fiscal environment and a wage formation process that would keep Irish labour competitive.' They say that the greatly improved external environment should not be underestimated, and admit that the fiscal turnaround after 1987 'took everyone by surprise'. They say that the devaluation in 1986 was especially timely because of 'the loss of competitiveness associated with a rapid depreciation of sterling', and Ireland was 'well-placed in terms of wage competitiveness to benefit from the accelerating economic boom in the UK and other trading partners countries after 1987'.

They place much emphasis on wage competitiveness and argue that in Britain, Thatcher attacked and undermined trade unions, whereas in Ireland 'there was no explicit government agenda to curb union power; on the contrary, the role of unions was greatly strengthened by the revival and deepening from 1987 of a centralised bargaining process that went beyond wages to cover taxation and other aspects of economic policy'.

Education contributed over many decades, as did the rule of law, quality of public administration, and the depth and efficiency of the financial system. They point out that the tax concessions for companies have become less attractive, but their 'continued liberality is obviously important' in an improved economic environment. Other factors were the demographic improvement, EU funds, devaluations of 1986 and 1993, boosting tourism and industrial investment.

Honahan and Walsh admit, perhaps reluctantly, that 'the importance of the *social partnership* from 1986 on cannot be dismissed. The partnership agreements did reflect a determination to set aside, for the time being, social class antagonism in favour of a joint effort to remove barriers to employment growth.' They argue for example that the income tax rate reductions, 'sometimes attributed to the partnership process, were evidently part-and-parcel of the fiscal normalisation'.

'A lucky period then, for Ireland, but one during which policy-makers and the social partners, shaken into realism by earlier disasters, seized the opportunities that were on offer with greater prudence, realism and restraint than before.'

A World Bank study[37] found that the EU rules on Structural Funds expenditure 'has had a significant effect on evaluation practice in Ireland'. This 'external push to promote evaluation has been a key determinant in systematising the approach to evaluation compared to what had been a very *ad hoc* approach previously.'

Alan Gray gathered eight international economists for an assessment of Ireland in 1997,[38] and he lists the reasons for the success. One was the labour force skills and education which Nobel laureate Keith Arrow focuses on, including child development and the influence of the family environment on cognitive development. This is a point made by Peter Sutherland and which Paul Krugman also emphasises in Gray's book. Krugman also focuses on FDI and the high productivity growth. He analyses why Ireland was so successful in attracting US FDI. One reason was transport costs, which, now reduced, no longer deter the long-range trade into Europe and the growth in traded services. A labour force which is well educated and English-speaking is also attractive to US firms, he found. Jeffrey Sachs praised the cut in public spending as a percentage of GDP from 51 per cent in 1987 to 43 per cent in 1993, which he believes supported export-led growth. These views are in line with many other commentators.

Ireland's leading independent economist, John FitzGerald of the ESRI, who had forecast the emergence of the Celtic Tiger, suggested the following reasons for the boom.[39] Firstly, there was the opening up of the goods and capital markets since 1960. Secondly, there was liberalisation of markets, but this was combined with the third factor, which was strong intervention by the state in investing in human capital. Fourthly, the state was strong in directly encouraging foreign direct investment, with both of these state interventions being pursued consistently over thirty years. Fifthly, membership of the European Union played a pivotal role as a force for change. He is highly critical of the state's failure to invest sufficiently in education in the first fifty years of independence, but the acceleration of such investment over the past twenty-five to thirty years is a key part of the success. FitzGerald says the social partnership approach to policy 'has made an important positive contribution to facilitating rapid growth' and it 'owes an intellectual debt to the experiences of countries such as the Netherlands and Germany' and to the European social model.

FitzGerald places strong emphasis on the role of education and points out that the rise in participation rates since 1980 were greater than in the first fifteen years of 'free education' and participation in third level continued to rise in the 1990s. The investment in education increased the supply of skilled labour, on top of the rapid rise in the supply of young people entering the labour market after the high birth rates up to 1980. FDI, favourable demographics and better management of public finances also helped the success. The increased participation of women also helped and he found that one-third of the 'very big rise in female participation rates since 1980 is attributable to the effect of investment in education'. He holds that the 1977 'dash for growth' involving a huge fiscal injection 'almost wrecked the Irish economy' despite warnings from economists.[40]

Which model describes Ireland?

It is worth examining a number of characteristics of modern Ireland to ascertain which political and economic model it belongs to. The issue of where to place Ireland in broad existing socio-economic paradigms is complex and elusive. Ben Tonra[41] believes that Ireland has evolved over four foreign policy narratives which attempt to define who we are, with the first being that of the Irish nation. The second was as a global citizen which is more internationalist and modernist, with the third as a European republic, not only in geography but in culture, politics, philosophy and religions. The fourth is that of the Anglo-American state, with the common English language, common law traditions and familial bonds with North America and the old Commonwealth. Tonra sees the possibility of a fifth, in the synthesis of that of the global citizen and the European Republic.

The view that Ireland is a model for the Right to follow may be correct if their objective is simply to have low public spending. However, high public spending does not define a successful Left political objective, especially in modern Europe. Ireland's public spending was at 45 per cent in the 1980s, largely due to the mismanagement of the economy from 1977. This was far from a successful economy for either a Left- or indeed a Right-wing government. The current low public spending is largely the result of the very rapid economic growth; strong revenue from economic success but, as growth slows, so public spending will rise as a proportion of national income. This will happen whatever the political hue of the governing parties, because the Irish public want better public services.

The Irish model has been held up as a beacon for the Right in many parts of the world, especially the USA. Yet the Left has been interested in it too, though not as enthusiastically as some right-wing American think-tanks. It is my view that the Irish model does not conform to either stereotype, but has tantalising features which make it attractive to an *à la carte* choice by either.

In a glowingly approving article called *Thatcherism Triumphant? The New Business Climate in Europe,* the very conservative Heritage Foundation in the US said that 'once viewed as largely socialist, the economies of Europe have changed'.

The *2006 Index of Economic Freedom,* published jointly by the Heritage Foundation and the *Wall Street Journal* said that Ireland is pro-market and the third 'freest' economy in the world. Ireland scored 1.58 in this Index. 'Ireland offers employers a flexible labour market and low social security payments, and it resists EU attempts to harmonise tax rates,' Heritage says. Ireland's economy got an added boost in the early 1990s, 'when the government slashed the corporate tax rate to 12.5 per cent and took other measures to unleash the nation's entrepreneurs to create wealth'. In another article, the author, President of the Heritage Foundation, Edwin Feulner, does not mince his words – on corporation tax, he says 'There's a worldwide race to the bottom going on,' led by Ireland. 'And if the United States doesn't get moving again, we might even lose it.'

Another laudatory piece by the Heritage Foundation's Marc Miles in early 2006 said, 'Take Ireland. Once known as a poor agricultural society, it's become a hotspot for foreign investment. . . Ireland gets good marks for its low level of government intervention in the economy. It posted a perfect score of 1 this year on monetary policy,[42] foreign investment, banking and finance and property rights. It scored 2s for low government intervention in the economy and low regulation and 2.3 on a low fiscal "burden".'

The Cato Institute, another of the many very conservative think-tanks in the US, also claims that Ireland's success is thanks to tax cutting, low regulation, the small size of the state and lack of intervention (interference) in the market.

However, the reality is more complex as this book demonstrates. As John FitzGerald argues, 'there was more to Ireland's belated success than merely a liberalisation of markets. There was also active intervention by the state in investing, also belatedly, in human capital and in directly encouraging foreign direct investment.' This two-pronged approach has been pursued with consistency by all governments over the last thirty years. He also argues that 'there were also a series of "enabling" factors that have facilitated the success of the last decade, as well as some policy mistakes.'

The Irish economic model is a mixture of market liberalisation, strong state intervention, tax-cutting, state shrinking, strong public investment, union involvement in key decision-making in partnership with employers and government and state-led industrial policy, etc. Where it lies on the political spectrum may be a matter for a political analysts, once they set out their analytical framework. On balance, the formula for its economic success has more to offer those on the Left than to those on the Right because of strong state intervention; high state investment; broad participatory policy formation and execution; and the consensus that social and economic objectives have parity. The latter point on parity of the economic and social objectives now peppers government ministers' speeches. 'Nurturing the complementary relationship between social policy and economic prosperity' is one of the first items in the current agreement, Towards 2016.

Globalisation and Ireland

It has been seen that globalisation is important to Ireland. Any small economy will have a large number of foreign firms which supply the domestic market, but more importantly also use it as a base to export to other countries. One of the themes emerging from this book is that Ireland has gained immensely from globalisation. It was late to open up to trade, but got in early to the first phase of real FDI globalisation and played its first-mover advantage very well.

The foreign multinational firms employ 150,000 directly in Ireland which is just 6 per cent of the workforce. However, these companies export a disproportionate amount of our exports, in very high productivity processes. They also generate high quality skills, have fairly strong linkages and have been investing more in research and development in recent times.

Ireland does very well in the competition for FDI as has been seen in the interviews. Ireland is not *dependent* on FDI, but is part of an inter-dependence in the globalised world, in a two-way process. Ireland is far from being an impotent state. It is a small but important part of a contract with the global economy and with the investing firms. One would not expect firms like Intel to invest several billion in Ireland and then walk. Ireland is very important in the globalised world and punches well above its weight.

It has been seen that the total stock of FDI in Ireland in 2005 was much bigger than its national income at 125 per cent of GNP – far above the average level in the EU at 33 per cent. It was pointed out that small countries have a higher proportion of trade and are more globalised but Ireland is in a league of its own. It was also seen that Ireland itself is now a major foreign investor. 2004 was a record year when total Irish FDI in other countries exceeded total FDI in Ireland, at over €15 billion. And this excluded huge investment in property abroad by wealthy individuals and companies, which are now major investors all over the world.

The growth in exports of services has been very strong, rising to €54bn in 2006, as the growth in trade in goods slowed. Irish exports of services are around the twelfth highest in the world. Ireland had 2.5 per cent of the world's exports in services in 2006.[43] A large part of these services exports was in computer services and business services. The 'visible hand' of the state has been very evident in Ireland in industrial policy and latterly in economic policy with the shift to services, especially internationally traded services. The completion of the Doha Round will assist Ireland's shift to export services, when new rules for trade are established.

The hard fact in the modern world is that a small economy in a globalised world is dependent on FDI. But it is not a passive participant. It can play a major role in attracting the kind of investment it wants, as has been demonstrated. Also, the outward investment by Irish firms and citizens is now very substantial. Irish firms employ almost as many workers in other countries as all the foreign firms employ in Ireland. Irish investors own large chunks of commercial property in London and in many other parts of Europe. Irish multinationals, such as CRH and Smurfit Kappa, employ tens of thousands abroad, but unlike the foreign companies in Ireland, they are not in such high value added businesses. Foreign firms have created more backward linkages and actually have a slightly longer average life than indigenous firms in Ireland. They are high value added, many are unionised, generally pay well and bring in skills in management and technology, which benefit the country. With fewer of these companies, Ireland would be a far poorer place but the debate is important and will continue.

In conclusion, our analysis has shown that there were many inter-related reasons for the Irish economic success. However, five factors were more important. These were a) membership of the European Union and at a fortuitous time, b) FDI, c) low company taxes, d) the young, abundant, educated and English-speaking workforce, and e) social partnership. Other factors were important too such as its small size, institutions and favourable demographics. We also examined Ireland and globalisation, and attempted to ascertain which economic model Ireland best fits. The final chapter will again examine the basic building blocks of economic prosperity for nations, lessons from Ireland, issues which are still outstanding and Ireland's future prospects, but the next chapter sets out the hard facts on what actually was achieved in Ireland in the twenty years from 1987.

CHAPTER TEN

The Hard Facts
on the Irish Economic Success

In Chapter One, a short overview was given of the extent of the Irish economic success. In this chapter, the main economic fundamentals over the twenty-year period from 1987 will be examined. It will be seen that on all key factors, especially employment, the hard data demonstrates unequivocally that Ireland had a spectacular economic performance.

The success: massive growth in employment

The greatest achievement of the Celtic Tiger years has been the staggering growth in employment. In the twenty years from 1987, the numbers at work in Ireland doubled from 1,090,000 to 2,120,000. This success has been particularly spectacular after hundreds of years of mass emigration.

Figure 1: Irish Job Machine

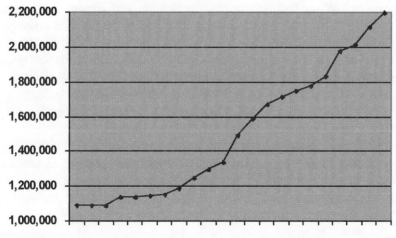

Source: CSO

The best way to appreciate Ireland's job success is firstly to compare it to its own history and then to compare it to other countries. Ireland had virtually no net new jobs between Independence in 1922 and the 1980s and this stagnation was accompanied by mass emigration. The growth in net jobs in Ireland really began from 1993 and between that year and 2007, it grew at 4 per cent each year, which is four times that of Britain, which also had one of its best job-creation periods for many decades. The US is lauded for its job-creation success and it has performed well, but Ireland was almost three times better in this fourteen-year period. Ireland was almost four times better than the average in the EU15's advanced states in this period and it was well ahead of Spain, the next best job performer in the period, which averaged 3.6 per cent a year. Ireland's job growth averaged 4.3 per cent in the decade to 2003 although it slowed slightly in the later years to 2007.

Characteristics of the employment success

The reversal of emigration

The curse of mass emigration is not just a recent memory, like in the 1980s or the 1950s. Ireland has had mass emigration since the late seventeenth century. It did not all begin with the Great Famine of 1845–48, but it accelerated after it. Almost one-tenth of the population (of 8.1 million on the island) emigrated in the decade after the Famine. There was a staggering fall in population – a halving in sixty years.[1]

In the nineteenth century, Ireland, one of the smallest European countries, contributed more migrants to the US than any other country. Ireland's emigration had an impact on many parts of the country, but unlike the dead of the two world wars in European countries, they are not remembered. While Ireland's population loss was far greater, the emigrants did not die. There has been no greater population shift in European history, which had many – too many. The population of the Republic was 6.5m in 1841. It fell to just 2.9m by 1926, just after Independence in 1922, and it reached its lowest level in 1961 at 2.8m. This was hardly the sign of a successful republic. By 1986, population had slowly edged up to 3.5m. By 2007, it was 4.3m and the forecasts are upwards, to five million by 2020, counter to many other European countries.

1989 was the peak year of emigration with a massive 70,000 fleeing Ireland.[2] When the economy began to recover, inward and outward migration began to balance from 1991. From 1994, when the jobs boom really took off, net immigration began and emigration declined. Net immigration peaked in the year to April 2006 with an inflow of 87,000 (net 70,000). Returning Irish, who had made up 70 per cent of all immigrants in 1991, fell progressively to just 26 per cent by 2004.

The admission of ten new member states into the European Union on 1 May 2004 led to many Central Europeans coming to Ireland. They made up most of the new migrants. Foreigners made up over 10.4 per cent of the population in Ireland by 2002, compared to 6 per cent in 1991. In early 2007, there were 320,000 foreigners aged fifteen or over in Ireland who made up 9.3 per cent of that cohort. Foreign workers made up 11 per cent of those in employment (229,000) in mid 2007. More Polish immigrants sought social insurance numbers, PPS numbers, than Irish in 2006.

The huge drop in unemployment
Unemployment had been over 17 per cent in 1985–7 inclusive (on top of the emigration) and fell each year from a peak of almost 18 per cent in 1987 to 4.2 per cent in 2002, where it hovered to the end of 2007. It is one of the lowest rates in Europe, where average unemployment in the Euro area was 7.4 per cent in 2007.

Good quality jobs
Contrary to popular myth, most of the new jobs have not been McJobs, but higher skilled. The quality of the jobs created has been high. Of course, as employment doubled, so the absolute number of low-skilled jobs has grown substantially, but the proportion of low-skill jobs has fallen and continues to fall. The forecast is for shortages of high-skilled people by 2020 and increased unemployment of the low-skilled.[3] The biggest increase in jobs was in services, where 1.4 million work, double the level in 1994. There has been very strong growth in professionals and also in the less quality, but sometimes lucrative, personal services, since the middle 1990s.

There has been a big structural change. In 1960 almost 40 per cent of all at work were in agriculture, whereas today it is only 5 per cent of the workforce. In the 1990s Irish manufacturing moved against the international trend of decline in employment, with a substantial growth in jobs. However, there was a decline since the 2001 peak of 251,000 and it was around 220,000 in 2007, though manufacturing output continued to grow. In four key areas of job quality, worker autonomy, work stress, job security and job satisfaction, a study[4] found that in the most rapidly expanding jobs, in professional and technical occupations, there were high levels of autonomy and job satisfaction but more intense work pressure. The other expanding group – personal and protective services and sales – 'were characterised by low levels of job autonomy and lower levels of job satisfaction, but also low levels of work pressure. The differences between the expanding occupations suggest some polarisation of job quality.'

Increased part-time work
There has been a substantial growth in part-time work which has been a conscious choice for many. This choice has been made far easier because

the economy is close to full employment, though work–life balance is also a factor. Employers and employees both like flexible working arrangements. Part-time employment more than doubled from less than 7 per cent of total employment in 1983 to over 17 per cent in 2006. However, the incidence of under-employment (those who would like a full-time job) fell substantially to 11 per cent of those part-timers in 2007, showing that most of those working part-time wish to do so. The decrease in involuntary part-time work has been striking. Only 6 per cent of men work part-time compared to 32 per cent of women, and women tend to have routine and lower-skilled part-time work.

Security of employment

Another popular myth is that there is no such thing as job security in the modern world except in the public service. Yet the vast majority of Irish employees, over 85 per cent, almost 9 out of every 10, are on secure contracts, which is the same as Europe at 85.5 per cent in 2005.[5] Where there is a trend to contract work and to longer contracts for employees, it does lead to stress and insecurity. Most employers know that if they want to retain good staff, they employ them directly and they still do this. The numbers on fixed-term temporary contracts actually fell in Ireland since the mid-1990s, which may be because of the weakness of employment protection laws in Ireland which employers feel gives them flexibility without the need for such temporary contracts.

Employment rates

The employment rate[6] was 68 per cent in 2006, above the EU15 average of 65 per cent. It rose rapidly from 54 per cent in 1995. It is now above the rates for France and Germany, where leisure is more valued than work but it is below that of the workaholics, the US and the UK at 72 per cent, but Iceland at 84.4 is tops and even socially-aware Denmark is very high at 76 per cent participation. Increased employment rates, particularly of women, have raised both living standards and growth rates substantially.

Women's labour-force participation rate in Ireland increased dramatically, from a low base of 46 per cent in 1994 to 60.3 per cent by 2005,[7] slightly below the EU15 average. In contrast, men's labour-force participation initially moved in the opposite direction, falling from over 76 per cent in 1981 to 69 per cent in 1998, but then up to 80 per cent in 2005. The overall labour-force participation rate[8] which was almost unchanged in the 1980s, rose to 70 per cent in 2005. Women are expected to account for 45 per cent of total employment by 2015.

There has been a substantial rise in the numbers participating in education – up from 200,000 in 1981 to 369,000 in 2006 which has helped on the jobs front, by reducing the numbers seeking jobs.

Monoculture to cosmopolitan in jig time

Perhaps the most remarkable features of the Irish economic success are two changes in the composition of the Irish workforce with a) the increased participation of women and b) the new immigrants. The Irish workforce has been utterly changed, grown cosmopolitan – from all-Irish to over one in ten workers being foreign – in just a few years. Over one-tenth or 229,000 of the two million workers in 2007 were foreign, with the largest group from the ten new accession states of the EU, which joined in May 2004. Ireland moved from monoculture to cosmopolitan in no time! While Germany, Britain, France and other European countries have absorbed many foreign workers since the Second World War, the numbers of foreign workers in Ireland's workforce rose dramatically in just six years. The stock or total number of foreign workers in Ireland is higher than that in many larger European countries.

The real achievement of the Irish economic success has been on employment and emigration. The numbers at work doubled in just twenty years. However, most of the increase was from 1994, so the great employment success was achieved in just a thirteen-year period to 2007. The other aspects of the employment success included increased participation of women; the increase in the total number at work; a shift in employment to services, to better quality jobs; the termination of involuntary emigration; and the absorption of large-scale immigration, in a very short time.

Economic growth: driving the economy

Economic growth has been very high in Ireland for many years. GDP averaged 7.1 per cent a year between 1994 and 2007 inclusive. This was way above virtually all other industrialised countries, where growth rates averaged 2 per cent in the EU, 3.2 per cent in the US and 2.3 per cent in Japan. China and a few other newly industrialising countries have been higher, with Singapore and a number of South American countries enjoying high growth in recent years. Some Central European countries like the Czech Republic, Poland and Estonia are growing fast, but only in recent years, and they are way behind Ireland in per-capita incomes.

Ireland, amongst all countries, will face challenges and also opportunities from a group of large emerging countries which are increasingly integrating into the globalised economy. These are called 'the BRICs' – Brazil, Russian Federation, India and China. From just 17 per cent of world GDP in 1990, they already accounted for one-quarter of world income by 2005. They are among the ten largest economies in the world and on current performance, they will get much larger and more important in future years. Between 2000–05, India created 11.3 million net new jobs a year on average. For China the figure was 7 million, 2.7 million for Brazil and 0.7 million for the

Russian Federation. This compares with just 3.7 million in the thirty richest countries, the members of the OECD, in that period.[9] India's increase in jobs of over 11 million a year seems huge – a rise of 15 per cent in the period, but Ireland's performance job creation in the period was slightly better with a rise of 15.4 per cent (see Appendix 1 for Ireland's employment data from 1983 to 2008).

Growth has been as high as a phenomenal 10 to12 per cent in a number of years (in 1997, 1999, 2000) in Ireland. Figure 2 shows how Ireland's growth, in both GDP per capita, and also the more informative Gross National Income per capita, was way ahead of all OECD countries in the decade.

Figure 2: GDP and GNI per capita growth, average annual growth 1994–2003

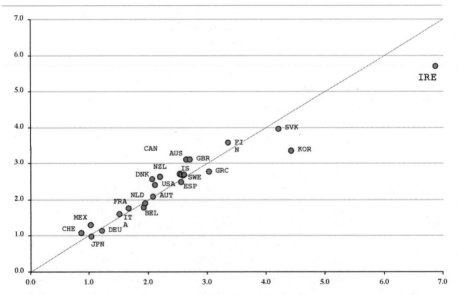

Source: Congress' *Coming Challenges in Productivity* and OECD, *Working Paper No 1 on Alternative Measures of Well-Being*, 2005

The very high sustained growth rates allowed Ireland to catch up with the rest of Europe and to overtake most countries. When Ireland joined the European Community, as the EU was then called, in 1973, its per capita income was only 55 per cent of the average GDP of the fifteen advanced European economies. Today it is 150 per cent, that is, it appears to be 50 per cent above the average. It appears to be the second highest – with only Luxembourg being higher. However, when Gross National Income, the income available to Irish people to spend, is used, Ireland is moved from second highest place to fifth. Fifth highest income per person in Europe, ahead of the UK (which has had ten very good years of growth), Sweden, Germany and France is no mean achievement in such a short period of time. However, regions like the south-east of England are still way ahead of Ireland.

Figure 3 shows that Ireland's economic growth in GDP terms exceeds all other countries in the decade to 2005.

Figure 3: GDP growth 1995–2005

Source: OECD in *Figures 2006*

Which measure of National Income – GDP or GNP?

There is a complication with the rate of the growth in national income measured by GDP of the Irish Republic. GDP exaggerates the income available to Irish people. The international comparator commonly used is Gross Domestic Product (GDP). For Ireland, there is an unusually large divergence between Gross National Product (GNP) and Gross Domestic Product (GDP), whereas for other countries GDP and GNP are very close. The difference between GNP and GDP is made up by 'net factor flows' which are mainly due to profit repatriations and transfer pricing by multinationals. In 2007, the gross outflow for Ireland was €26.3 billion, from which inflows should be deducted. Repatriated profits and royalties and 'reinvested earnings' might be added to this, which are profits made by multinationals but not yet repatriated. There are interest payments on the national debt too. Many Irish companies are now major investors abroad and repatriate profits, but back to Ireland. The bottom line is net factor flows (or payments) which amounted to €27bn in 2007 and this is deducted from GDP of €195bn, giving GNP of €168bn, which is the unique Irish difference.

Transfer pricing or transfer price-fixing is where multinational companies transfer profit to countries with low company taxes by inflating the prices of materials or other inputs in high-tax countries and reducing them artificially in the low-tax countries. It exaggerates the level of real economic activity in the low-tax country. In the case of Ireland, total factor payments, which include transfer pricing (and other payments), are very large – 18 per cent of GNP or €27bn in 2007 and this is why GNP and GDP diverge.

There is a major upside to transfer price fixing. By locating the profits in Ireland, MNCs are paying company tax there that would not otherwise be received, and thus they are boosting the Irish Exchequer.

Investment

A major driver of economic growth is investment and both public and private investment in Ireland has been very high for many years. Ireland's cities are dominated by cranes and there is construction everywhere. Economic growth is driven largely by productivity, which in turn is boosted by investment in plant, machinery and people. Ireland has been investing at about twice the level in Europe as part of its catch-up. It is recognised that it still has a way to go and much investment is public investment through major government spending plans, with the 2007–13 National Development Plan (NDP) hoping to invest €184bn by 2013, of which €78bn is capital spending and the bulk of it is public investment by the taxpayer.

The roads, water, waste infrastructure, public transport are well behind those of most of Europe and new public buildings (schools, hospitals, clinics, universities, libraries, courthouses, etc.) are only now being built and others modernised.

Private sector investment has been high too, with gross capital formation by the private sector in Ireland peaking at 28 per cent of GNP in 2005, the highest in the EU, but 75 per cent of the total was in construction. Gross investment in real prices has averaged 5.5 per cent since 2000 compared to just 2.2 per cent in the EU15, and it was 8.4 per cent in the 1990s compared to the same steady 2.2 per cent for the EU15.[10]

Productivity
Productivity underpins economic growth and there has been very strong growth in Irish productivity over two decades. The aggregate productivity in Ireland reached the levels of other industrialised countries in the late 1990s, mainly due to the contribution of the manufacturing sector. This very strong productivity growth and Ireland's robust employment growth over the 1990s practically wiped out unemployment, which fell from 13 per cent in 1990 to around 4 per cent in 2001. It has remained low at around 4.2 per cent over the following six years. Unemployment was the lowest in the EU27 in 2006 compared to an average of 7.9 per cent in the Euro area, or as high as 9.4 per cent in France and 8.4 per cent in Germany that year.

Ireland attracted foreign investment because it was a low-wage economy in Europe in the 1960s and 1970s. This was to change with the boom years, but not dramatically. Under the social partnership agreements, there were relatively low wage increases initially, but with substantial rises in take-home pay, due to cuts in income tax.

Ireland's productivity growth has been spectacular and its level is now one of the highest in the world. In 2007, it cost only 61 per cent of what it cost in 1995 to produce the average widget.[11] The level of productivity – per person at work, defined as GDP per person employed – was the second highest in the EU27, after France in 2007. However, as GDP exaggerates Ireland's performance, Ireland is somewhat lower down, but it is still quite high on the league table.

Like all economies, some sectors of manufacturing have high productivity while others do not. Ireland has a 'dual' economy, with foreign firms being highly productive and indigenous firms having lower productivity in general. Ireland is a major producer of information and communications technology (ICT) and this and 'chemicals' boosts our productivity substantially. Our productivity in the use of ICT in offices and services is not so high and this is an area to address through education and training.

However, productivity has hardly risen since 2000, due to the slowdown in manufacturing; the increased size of the construction sector in the economy, which has low productivity and the continuing shift to services, which also generally has lower productivity. This could be a serious issue, though there were indications of improvement in late 2006 and early 2007, generated in an upturn in manufacturing. As productivity is at the heart of economic progress, it is an area which has to be addressed constantly and Ireland cannot rest on its past success in the area.

Earnings
In the twenty years from 1987 to 2007, average industrial earnings rose from just over €13,000 to €33,000 a year before inflation. Taking account of inflation and the large reductions in income tax, single earners' net income rose by a substantial 83 per cent in real terms in the twenty years. Married persons saw their income rise by 73 per cent in real terms in the twenty years.

Put another way, there was an annual rise in real incomes of 3.7 per cent above inflation each year over the twenty years or of almost 4.2 per cent rise for single people.[12]

Contrast this to the very slow growth in wages in the US where there was around a 14-per-cent growth in wages between 1997 and 2000. Then wages failed to rise for typical workers between 2001 and 2006 'even as half of the productivity growth of the 1995–2005 period occurred since then', according to the independent Economic Policy Institute.[13] Hourly wages, in inflation-adjusted terms, actually fell by 0.1 per cent annually between 2000 and 2004 in the US. The EPI found that 'the typical, or median, workers' hourly wage was just 8.9 per cent higher in 2005 than in 1979, with almost all of the growth (7.7 per cent) occurring from 1995–2000. In contrast, productivity has grown by 67 per cent since 1979' in the US. Another study[14] found that the top 1 per cent population in the US has had an increase of 43 per cent in incomes as against a real gain of only 14 per cent for the lower 80 per cent of families, between 1979 and 2004. The authors found that income gaps 'are also observed in other industrialised countries – in particular the English-speaking countries'. While income and wealth inequality increased in Ireland in the boom, Irish workers fared far better than workers in many other advanced countries, especially in the US.

Using different dates and for a smaller category of workers, real earnings of Irish employees in the business sector increased by substantially above the EU15 and all other countries.[15] While the earnings of Irish industrial workers were well behind most other European workers ten years ago, when adjustments for tax reductions are made, they improved their living standards far faster than all others and surpassed those in many countries in take-home pay. Their social wage is, however, still well behind most Europeans in terms of healthcare, childcare, welfare, education, public transport, etc. There were substantial improvements in public provision of services in Ireland in the boom, too, but it will still be difficult to catch up.

While real take-home earnings increased substantially and Ireland is no longer a low-wage economy, the cost of labour to an employer is still relatively low compared to most other advanced European countries. Total hourly industrial earnings were close to both the US and UK, but substantially below those in Germany, Netherlands and Denmark in 2004.[16] Under social partnership, there was agreement to reduce the 'tax wedge', that is, the total cost to an employer of hiring employees. This means that it is still much cheaper for Irish employers to hire workers in Ireland than in many other states, measured by total labour costs, and this is reflected in the above data and in other comparators of labour costs.[17]

The effective rate of income tax paid by average single industrial workers was reduced by half in recent years. It was reduced from 25 per cent of average earnings in 1994 to around 12 per cent in 2001.[18] The big reduction took place around 1999, with so many additional people at work and increased economic activity, which boosted tax revenue and allowed the reductions in income taxes to be made.

Those without earnings
The massive increase in employment had a dramatic impact on reducing poverty and this is reflected in the rapid increase in real household incomes. The poorest households with several unemployed people saw a dramatic improvement in their situation as one or more unemployed persons found work.

However, not all gained in the boom and the 'at risk of poverty rate' in Ireland in 2005 was 19.7 per cent, the second highest rate in the EU15, just behind the UK. It compared to 9 per cent in Sweden or 10 per cent in Denmark. It was significantly higher than the EU25 'at risk of poverty' rate of 16 per cent.[19] People living in consistent poverty in Ireland was 7 per cent of the population in 2005, though a higher 10 per cent of children were in this situation with 17 per cent of disabled people being in consistent poverty.[20] Income gaps and overall welfare will be explored further in the next chapter.

While the boom in the economy and the corresponding doubling in employment level had a dramatic impact on most people's fortunes, coupled with real rising take-home pay, some people, many of the poor, the disabled, discouraged workers, single parents and others did not share in the boom. Welfare payments did increase above inflation in the boom, but not sufficiently to really reduce high levels of poverty.

On the other hand, in terms of *quality of life* Ireland ranks fourth overall on the UN's Human Development Index which is a combination of education, health and income. It had improved substantially in 2004 over 2000. Life expectancy in Ireland had increased by three years for males and females since 1990, but it is slightly below the OECD average in 2005.

The government finances
Day-to-day public spending amounted to 50 per cent of GNP for several years in the 1980s in Ireland, but it fell to only 29 per cent by 2000 and has remained in the low 30 per cent area since; the lowest in the EU15 advanced economies (see Appendix 3). Public spending had been running out of control in the 1980s. This was a result of the economic policies introduced after the 1977 election victory by Fianna Fáil, where taxes were cut substantially and spending was increased! There was an iconic tax cut – the abolition of taxes on residential property. This has had a major impact on local democracy, on fairness, on property prices and in the longer term, on Irish people's hostile attitude to property taxes.

Taxes had to be raised very substantially to pay for the excesses of those election promises which had led to a mountain of debt and massive interest repayments. The interest payments alone were taking all income tax levied in the country for some years. The top rate of income tax had risen to 65 per cent and even those on low incomes paid high income taxes. Evasion and avoidance was widespread, which generated stronger dissatisfaction.

From 1983, government revenue (from all sources) peaked at 45.3 per cent of GNP and it was reduced by slightly below that (to around 40 per cent of GNP) until 1995, when it was reduced further. It has been around 35–37 per cent of GNP since (see Appendix 3). The Irish National Debt is the second lowest in the EU15 at 24 per cent of GNP, having been the highest in the late 1980s. On the other hand, private sector debt has soared and rose to €300bn in 2007. This was the most indebted per capita in the Eurozone, bar Luxembourg. In 2006 private sector credit grew by 25 per cent, in spite of rising interest rates. The General Government Balance has been in surplus for ten years. If the capital spending and the money put into the National Pension Reserve Fund are added back, there would be a substantial current surplus each year since 1995, running as high as 8 per cent of GNP.

There has been a remarkable turnaround in Irish public spending in the twenty years, from a highly taxed, highly indebted, under-investing economy to one with the lowest income and company taxes, a low national debt, and high public investment. Conversely, Ireland also has the lowest public spending on day-to-day public services in the EU15, just below that of Spain in 2007.

Public spending – down but still up!

The main political parties in the 2007 general election promised to reduce Ireland's already low income taxes even further and simultaneously, to increase public services. Ironically, if economic growth levels were maintained at over 4 per cent a year for several years, it was possible that the parties could do both. Most of Ireland's politicians boast of the low tax regime. Conversely, few boast that Ireland's public spending is one of the lowest in the world's advanced economies, not far off the level of the US and well below the EU15. Current or day-to-day public spending as a percentage of GNP was cut dramatically from 42 per cent in 1994, to remain at 31.4 per cent on average between 1998–2005.

Yet in an apparent paradox, at the same time, the level of public spending rose substantially in that period from 1995 to 2006 inclusive – by a very substantial 8.9 per cent on average per annum and it had soared to almost 16 per cent in 2001 because there was to be a general election in May 1992. Strong economic growth means that public spending can rise in absolute terms, while remaining low as a proportion of national income. The benefits of a balanced, growing economy allow politicians to have the best of all worlds. This is the reason why even the more socially conscious Irish politicians were unembarrassed by promises to further reduce taxes in a country with already very low public spending as a proportion of GNP.

The very benign scenario for the Irish public finances has also meant that at the same time as reducing the national debt, the government has also been able to save. Since 2001, it has been putting 1 per cent of GDP into a pension fund for its civil servants' pensions and for other pensioners. In May 2007, the National Pension Reserve Fund stood at €21bn, not far below the national debt of €25bn in 2007. It is invested in firms all over the world. The virtues of an economic boom are many and explain the apparent paradox of reduced taxes, and some increased spending, debt reduction and savings. Massive employment growth, rising incomes, rising profits underpinned by strong productivity growth and then by domestic consumption boosted revenue so much that it also allowed taxes to be reduced simultaneously, and debts to be repaid.

The level of *capital* public spending has been very high at 5 per cent of GDP for many years – about twice the level of Europe. While the government has plenty of money to undertake all this investment, it also has a major public–private partnership (PPP) scheme to involve the private sector in the massive investment in public infrastructure. The 2007 National Development Plan, the fourth, is overseeing a further investment of 5.5 per cent of GNP to 2013.

So it has been seen that various Irish governments have been both shrinking the size of the state (when judged by current spending as a per cent of GDP), a major objective of the Right, and substantially increasing its day-to-day spending on public services, which is generally ascribed as an objective of the traditional Left. Yet governments could have still tipped the balance either way, if they so chose. They could still have reduced public spending as a percentage of GDP by less, but greatly increased spending on public services, without many problems. On the other hand, they could have cut public spending and taxes by even more than they did.

In practice, increasing public spending very rapidly might have met capacity problems and it may have boosted inflation too. While most Irish people appear to like the low-tax regime, they are also unhappy with the poor level of public services, especially in health, education and public transport. The connection between taxes and public spending has been blurred by the boom and all the main political parties clearly reflect and follow the mainstream public's choice and favour low taxes, while espousing better public services.

Only with such a buoyant economy can public spending as a share of GDP be cut so radically while simultaneously boosting it above inflation each year. When the downturn comes, which it will, public spending will be under pressure and taxes may have to rise. Getting better value from public spending is and will continue to be the major challenge to politicians in all advanced economies into the future. Public spending rose – seemingly inexorably – in the developed economies since the Second World War, and it was only from the mid-1990s that the upward rise was halted and slightly reversed.

The growth of privatisation, outsourcing, PPPs and other attempts to shrink the state and shift the provision of public services to the private sector may seem to be inexorable, but the figures show that the modern capitalist state is still spending a large proportion of national income in most countries. Current spending is somewhat lower than some years ago, as a proportion of GDP (especially in Ireland), but it was still at 42.5 per cent in the EU15 in 2007 (which was the same as in 2000), just over 40 per cent for the EU25 states and 33 per cent of GNP in Ireland. It is as high as 46.7 for Belgium and almost 48 per cent for France and Sweden. Current spending in the UK is 40 per cent – the same as in the mid-1980s – and it never moved by more than 3.2 percentage points below this in decades, in spite of Thatcher's ambition to roll back the state, as defined by such public spending.

Public spending is necessary to build the modern economy where education is a key input and the public is increasingly demanding better public services. Even in the US, the demand for public provision of basic healthcare is now rapidly gaining ground, particularly as even the largest firms belatedly realise that they cannot afford to pay for a system that is reeling out of control. New innovations and systems of organisation of the public service will be required.

The rapid growth of the economy generated increased revenue and this allowed reductions in tax rates, while simultaneously, there was a reduction in current public spending as a proportion of GNP. These two decades have been unusually benign for the governments' public finances since the mid-1990s. This period will, in time, be seen as a *golden era*.

Ireland – one of the most globalised economies in the world

Ireland has become one of the most globalised economies in the world. While it is twelfth in the overall country ranking in 2007 of the Swiss KOF Index,[21] it was third as the most globalised *economically*, after Luxembourg and Switzerland. The other two criteria that the Index used are *social* and *political*, where Ireland does not perform so well. Small countries are generally more trade-dependent and globalised than large economies and Ireland's imports and exports amounted to 147 per cent of GDP in 2007. Its exports were 79 per cent of GDP compared to the US where exports were only equivalent to 14.5 per cent of GDP, or the UK, with exports accounting for 66.6 per cent of GDP. Globalisation, which is criticised and feared by some, has been very good for Ireland. This huge interdependence with the rest of the world does have its downsides. A large and important part of the Irish economy is controlled outside the state and the Irish economy is inexorably entwined with the world economy.

An increasingly competitive economy

According to the World Economic Forum, Ireland was the twenty-first most competitive economy in the world in 2006, out of 125 countries. It had been ten places higher in 2001. This score is subjective as it reflects the views of top executives of large companies, but as the criteria are applied consistently, it is worthy of analysis. Switzerland is tops, followed by the Nordic countries. So, even in spite of their high public spending, the Nordics are generally close to the top of the competitiveness league. Singapore and the US follow.

The criteria include a sound institutional environment, infrastructure,

R&D, transparent and stable public institutions. The US has been demoted from the top position because of its large fiscal and trade deficits. The major reason Ireland is lower is because of our poor infrastructure, low scores on 'innovation and technological readiness' and because the 'quality of the national business environment' is poorly ranked. The latter is surprising as Ireland scores higher on being very business-friendly in other indices. For example, the Economist Intelligence Unit rated Ireland as the sixth most friendly business environment in the world.[22] In time, the huge public investment in infrastructure and in innovation and science should raise Ireland's standing in these leagues, which is far from bad already.

In a paper on Ireland's competitiveness, two Central Bank economists[23] found that its position at the beginning of the current decade was 'extremely favourable' and deemed to be 'probably unsustainable' at that high level. Ireland fares quite well by international standards in the high-technology intensity of output and exports, the percentage of the young workforce with third-level qualifications, the relatively light regulatory burden facing business and a taxation environment that is supportive of enterprise, investment and labour. Irish economy subsequently lost competitiveness due to factors like rising prices and production costs relative to our trading partners, an appreciation of the effective exchange rate and weaker productivity growth, the bank economists found.

The reports of the National Competitiveness Council give an excellent overview of the competitive position of Ireland on a multitude of criteria every year and it also publishes reports on issues like the *Cost of Doing Business in Ireland*. Overall Ireland has performed very well on many criteria, but could do better on others.

Trade

The rate of growth of Ireland's exports had been exceptional in the early take-off phase to the end of 1993, at just over 10 per cent annual average increase in volume. 'Very strong productivity growth over two decades', especially in trade fuelled 'rapid real convergence', according to the European Commission.[24] In the boom years 1994 to 2000 it was at a very high annual average of almost 18 per cent a year, but this dropped to under 5 per cent a year between 2001 and 2008 inclusive, that is, in the third domestic consumption-driven period of the boom. However, the exports of services doubled between 2000 and 2007 and this growth is likely to continue.

Manufacturing, an important driver of productivity and of exports, is accounting for a declining share of national output as the economy shifts to services, with employment (which grew against the odds in the boom years) now declining, though output is still increasing. Productivity growth resumed in 2006 and 2007, probably due to a pick-up in manufacturing.

Ireland's main export markets for goods in 2006 were the US, Belgium and the Netherlands at 20 per cent of the total, with the UK at 17 per cent and Germany at 8 per cent. The level of Irish ICT exports declined from €37bn in 2001 during the 'tech bubble' to €23bn in 2006, but exports of chemicals rose from €27bn in 2000 to over €40bn in 2006.[25]

Ireland's exports of services had boomed in recent years, rising from €20bn in 2000 to €55bn in 2006. Software and business services are the largest sectors followed by financial services. The rise in foreign earnings from export services has been very high. Some of the service sectors' exports have a much higher value added than goods exports and also have a lower import content. The relative prices of services have increased faster than the price of goods, which have fallen in real terms. The ESRI estimates that 'the impact of a unit increase in services imports on the economy may be substantially greater today than it is for a comparable increase in the export of goods.'[26]

Foreign direct investment

Ireland gets a greatly disproportionate amount of greenfield FDI for its size within the EU and is the world leader along with Singapore on a per capita basis. The stock of inward FDI in Ireland (in investment in factories, plant and offices) is very high at $211bn in 2005, or 106 per cent of GDP. This is the highest in Europe as a percentage of GDP, and is triple the EU average. The Netherlands is next at 74 per cent, Sweden and the Czech Republic follow with 48 per cent and the UK with 37 per cent. The level of FDI in Western Europe is slowing as it shifts to Central European countries with lower costs now in the EU, and to the Far East. Yet Ireland remains attractive for FDI and for product development and R&D.

US firms have made exceptionally high profits in Ireland for many years, according to the US Commerce Department. This is because of the type of product made by firms in Ireland – modern, high-tech and often capital intensive, that is, highly profitable, such as Pfizer's Viagra, Microsoft's software, Coca Cola's concentrate or Intel's chips. Secondly, transfer-pricing by the firms in favour of Irish subsidiaries boosts the profits declared here. The average return on investment in US firms in Ireland between 2000 and 2005 was 16.8 per cent. While it had fallen from as high as 23.5 per cent in the previous five years, it was rising each year, from 13 per cent in 2001 to 20 per cent in 2005.

US FDI is important to Ireland comprising 47 per cent of IDA-supported firms, but 70 per cent of employment in these firms in 2005.[27]

The number of all foreign-owned plants peaked in Ireland in 1999 at 1,500 and was down to 1,167 in 2006, with the number of jobs peaking in 2000 at 165,000 and down slightly to 153,400 by 2005. The numbers employed by US firms has remained fairly stable at around 100,000. Interestingly, 38 per cent of employees of US firms in Ireland had third-level degrees.[28] This 2007 Indecon survey found that while some firms were considering shifting some plants and parts of plants to lower-cost countries, many were considering replacing these with alternative activities in Ireland.

Chemical/pharma firms have very high levels of value added in Ireland by net output, reflecting high R&D, and the sector employed over 1,400 research personnel in 2005. Electrical and electronic equipment firms employed over 2,600 R&D personnel in 2005.[29] The exceptionally high valued added in the sectors perhaps includes some transfer pricing, undertaken to avail of the low corporate taxes in Ireland.

Outward investment by Irish firms

One of the leading indicators of the Irish economic success is the rapidly growing and high level of foreign investment by Irish firms (and by individuals in stocks, shares, and commercial and holiday property abroad). The peak in outward foreign investment by Irish firms was in 2004 when a staggering €15bn was invested, and it was a still substantial €3bn in 2006.[30] Most of the greenfield investment was in the EU at 63 per cent and 16 per cent was in Central Europe, with 9 per cent in North America. The cumulative stock of Irish foreign investment abroad is equivalent to 60 per cent of GDP, second only to the Netherlands at 103 per cent of GDP in 2005. The numbers employed by Irish firms in other countries is over 100,000, compared to 153,000 in 2005 by foreign firms in Ireland.

Low interest rates

Real interest rates were exceptionally low since Ireland joined the Eurozone in 1999 and this helped drive the domestic investment boom. It also helped new and many existing businesses. The number of new houses built increased substantially with the economic boom (see Appendix 5). In 1980, 27,000 new houses were built and this fell each subsequent year in most of the lean 1980s to just 15,600 in 1988. But by 1990 it had risen to 19,600; by 2000 it was 50,000 and in 2006 it was 93,419 (see Appendix 5). There was a substantial rise in population and people responded to the very low real interest rates and to a lesser degree, to state subsidies for investment in housing, which remained throughout the boom. In spite of this rapid increase in new housing, house prices continued to soar way above inflation and above the growth in earnings.

The average house price in Dublin in 1995 was €89,000 – ten years later it was €439,000 – an almost fivefold increase!

Inflation

Inflation, which peaked at 20.4 per cent in 1981, was reduced to 3.2 per cent in 1987 and has remained in the 1.5 to 5.6 per cent range since. It tracked the level of the EU in the late 1990s. However, it has been high since 2000, and higher than the average in the EU, at double the average for a number of years. This has contributed to the fact that the level of consumer prices in Ireland was 17 per cent above the average in the EU15 in 2007, as most tourists would confirm! The high level of prices is due in part to catching up with Europe, to the high cost of services in Ireland, the strength of the euro and the shift in tax policy from incomes and profits to spending taxes and to use charges, and in recent times to the rises in interest rates set by the ECB.[31]

The only way to reduce Ireland's high price level, second only to Denmark in the EU27, is to curb inflation for a few years to a level below the average. This has not proved possible in recent years, in spite of the efforts of an anti-inflationary group established by government.

Conclusion

Ireland had a very sad economic history, dominated by two centuries of huge emigration. In the nineteenth century there was little progress and while incomes per head rose, this can be ascribed to emigration and not economic progress. It was the move to embrace globalisation in the 1960s which finally gave many Irish people a real rise in their incomes and in opportunities and which helped to cast off the yoke of cultural oppression which had dominated the people for so long. From 1987, consensus was developed and the economy picked up after a new national agreement, the appropriately named Programme for National Recovery, was implemented.

The greatest success of the Celtic Tiger has not been the rapid economic growth, the rise in incomes and in wealth, but the stunning rise in total employment. It doubled in just twenty years. That was the real success of the Irish boom. Furthermore, these jobs were of better quality than before, as well as paying more. There was much greater participation in the workforce by women and the employment rate also increased substantially. Irish living standards rose very substantially in real terms and, on a per-head basis, appeared to be well above the EU average and ahead of the UK, Germany and France.

While some owners of assets and business people made fortunes over the boom since 1994, incomes rose substantially for most workers and welfare was kept ahead of inflation. The level of productivity rose to one of the highest in the world per employee, per hour worked, underpinning economic growth, along with the employment growth.

The government's finances were dramatically turned around, with surpluses and a reduction in the national debt, once one of the highest, to one of the lowest in Europe. While income and corporate taxes (for most businesses) were cut substantially, the huge rise in economic activity and in the numbers at work meant that the Exchequer's revenue grew substantially each year. This meant that, while current public spending was reduced very substantially as a proportion of a rapidly growing GNP, to the lowest in the advanced EU countries, it still rose in real terms every year. That is one of the real bonuses of a booming economy. Capital spending was also high, but it was catching up on long decades of low investment. Inflation has been high since 2000 and the consumer price *level* is very high in Ireland, but unemployment was low, at around 4.2 per cent until 2007.

A prolonged economic boom leads to a virtuous circle, provided policy is reasonable and rational in the broadest economic sense.[32] It is a wonderful time for those in government, allowing them to cut taxes and to increase spending – at the same time. But it does not last. Every boom is followed by a slowdown, but politicians can, with informed policies and consensus, mitigate the extent of it. As Ireland has never been so globalised as it now is, it will feel the cold winds from offshore when that international downturn comes.

Thus, it can be seen that since 1987, but particularly since 1994, Ireland saw an economic boom unparalleled in its own history or in any other advanced country. Growth soared, the number of jobs doubled in a remarkably short time, incomes rose, living standards rose substantially, and the economy was modernised. Most commentators were in awe of the Irish economic success.

CHAPTER ELEVEN

Building Blocks of Prosperity

This book has sought to ascertain the reasons for the spectacular economic success of Ireland in the twenty years from 1987. The Celtic Tiger period, the six years in the middle, 1994 to 2000 inclusive, when every economic indicator was booming, was especially remarkable. This boom was followed by another boom, which, while enviable compared to any other modern economy, was one based largely on domestic demand. At the time of writing, the economy is slowing down, but will maintain levels of growth that are higher than most other advanced countries. It is possible that there could be an external shock. But a shock is just that. No one predicts shocks.

This chapter examines a) what makes nations prosperous – the basic building blocks and the more elusive factors which contribute to the wealth of nations. It also explores b) the lessons for other countries/ regions from the Irish success, including countries like Scotland and Northern Ireland, where politicians believe that independence gives freedom to pursue economic policies more vigorously and perhaps more successfully. It then, c) examines the issues which are still outstanding in Ireland and which need to be addressed. It concludes by, d) attempting to look to the future. While nobody knows what will happen, on the basis of current trends and Ireland's current state of economic development, the future for Ireland does look bright.

a) Basic building blocks of prosperity

Since Adam Smith's famous economic treatise, *The Wealth of Nations*, was published in 1776, thinkers and economists have systematically tried to ascertain what makes some countries more prosperous than others.[1] A major contribution to understanding this was his theory of *comparative advantage*, which says it is to the advantage of two countries to trade, if one has a lower relative cost of producing one good over that of the other country, which might be better at producing another good. This was the basis of modern trade theory, and of globalisation, which Ireland was to embrace so warmly.

Many others since Smith have tried to understand the key factors which are important for prosperity. In *Capital*, Marx developed Ricardo's labour theory of value, which stated that all value comes from work; from labour power. More important was his theory of economic development; his contribution to economic history, which showed that economies have developed through different phases, from slavery, feudalism, mercantilism, to capitalism.

More recently, in his *Wealth and Poverty of Nations*, David Landes[2] explores history in an effort to see why some countries have been wealthy and others poor. He considers a broad sweep of issues like war, which can be a real destroyer of value (but can boost innovation), the role of natural resources, religion, culture, technology and organisation. He also shows the importance of small factors, for example, the invention of spectacles (which doubled craftsmen's working lives and had a profound impact on productivity and output), the role of the clock in productivity and of hygiene in increasing life expectancy and human welfare. His emphasis is on 'Western civilisation and its dissemination: the knowledge, the techniques, the political and social ideologies, for better for worse.' Landes unashamedly argues that this dissemination flows from Western domination, Western teaching and from emulation of Western ideas.

Another influential book on economic success was Paul Kennedy's *The Rise and Fall of Great Powers*[3] which is more a study of the very largest countries or great powers over the last five centuries, with a particular focus on the impact of wars and conflict. From the time of Greek philosophers, there have been numerous other books exploring what makes countries prosperous. Even children's fairy stories dwell on the role of wise kings and queens in 'creating' prosperous countries for their subjects. Gibbon's *Decline and Fall of the Roman Empire,* published in the same year as Smith's *Wealth of Nations,* was perhaps the first systematic analysis of the fall of a great power, an empire. Rome was ruled by autocrats and based on slavery, but still impresses with its vastness and its legacy in roads, arenas and sewers and the centuries over which it lasted. The point is that Rome declined and mankind failed to retain most of its many inventions, systems and ideas. The lesson of the decline of Rome is that progress is not linear – it is not guaranteed. Today there are differing models of capitalism, from highly participative democracies; barely functioning democracies; autocratic oil nations; economies which are dynamic but unequal, such as the US and Britain; and others which are dynamic and much more equal, like the social democratic Nordic countries and the *old* European countries, Germany, France, Belgium, Luxembourg, the Netherlands, etc. Then there are the remaining socialist nations; China, Cuba and North Korea, with China being the fastest growing economy in the world for many years, albeit from a low base.

Some more building blocks
Economics has helped us to a much better understanding of what makes a modern economy prosperous, but the role of politics is also important, as are philosophy and the other social sciences. There are a number of basic building blocks upon which a country must start, if it is to be economically successful. Ireland was well endowed with these basic blocks of economic progress at its Independence. There must be a good administration, the rule of law, with a genuine separation of the judiciary and the executive. The rule of law is important, not just for dealing with crime and political corruption, but also because it sets the rules for markets and property rights. Without rules, which are made by man, markets would not function, a point poorly understood by some free-market economists.

A corruption-free administration is more important for sustained success of economies especially for those which are not particularly resource-endowed. In recent years, the OECD, World Bank, IMF and international agencies have finally come to recognise that corruption is a major impediment to economic prosperity. Nigeria is a classical example of how corruption means that immense oil wealth can be squandered away.

Free and fair elections, independent political parties, a civilian-controlled police and military are important too, as are independent trade unions, individual civil rights, and, not least, a free media.[4]

Thus, property rights, politics, good institutions, sound banking, insurance and finance sectors, lack of corruption, an independent media and a separate judiciary are essential to enable economic progress, as several failed African states today attest. But these factors are not sufficient in themselves and there are many other vital ingredients to economic success, as we have seen. Ireland had many good public and private institutions during its first seven decades, but it did not prosper.

A country which is democratic can be successful, but the non-democratic can prosper for decades. The oil states, like Saudi Arabia, and the seventy years of the Soviet Union, demonstrate that democracy is not necessary for substantial material progress. However, in the long term, democracy proves necessary if economic success is to be maintained in the modern world. The shocking decline of the once-prosperous and well-endowed Zimbabwe under the autocratic Robert Mugabe shows how important is the rule of law. The once prosperous states of South America failed in the twentieth century, with Argentina being the most remarkable economic failure. It was as wealthy at the beginning of that century as the richer European countries, but had a system of property rights biased strongly in favour of those old elite who seized the land in the first instance and against the poorer farmers and others. This worked as a strong disincentive for prosperity, wealth generation and distribution. Several South American countries are finally making excellent progress, having got rid of their dictatorships and adopted more rational economic policies.

China, the fastest growing economy in the world, is neither democratic nor capitalist; there is no separation of judiciary from the permanent executive, no free trade unions, nor is there a free press, nor even a free internet. The Russian economy is booming, thanks to the high price of oil and political stability, but the failure to develop the rule of law originally promoted by Gorbachev means that if businesses fall out of favour with the state, Putin's men will ensure they do not survive. It is not a recipe for success, but with the vast reserves of gas and oil, it may prosper for decades.

Saudi Arabia, a country owned by a family, is immensely successful economically, largely due to its immense oil wealth. Yet its leaders are aware that it needs sound economic policies to maintain success beyond oil. Thus, it is planning to promote indigenous industries such as car manufacturing, building materials, household appliances and metals. In early 2007, Ali Al-Naimi, the oil minister, outlined a plan for a new phase of investment beyond the vast infrastructure investment of its four multibillion dollar 'economic cities', to diversify its economy. Asian investors are helping to develop the downstream industries with the Saudis.

b) Lessons from Ireland

Perhaps the first lesson from Ireland is that the country gained greatly from globalisation, once it decided to open up. Had Ireland opened up to the second wave of globalisation[5] immediately after the Second World War, it would have become wealthier much sooner and so many would not have had to emigrate over four decades to the mid 1990s.[6] The integration of the world economy has led to great rises in incomes etc., but the impact of globalisation is uneven, and smaller and weaker economies need to step carefully into the globalised world, where the biggest fish compete best. New rules on trade under the WTO and other world organisations (IMF, World Bank, etc.) and their enforcement generally reflect the views of the bigger economies, their larger companies and farmers and free market economists. However, there is a growing recognition that the rules should be fairer and accommodate not just corporations, but also workers, consumers and all citizens of the world, wherever they are. Ireland was well prepared and also fortunate in its shift to globalisation.

A second lesson is that membership of an economic area is of immense benefit, particularly one such as the European Union, which aspires to embrace a wider political and social agenda, even if slowly and, in recent times, half-heartedly. The Central European countries may have taken note of Ireland's experience of the benefits of actively embracing the global economy and membership of a large economic club, the European Union. The main benefits of membership of the Union were:

1. membership of the vast Single Market; up from four million in Ireland to over 300 million overnight;
2. the enforcement of its rules on competition, so that the smaller countries and firms were not bullied, or big firms subsidised, nor allowed to abuse their power;
3. establishment of EU funds as a counter to the adverse effects of the Single Market, together with the Social Charter. Additionally, the timeliness of the funds was most important to Ireland;
4. introduction of new appraisal methods according to the rules around investing such funds, which was very helpful.

It was seen that the EU funds are now only a fraction of what they had been in the earlier decades, then under the regime of greater social solidarity within the EU in the Delors era. Most of the transfers still go in agricultural support under the Common Agricultural Policy (CAP), which has had less economic and social impact per euro in Ireland than the other transfers, from Structural, Regional and Cohesion Funds. Further, while some of the transfers may not have been effectively spent in some countries, most were and they contributed to economic progress in the recipient states. Ireland's overall imports from Germany, the main benefactor of the EU, are today much higher than in the mid-1990s,[7] and so all benefit in time. Today's wealthy Irish clamour to buy BMWs and Mercs from their old aid sponsor, Germany.

Thus, if an international trading bloc is established as an economic unit, its new internal market has to be governed under strict rules on competition, against subsidies and the abuse of market power by larger firms or countries. It is clear that transfers from the wealthiest to poorer countries are worthwhile, not just to the recipient country or region, but ultimately in benefits to all in the union.

A third lesson is that while fiscal responsibility is a given for any economy, it is often difficult to achieve and maintain. It was seen that in Ireland, the new system of social partnership devised in the late 1980s assisted in achieving difficult fiscal adjustment, where all major players signed up to tough decisions and participated in overseeing their implementation. Fiscal policy is difficult to get right because when things go well in an economy, revenue rolls into the state's coffers, but when things go badly, revenue dries up, just when the state needs more for welfare, education, etc.

The fourth lesson is that social partnership is one way forward in a more competitive world, where winning support for difficult actions from unions and employers can prove very worthwhile. It is part of a more participative decision-making process where people are increasingly better educated and more demanding of better public services. It reflects a more inclusive, less elitist and more accountable administration and generates better outcomes. It is not just about wage determination and taxation, but includes public-sector reform and change, investment, social programme reforms, etc. The process of social partnership does not grow overnight and it is still evolving in Ireland. In some countries it may not be possible to develop social partnership due to weak unions or to ideological hostility to sharing some power, however limited and consultative, with workers' and citizens' representatives.

Another lesson is the role the state can play in the economy. In the era of globalisation and the apparent power of multinationals, the power of the state is often perceived as diminishing. The role of the nation state is less than it was some years ago, but it is still dominant in most areas of the economy and society and it played a very important role in Ireland's economic success. In Europe, member nation states determine the laws and institutions of the EU and in that sense, are collectively more powerful. The Irish state invested in education in the 1960s, it determined tax policies, it set the laws and influenced those laws set by the EU and it encouraged social partnership to develop. A high level of public investment by the state can generate high returns, particularly when there is a long way to catch up. Again some political parties in some states may object to such state intervention.

Consistency in policy by the state is another major feature of the Irish experience over a long period of time – since the late 1950s. It pursued pro-business policies which simultaneously did not diminish consumers' rights nor trade union rights and it funded many state promotional and marketing agencies generously, staffed with highly motivated professionals. These state bodies originally paid out hundreds of millions in grants and subsidies to firms annually, but, in later years, gave advice and assistance in every area, under coherent, informed and developing policies. The state greatly boosted public capital investment. Public policy also played a vital role, and became more rational under the aegis of think-tanks like NESC and tripartite bodies on industrial policy, skills, competitiveness, company law, etc. established by the state. The move to more rational economic policy-making has been assisted by many public-spirited people from business, unions and the public on once-off tripartite bodies on economic and social areas, a recent one being the High Level Group on Manufacturing. While their reports may not be fully implemented, their analysis does inform policy, over time.

Not all state policies were successful, nor contributed to economic success. There were large tax breaks for all kinds of business and particularly property-based investments, which were highly regressive and boosted an already overheating market for decades. These property 'tax reliefs' are now being phased out, slowly, after economic reviews, with the exception of private hospitals, clinics and nursing homes. The big spending cuts in the late 1980s were in capital projects, but the state was slow to reverse these cuts. It is still slow to recognise that areas of capital investment generate high returns, such as in pre-schooling, education in general and integrated public transport in crowded urban areas. Yet policy is evolving to become more rational, more evidence-based, more participative, over time. Again some politicians in other countries might have difficulty in following Ireland's strong state interventionist policies and evolution to a more participative democracy.

Richer by secession
In recent times, there have been occasional revolts by the richer regions in European countries against their taxes being used to subsidise the poorer regions of their own countries in social solidarity. The rich Lombardy region in Italy was one of the first to wish to end subsidies to the poorer south. With the break-up of Yugoslavia in the 1990s, the wealthiest part, Slovenia, was quick to seize the opportunity to secede and so end paying part of its taxes to support the poorer parts. The Czech Republic did likewise, seceding from the poorer Slovaks. In Spain, some parties in wealthy Catalonia, with its capital Barcelona, are grumbling at paying taxes which subsidise the poorest of Spain's seventeen regions. They are looking to the Basque country, which only pays for those services it gets from Madrid, though most admit that pushing too far might mean the end of Spain. In Belgium, some politicians in wealthy Flanders in the north, would like to break from poorer Wallonia. The European Union itself is based on social solidarity between the richer and poorer regions, and one of the greatest successes of this policy has been the prosperity of Ireland, followed by Spain, assisted by membership and EU transfers. However, today, European solidarity is much less and subsidies to the new accession states are a fraction of what Ireland, Greece, Spain and Portugal received.

A richer, independent Scotland?
The Irish economic success has been praised by many of Scotland's independence-seeking politicians over the years and used as an example of

what an independent state can achieve. Some have focused on its oil wealth, arguing that an independent Scotland would retain more of its wealth, while others have argued that as the oil revenue is falling, it would have to raise taxes or cut public spending. The Scottish Nationalist Party, which became the largest party in the 2007 election, hoped that the country would be economically independent of Britain and planned to set up a stg. £90bn oil fund. However, all the oil revenue would have to be used to fund public spending and while high oil prices have boosted revenue considerably, oil production is set to fall from three million barrels a day in 2007 to under one million by 2020. Some have argued that if Scotland was independent, it would be able to set its own taxes, perhaps emulate the low corporation tax and attract industry, as Ireland has done.

However, Scotland's economic performance in terms of gross value added has tailed that of the UK over the past decade. No separate figures for the origin of UK tax revenue mean that a proper analysis of Scotland's economy is difficult. Scotland has 'continental European public expenditure levels with UK tax rates, but Wales, Northern Ireland and north east England have bigger subsidies', according to the *Financial Times*.[8] Scotland's five million people get a much better deal from Westminster than English citizens, through greater subsidies and representation in parliament.

While the oil wealth is unlikely to bridge the gap in the longer term, a dynamic, independent Scotland would be a more aggressive competitor to Ireland for foreign FDI. It is highly unlikely that a cut in its corporation tax would be enough to encourage sufficient investment and, as has been argued in this book, such a reduction in company tax would probably be too late to be effective. Any advantages of reductions in company taxation to attract FDI are already being eroded by reductions by most countries, with increased tax competition. Scotland would need more than tax cuts to replace the subsides from the UK when the oil runs out. Nevertheless, some lessons may be learned from Ireland.

Spain, for a long time run as a dictatorship, 'has managed a remarkable performance in terms of growth, employment and public finances over more than a decade' in the words of the OECD.[9] The OECD found that 'a combination of expansionary monetary conditions, fiscal prudence, beneficial structural reforms and the positive supply side effects of the strong rise in immigration has contributed to these outcomes'. It has enjoyed strong employment growth and immigration, but inflation and the resulting low real interest rates, combined with high household debt, led to a construction industry boom somewhat like Ireland's. Ireland, Spain and the UK were among the leading economic performers in Europe over the decade to 2007.

A poorer, independent Northern Ireland

Northern Ireland and the Republic should benefit from the outbreak of peace and the establishment of the power-sharing executive in May 2007. From being an industrial dynamo at the beginning of the twentieth century, Northern Ireland is now a highly dependent economy, getting more subsidies per head of population than any other region in the UK. Public spending was at £10,000 per head in 2005 compared to £7,600 for the UK as a whole. London and the South East contribute most in taxes, with Northern Ireland at the extreme other end. While the London area is a net contributor to UK public finances, Northern Ireland is one of the biggest recipients per head.

Of gross value added, public spending on the rest of the UK outside London is 53 per cent, close to the Nordic countries, but in Northern Ireland it is a staggering 73 per cent.[10] The ultimate objective of many nationalists, particularly Sinn Féin, for Northern Ireland, is for a united Ireland. Most political parties in Northern Ireland and all business lobbies have sought some independence from Britain on tax setting – all sought to reduce the rate of corporation tax to match that of the Republic in 2007. Not surprisingly, this has not been agreed by Westminster.

It is clear that a Northern Ireland independent from the UK would be a much poorer place. In essence, it would be a non-viable region. If it were to re-unite with the Republic, the subsidies required to maintain it at today's levels would impoverish the Republic. As the voters in the Republic in 2007 indicated that they did not wish to pay more income taxes and yet complain endlessly about poor public services, it is unlikely that they would be willing to fund a united Ireland at such a high cost in the foreseeable future.

However, the peace dividend gives Northern Ireland the opportunity to greatly boost its economy and this it will do in the coming years. It was an industrial powerhouse less than a century ago, with the *Titanic* having been built in Belfast, which was then a mighty industrial hub. Northern Ireland has many of the attributes for economic success and has the potential to grow very rapidly in the new era of peace.

c) Issues outstanding to make Ireland a better place to live

The falling dependency ratio gives Ireland an opportunity that will last for fifteen or twenty years, according to independent economist Professor John FitzGerald, and after that, the aging process will change the character of the economy and of society. From around 2015, the economy will slow down as greater numbers age. This perhaps once-off golden opportunity, presented by our prolonged period of economic success, was also a point made by David Begg. Indeed most of our interviewees had recommendations on what needs to be done to both a) extend the economic success and b) make Ireland a better place to live.

Steps to maintain the economic success are first examined and then some of issues which should be addressed to make Ireland a better place to live in are dealt with.

1. Maintaining the economic success
Investing wisely in education
Education is the most important area for future action. It now recognised internationally that all countries will 'have to run to stand still' in the so-called *knowledge economy*. It was generally agreed that Ireland has been 'good but not great' in educational performance. The Taoiseach cited education as one of the four or five key factors in the success, but Peter Sutherland was quite critical about Ireland's achievement on education and he was not alone of our interviewees. The analysis in Chapter Nine showed that we do need to invest much more in the area. Spending on education and on training, even if designated as current spending, is a form of investment or capital spending, because it brings returns for individuals, for firms and for the economy.

Education contributed to Ireland's competitive advantage, but as suggested by the interviewees, the standard could and must be improved. To date, educational performance in many areas is good and this is in spite of the low input in public spending relative to GNP. Garret FitzGerald[11] estimated that with low spending, especially in primary and secondary, the output was still high. Public spending appeared to be on a par with other countries, but when adjustments are made for the lower public spending relative to Irish GNP and the relatively high number of students, Fitzgerald came to the conclusion that both high student and high teacher motivation may be the key to the achievement. While quantitatively we have not provided students with resources at the EU standard, we appear to have made up for this qualitatively, which delivered the well-educated, flexible and motivated Irish worker which has been praised by many foreign investors.

Garret FitzGerald argued that the high status position and the pay of Irish teachers has motivated them well and there is a strong pro-education streak in the Irish, especially in rural areas. Parents and students responded very positively to free second-level education introduced by O'Malley in the 1960s. However, much as education is valued by Irish people, it is well known internationally that it is the one investment which will now generate the future returns for modern economies. Educational spending is no longer seen as a *cost*, but as a valuable, worthwhile investment at all levels by most countries.

Ireland is a very poor performer in pre-schooling, where state investment is virtually non-existent, in spite of widespread recognition of its importance. The University of London study on three-year-olds cited in chapter nine showed how important early education is in eliminating disadvantage, which, in turn, boosts economic growth in the modern economy. One-third of Irish people of working age do not have a Leaving Certificate and half a million are functionally illiterate. The Irish adult education system should be one of the best in the world to deal with this, but it is not.

It will be the real challenge to governments and educational professionals to ensure that a) there is adequate funding for education at all levels from pre-school to fourth level and, most importantly, for upskilling all those at work, and b) that the money is as well spent per euro as it has been in the past. Investment in education, at every level from pre-primary to life-long learning, is the key area where investment and a sharper focus must be made, if Ireland's economic success is to continue.

Public capital investment is important

A lesson for other countries is that a high level of public investment generates high returns, particularly when there is a long way to catch up. Each euro can deliver a very high return in the early phase of investment. While there can be criticism of some areas and of the effectiveness of some investment, overall, it has been impressive and continues to be so. Indeed, the Taoiseach, when responding to the question 'With the benefit of hindsight, what would you have done differently?' immediately said he would have made much greater investment in infrastructure, earlier. Yet his response showed that this is not easy. He said if he had decided to borrow more in order to increase investment levels by a few percentage points, some critics at that time would have said he was an 'eejit'. The Irish experience also demonstrates that cutting capital investment in tough times is counter-productive. Ireland's infrastructural deficit held back economic development for some years. Serious economic analysis should determine if it is worthwhile for a cash-strapped state to borrow to invest. In most cases, the answer should be positive, provided it is effective investment.

It is well known that effective capital investment is very important but what is not widely understood is that it generates returns usually far beyond the investment. Much of Ireland's capital investment (under the national development programmes) has been monitored and assessed by the ESRI, which found it to be worthwhile and generating good returns, though the Institute was not so sanguine about some planned investment under the current NDP to 2013. While the overall success of investment in Ireland is good, again, it could be better. For many years, the level of investment has been at double the EU average, but under the last NDP to 2006, the difficulty was in getting the money spent each year.

Public investment attracts corruption and it is important that systems are in place to prevent it. While Ireland was relatively free from corruption, with the exception of planning around Dublin, there is poor project appraisal by the central economic departments on much major capital and current spending. Much major spending appears to be undertaken on an *ad hoc* basis, or even does not take place. A number of interviewees pointed out that the quality of economic evaluation of most areas of the public service is below best international practice.

The system of appraisal before, during and after investment, introduced by the EU, appears to have been dropped for many state-funded investments. The ESRI has examined the NDPs overall, but neither it nor any other body examines individual projects. Huge investments are being made without proper evaluation. Such evaluation should, in turn, be assessed independently by a body other than the one investing. It would make sense for governments to have such a body established because it would also take the political flack away from their over-pricing, cost over-runs and delays.

On the current spending side, systems need to be put in place in all government departments to enable early detection of any possible unanticipated expenditure which may result from policy errors, especially those taken in the, perhaps, well-intentioned belief of 'saving' money, like the nursing homes scandal. The Auditor General, with limited resources, appears to do a good job in ex-post evaluation – after the event. We need ex-ante and continuous evaluation of all major public spending, with new systems and new teams of experts.

The need for a repository of professional expertise within the public service, with a corporate memory and a public-sector ethos, is urgent. Even with the outsourcing of much work, the public sector, as the client, requires a cadre of expertise to oversee all contracts professionally, to ensure quality and high technical standards are being met and also to ensure there is value for the public purse. Private consultants can offer expertise with an international perspective or, in times of shortage, supplement in-house talent, but should not replace it. This body or repository of professionals could advise all areas of the public service, from central civil service to the many quangos, regulators and local authorities on engineering, project appraisal at all stages, legal issues, negotiation, financial accounting, economics, etc. A tentative first step, long overdue and rather too conservative, has been the establishment of an Evaluation Unit in the Dept. of Finance to evaluate public spending.

Successive governments admit the 'infrastructural deficits', and have invested in a large public investment programme. For over a decade it has been clear that investment in public transport is the best way to spend money in all major urban areas and interlinking the main cities. While the need for a shift to public transport has now been recognised, under the new NDP what is planned and the long timeframe for achievement is very disappointing.

New car sales rose from 83,000 in 1990 to 126,000 in 1997, to peak at 225,000 in 2000, and were at 166,000 in 2005. Yet the number of cars per 1000 of population, while rapidly rising, was still below the average in Europe, at 439 in 2005 compared to between 550 and 650 for most countries,[12] which means that it is inevitable that the number of cars will still increase for several years, in spite of congestion and rising oil prices. The sales of expensive cars – BMWs, Mercs, SUVs – have been soaring over many years. SUVs are a 'must' in Irish suburbia; the growth in their numbers, in spite of the acute awareness and recognition of the reality of global warming, may reflect the ultimate, selfish, last hurrah before they are required to behave more environmentally responsible by the state in the face of climate change.

The rule of thumb for the price of oil for the past five years has been to take the last digit of the year and add a zero. In 2002, oil prices were in the $20s, but in 2003 were in their $30s and by 2007 oil prices were in the $70s. While not a logical rule of thumb, it is nonetheless frightening. A real working, integrated public transport system in every urban area is the only alternative to the obsession with cars. The huge benefits of an integrated public transport network in all urban areas has still not grabbed the politicians nor most policy-makers, in spite of the success of a very limited new tram 'system', which was immediately overcrowded at peak.

Yet lessons can be learned. For example, the cost over-runs on roads is one area which is being addressed by the National Roads Authority (NRA), which is now delivering roads within budget and on time, if not before. Irish politicians love to cut ribbons on a few kilometres of new road, or a partial tramline, but have not learned to 'let go', to set up adequately funded, competent agencies to plan, execute and deliver a network of public transport systems. The NRA is now such a body for roads, but the RPA, CIE and the myriad of other public transport service providers, publicly funded by millions of tax euros, do not work with each other, do not appear to even talk to each other, and are unable and unwilling to provide integrated ticketing, integrated services or meet performance criteria. The establishment of an effective Dublin transport authority is long overdue.

The contamination of the water supply in the city of Galway in 2007 where the citizens could not drink the city's water due to cryptosporidium contamination showed two things. First, there is a need for continuous public investment in all kinds of 'invisible' infrastructure such as water and waste to enable a modern society to develop. In spite of strong tax revenues, such investment had not taken place in this city and also in many other parts of Ireland. Inadequately treated sewage flows into surface water and increases the risk of contamination. The second lesson demonstrates the difficulty in making good political decisions. The spread of one-off housing in Ireland means that as many as one third of all new houses are 'one-off', whose own septic tanks too often contaminate ground water for themselves and others. Olivia O'Leary made the point that many Irish feel that they have a right to build anywhere, if they own the land. The political system has failed the majority in the face of a short-sighted, vocal minority, which has, in turn, been aided by the lack of residential taxes. Such taxes would improve local democracy and would generate greater interest in house size and location if they reflected true economic and social costs.

Public investment is very important for economic growth and for social progress too. Ireland cut back in investment in the lean 1980s and it is still feeling the consequences in daily commuting, and poor hospitals and schools. Such investment has generated high returns but the systems of oversight in project appraisal are poor for a modern economy, leading to delays, a less efficient economy and loss of tax euros.

Low corporation taxes

It has been seen that several interviewees argued strongly that low corporation taxes were a major factor in the attractiveness of Ireland for FDI, especially tax-conscious US corporations. Ireland has been a tax innovator. It was the first country to introduce a tax-free industrial zone (Shannon Airport Duty-Free Zone) which was emulated in many parts of the world. But when, eventually, tax incentives multiply, as happened with the tax free zones, the diffusion of tax incentives means they become ineffective because so many compete, the cost of them rises and their impact diminishes.

Similarly, Ireland's low corporation tax regime is under threat with a) corporate tax rates being reduced elsewhere, b) the possibility of a change in the law in the US, c) the possibility of a decision by the UK to change its stance and to support tax harmonisation in Europe, and d) the EU's continuing attempt to introduce tax harmonisation in its Single Market. While government cannot admit that the policy may be in terminal decline, policy must shift to more sustainable comparative advantages, such as education. It must also plan for the time when the large tax revenues from transfer-pricing by multinationals decline substantially. Ireland did benefit immensely from its first-mover advantage with its low corporation tax regime and continues to do so. It greatly helped boost FDI, especially from the US, and generates additional company tax revenue.

Globalisation itself may be under threat

It has been argued that Ireland was a major beneficiary from the current phase of international economic integration or globalisation. Most small, flexible states gain from globalisation, from trade, FDI and migration. However, globalisation is not inevitable[13] and just under one hundred years ago, the first wave of globalisation ended and the world lurched into protectionism at great economic and social cost to its citizens for the following thirty years. At the beginning of this wave of globalisation, there were rules and codes of behaviour under the Bretton Woods Agreement[14] and such international governance rules can and should be agreed again to suit the needs of the modern world. Indeed, there is an imperative for completion of Doha and for new international rules on governance because there are a number of threats to globalisation, with perhaps the least coming from the anti-globalisation protestors.

While some countries are flirting with protectionism today, when the Asian economies begin to dominate and impose their political and economic models on the world stage, there could well be very negative protectionist reaction from the West when the next recession begins to bite. Another issue is that sovereign wealth funds, the state investment funds of the excess foreign reserves of many Asian and oil countries, may be used to buy up firms all over the world. These reserves are not a bulwark to defend their currencies but may be a mercantilist desire to keep down their currencies in order to promote their exports. As they shift from low-yield dollar bonds to equities, they pose major challenges.

The Chinese foreign reserve agency bought $3bn of equity in the private equity firm, Blackstone, but with limited rights, in June 2006, ceding control of its shares to the directors. Such actions pose challenges in corporate governance. Germany is establishing an agency to vet acquisition by state-controlled foreign funds from Russia, China and oil-producing states. The US already has a Committee on Foreign Investments to block foreign direct investments which the President does not like. Blackstone and the Chinese state each have a small shareholding in Deutsche Telkom, and Russia also sought a stake in Deutsche Telkom. Dubai has a small stake in Deutsche Bank. These moves have led to the German government's being concerned about the might of state-controlled funds.[15] These protectionist actions may herald a greater move to insularity to come.

This form of counter-privatisation, where huge state-owned firms from

Asia, the Middle East and Russia are buying up firms in many countries or taking large equity stakes in them, may induce protectionism. One example was the Dubai Port's attempt to buy several US ports, which was blocked by the US government for 'security reasons'. It also blocked the attempt by the huge Chinese state-owned CNOC to buy US oil company Unocal. The purchase of the stake in Blackstone could be a move by China to gain access to management skills and intellectual capital. The US is paranoid about this whole area, initially about access to intellectual capital, patents etc., but some US politicians have also shown a hostility to what they consider to be too much foreign control of its corporations. It is likely to react in a more protectionist way if these back-door, 'part-nationalisations' continue. The growth of 'sovereign wealth funds' or state-owned investment funds was estimated at $2,000bn in 2007 and is expected to grow to up to $9,000bn by 2015.[16] Western governments were happy when these funds bought government bonds (i.e. lent to them) but are unhappy with their buying big stakes in some of the world's largest companies. While the Norwegian Norske Bank and indeed Ireland's own pension fund are regarded as blue-chip investors in major multinationals, Russian, Arab and Asian funds do not seem so welcome, for whatever reason. Angela Merkel, the German Chancellor, was trying to get the EU to impose some form of regulation on these funds in 2007, but it could hardly do that without imposing higher standards of transparency and governance on hedge funds, private equity funds, etc.

There are also many issues with the growing global corporate influence of private equity firms, which are unlike most firms which have relationships with the country and region in which they have operations and with their employees. These firms have little allegiance to anyone and seem to inhabit a world far removed from that of most people. Assisting this unreality are the 'rewards' paid to the directors of some private equity firms. Blackstone paid Stephen Schwarzman $398.3m in 2006, and $212.9m to his partner, Peter Peterson. Each sold stock at the IPO for €677m and €1,880m respectively and also retain large stakes, making both stratospherically wealthy. The *Financial Times* said that while US trade unions may have failed to stop the listing of Blackstone, 'their concerns speak of a wider public unease at the wealth being accumulated by the new masters of the financial universe'. The *FT* continued, 'As America grapples with a yawning gap between rich and poor, buy-out executives have not dispelled the public perception of a clubby industry of jet-setting billionaires who grow rich by cutting costs and making workers redundant.'[17]

The other threat to globalisation is from within; from the losers. When the conservative OECD and the *Financial Times* came out strongly in favour of steps being taken to assist the losers of globalisation in 2007, this indicated a major change in official attitudes. Extolling the virtues of globalisation, the *FT*[18] then said 'it has also created losers, particularly among the middle and lower classes in rich countries'. It said 'government needs to do more to help the groups most hurt'. It argued for more retraining and help for those who lose their jobs, for a more progressive income tax and benefits, though it concluded with the firm belief that 'globalisation is inevitable', a view with which the author does not concur. The OECD[19] said the dangers of globalisation are overblown, but admitted that the share of output going to labour worldwide has declined over the past decade leading to a rise in earnings inequality in the rich countries. Its Secretary General, Angel Gurría, accused employers of using the threat of offshoring as a bargaining chip in pay talks.[20] The OECD also concluded that more steps must be taken to protect the losers of globalisation.

2. Social progress and economic success
Growth for growth's sake or sustainable development?
Why and how the economic success occurred has been at the heart of our analysis. What has not been examined is the *social* progress of Ireland. While much social progress has been made, it lags behind the spectacular economic success. That in itself is a lesson for any other country. Yet there is now a fair consensus that the economic and social should go in tandem in Ireland. The old argument that the social progress has to await the results of economic progress is no longer accepted by the Irish government. Employers, unions and the social groups who make up the fourth pillar of social partnership accept this policy. However, government has not yet been able to put this into practice. It is difficult and, like a big ship changing direction, takes time.

A lesson of the Irish economic success was that it was time to take the foot off the economic growth accelerator and focus on development. A slowdown began in 2007. Strong growth fuelled congestion, inflation, difficulties in access to schools and hospitals and over-development in some areas. Instead of the pursuit of economic growth, government should shift its focus to economic and social development. Such development includes some economic growth, but focuses on the socio-economic, on building working communities, viable transport, reducing congestion, urban and rural blight, more focus on the environment, some redistribution of income and wealth and much more.

The downsides of rapid economic growth were the prolonged period of rising and very high house prices, housing shortages, growing income and wealth inequality, difficulties in access to schools and hospitals and the inability of governments to provide modern public services. Price *levels* are much higher than the average in Europe (at around 17 per cent higher than levels in the EU15 in 2007 for consumer items) and inflation continues at higher rates than elsewhere, which makes it is difficult to bring down the high price levels. At the level of the individual, confidence has turned to brash aggressiveness in some – widespread binge drinking, increased drug-taking – and the 'Ireland of the Welcomes' is under some threat.

Greater social development requires far more rapid access to schools and hospitals than we have at present, provision of modern public transport systems to ameliorate traffic congestion and improve mobility for all, reduction of housing problems, as well as the integration of the existing migrant population, combined with continuing inward migration. The shift in gear from growth to more balanced development would be a key policy change and could bring many benefits.

Reducing relative poverty

It has been seen that the Irish economic success has generated a substantial rise in real incomes for most working people. The average industrial worker has seen their standard of living, measured by earnings, increase by 80 per cent in twenty years and some have done much better than this. All home owners (and mortgage holders) gained increases in their wealth with the huge rise in house prices. The doubling in employment has had a major impact in reducing the level of poverty especially, boosting household incomes dramatically, as more people in households have found jobs. The numbers on welfare have fallen and welfare increases have been above inflation.

The comprehensive study of the impact of the Celtic Tiger on Irish society by sociologists from the ESRI and some universities, edited by Tony Fahey and others,[21] found that 'a long list of social fundamentals' are 'stronger today than they were before the Celtic Tiger arrived'. These include 'subjective well being and national morale, which are among the highest in Europe', living standards which have risen and 'have done so more or less for everyone', jobs which have 'become astonishingly abundant and have improved in quality; people are now flocking into rather than out of the country', and people are healthier, and 'feel good about themselves and the society around them'.[22]

The Taoiseach said that 'social policies, aimed at promoting equality and tackling problems such as poverty and educational disadvantage, were key to a healthy society and were eminently desirable in their own terms'. He also argued that such policies have a 'very strong stabilising effect on the economy'. Thus he shows a strong appreciation of the benefits of reducing poverty. While our interviewees and especially the business people were mainly discussing the reasons for the economic success and not social issues, yet Gary McGann of Smurfit Kappa stated, 'There is money to deal with social inclusion, to make a better society for all. But why do I see more people sleeping rough than I did twenty years ago?' David Begg focused on the impact of social welfare on the labour market and argued that the Irish welfare model was out of date. He argues there should have been greater spending on welfare, health, education and investment – funded by smaller cuts in income taxes.

What is the real picture on poverty in Ireland? There has been substantial progress, but more needs to be done. The economy has been so strong that it could have wiped out most poverty with little effort. There is relative and absolute poverty and the latter is easily dealt with by ensuring all have basic necessities such as food, shelter and clothing. Dealing with relative poverty is more problematic because we are talking of comparing those at the bottom with those in the middle or at the top, and it is a moving comparison, as society's material income and wealth improves. However, there are internationally accepted standards in measuring relative poverty. Unfortunately, Ireland is still one of the more unequal societies in the developed world.

The ESRI found that one in five people in Ireland was economically vulnerable and could find themselves living in poverty in the future. The Institute study[23] was critical of those who talk of 'an underclass' in Ireland because multiple deprivation and multiple disadvantage are fairly rare. However, 7 per cent of the population is at serious risk of poverty in important areas such as consumption, housing, education and neighbourhood and environment. Six per cent of people were at risk of current lifestyle deprivation, that is, unable to meet day-to-day basic expenses. While few suffer absolute poverty, many suffer relative poverty. This is not a comparison with well-off people, but about what one would basically expect to be able to afford in our society.

While all boats were lifted and virtually all gained, those at the top did very well. The Fahey study is highly critical of the naysayers who cannot see any improvement in Irish society and it presents a good overview of evidence-based analysis to show that most peoples' lives have been greatly improved in the period. Its contributors found that both the levels and depth of poverty 'are a good deal more modest than suggested by radical critics of the Irish experience of globalisation'.[24] Further, they conclude that income distribution has remained fairly stable over the Celtic Tiger period. In short, income distribution had not got worse. However, they do point out that it had disimproved between 'older people and those of working age and between those at the top and the bottom of the income distribution'.[25]

A chapter on income inequality in the Fahey book did also find, from income tax data, that 'there was a marked increase in total income to the very top – the top one per cent or even half per cent – of the distribution'.[26] However, the problem with income tax data in Ireland is that a number of the very top earners, some of whom have gained massively in the two decades, are tax exiles and so do not pay Irish income tax and are excluded from the data analysed. The inclusion of these billionaires in Irish income tax data would dramatically skew the distribution information. Further, while tax evasion has been reduced, it is still high in Ireland. The data may be further complicated because a number of top earners did not pay or paid very little income tax on large incomes, due to the use of tax shelters. Many of these tax shelters are in the process of being abolished, thanks to the slow shift to more evidence-based or rational economic decision-making where eventually economic appraisals were commissioned which showed they had little or no economic value.[27]

What is remarkable is that the overall gap in incomes between the top and those on the bottom has not narrowed. It appears that over a long period, the Irish people, or more importantly, most of their political leaders, have not sought, *actively and persistently*, to bring about a more fair society. In the academic words of the authors, 'a low redistributive "effort" is a long-standing characteristic of Ireland's welfare state'.

While Ireland is not one of the most unequal societies in the world or Europe, it is one in a group of rich countries 'that have relatively high levels of income inequality'. Nolan and Maître conclude by saying that the new prosperity opens up choices for the Irish about whether such a 'high level of income inequality and such widening gaps continue into the future'. The fact that the incomes gap has not widened, overall, is welcome, but it is a poor reflection on Irish society and on the Irish people that they have not sought to address poverty over a period when it would have been painless to do so. A smaller reduction in income taxes, which are very low, could have led to a more equal society.

Substantially increased spending on welfare (which did increase in real terms every year) and on general public services like health, education and public transport would greatly improve the lot of those at the bottom of our booming economy. Those who suffer most from poverty are the poorer farmers, those with little education, lone parents and the unemployed. In the face of high levels of conspicuous consumption in Ireland, the least that should be done is to boost welfare spending per head substantially, and to put more money into public services.

A very high proportion of luxury-end cars have been sold in recent years compared to other advanced economies. This country with 4.2 million people boasts over ten billionaires and is estimated to have tens of thousands of millionaires. In the face of Ireland's wonderful economic success, the failure to reduce relative poverty should be a source of embarrassment to most Irish citizens and should be top of the agenda for future action.

Wealth and incomes

There is a distinction between income and wealth. Ireland has amongst the highest incomes per capita in the developed world, but it has some way to go to build up substantial wealth. The wealth of nations is built up by investment in public and private assets.

With relatively low incomes for many years, Ireland did not invest in public assets – in roads, schools, public buildings, etc. The strong economic growth over the twenty-year-period from 1987 led to an upward shift in incomes, in profits, to a doubling of the numbers in work and this, in turn, is now leading to an upward shift in public and private wealth. There is a rapid increase in both publicly funded assets – roads, bridges, hospitals, schools, etc. – and in privately owned assets – houses, flats, holiday homes, shares, pensions, bigger cars and foreign properties. This is a key part of the shift in the nature of the Irish economy. Ireland now has a modern housing stock, near adequate inter-urban roads and many people have wealth and incomes which allow them to build savings and other assets.

The 1960s may have seen Ireland's first economic boom, but at the end of that decade, while incomes rose substantially, everyone was still relatively poor, with little discretionary income. Today, the middle classes – certainly the upper-middle classes – have discretionary incomes based on substantial wealth that they never dreamed of. Many of the newly rich do engage in conspicuous consumption, in the vulgar display of their new wealth. Many do not invest quietly in new enterprises but spend it. The Celtic Tiger boom greatly expanded the Irish middle class and it is this group which is spending and thus generating the domestic consumption boom since 2001, fuelled by the wealth-effect of increased house values.

Many of the comfortable middle class have valuable pension assets, some shares and other wealth, like savings or second homes. The growth in the value of the assets of the middle classes and in the size of the middle classes itself has been a key driver in domestic demand and in the escalation in imports as they have bought new cars, TVs, etc. in recent years. The rapid escalation in real-estate values and the multipliers generated have boosted the 'wealth effect' where people feel richer, are richer and go out and spend. Their spending on home extensions, etc. had a strong domestic multiplier generating €69 on every €100 invested.

Irish banks and accountancy firms have established 'wealth management' divisions in recent times to woo the 'mass affluent cohort of the economy' which is a 'significant and growing demographic that has enhanced its wealth through the Celtic Tiger and the rise in property values of the past decade or more'.[28] There has been massive spending by Irish businesses and individuals on foreign assets, buying up tracts of commercial property in London and homes all over Europe. It is estimated that Irish-owned foreign assets amounted to €330bn in 2006, up 50 per cent on 2002, generating significant flows of dividends, rent and profits from abroad.

Public capital spending, that is, public investment, actually fell as a proportion of GNP between 1987 and 1999. However, it grew strongly in absolute terms from 1992. Since 1999, public capital spending has grown even more strongly. The new public investment programme to 2013, the NDP, plans to increase spending over the next seven years which will build public assets.

This growth in wealth has also changed the political landscape. While the poor are still with us, the growth in the size of the middle classes has meant that all major parties focus on their perceived needs. Hence in the election of 2007, all major parties promised further income tax cuts even though Irish income taxes and Irish public spending was the lowest in the EU15. In an *Irish Times*[29] poll, the middle-class view predominated, with 72 per cent against increased taxes to fund better public services. However, the view was more sophisticated than first appeared because 83 per cent believed that in 2007 increased taxes were not required to fund better public services. This was probably correct, if it meant only marginally better. The question is – are the swelling Irish middle classes so confident of their own futures and their own abilities that they feel they can fund their own and their children's education, healthcare, childcare and welfare privately into the future?

d) Prospects
The future economic outlook for Ireland in the medium term is very positive, on the basis of current trends, providing there is no major shock. Secondly, the extraordinary boom of the Celtic Tiger years 1994 to 2000 inclusive lifted the Irish economy onto a new plane and Ireland's economy is modern, productive and well balanced between sectors, industries and firms, with a good skill base etc. Like all small countries, it is highly dependent on foreign investment, on the vagaries of the globalised economy and on its neighbours' welfare. While the level of investment in infrastructure is high, a lot of ground has still to be made up. A slowdown from the high economic growth levels will provide an opportunity to focus on economic and social development.

Will the economic success continue? Ireland is a victim of its own success – it is now a relatively high-cost economy. Consumer prices *levels* are way above those in the EU and while wages are not as high as in the leading countries in Europe, they have moved up closer. This is not a problem if productivity remains high, but its growth has slowed and this may be a problem if it persists. Ireland has a tight labour market too, in spite of strong migration. Ireland does seem to be moving up the value chain to more modern jobs, but investment in education, training and developing productivity in all areas is crucial for sustained economic success. Manufacturing will continue to be important as a driver of productivity and innovation.

The economy has reached a high level of development and one economic model[30] shows that if exports fall (which has occurred in recent years), the economy will not decline as quickly as it grew. A major constraint to growth has been the difficulty in increasing the proportion of the population at work. This constraint has been overcome somewhat by immigration. It would be further eased with better childcare programmes and the provision of pre-schooling, which would facilitate working parents.

As always, the external environment is crucial and a downturn or major shock elsewhere will impact on this little globalised economy. At present, the world economy is doing very well, recording its fifth year of sustained growth in 2007. A major trading partner, Germany, has recovered rapidly and, aside from the US, most trading partner economies are performing well. Maintaining Ireland's position close to the top of the world in GNP/GDP per capita should not be an insurmountable challenge for Ireland, even if it shifts policy from the strong emphasis on the pursuit of economic growth.

Ireland is, however, the most oil-dependent economy in Europe and if we are close to 'peak oil' and prices are sustained or increase much more, there will be adjustment problems. The use of public space, construction and transport is based on cheap oil and the motor car. As mentioned before, public transport is poor and very much subservient to the motor car. Ireland could have a serious problem in adjusting to expensive oil in the coming years, unless it begins that adjustment now.

It is widely agreed that education and the upskilling of existing workers is crucial. Education is the key to continuing economic success and will contribute greatly to social success. It will require increased investment, increased current spending and change. The past investment in infrastructure is beginning to show in improving productivity and that planned under the NDP to 2013 will help improve it further, but it needs re-orientation.

The economic growth in this third phase – the domestic boom, from 2001 – has been based less on export-led demand than on domestic demand. The high dependence on construction cannot be sustained, and while the new NDP may mitigate a downturn, there could be a hard landing, impacting on many other sectors of the economy. The public finances are strong and the national debt has been greatly reduced, providing some leeway for the Exchequer when the inevitable downturn comes.

On future prospects, the Taoiseach said we have taken the right steps to prepare well: 'Looking to the future, we now have almost 40 per cent of our twenty-five- to thirty-four-year-olds being educated to third level. We are still getting in really good foreign direct investment; we're educating people now to a high standard, and we are spending lots of money on Science Foundation Ireland and the R&D programmes.' Professor Frances Ruane said the stage of globalisation we have gone through has favoured us, but 'the next stage will favour others, who were late in recognising how globalisation was changing the world. We had first-mover advantages and the challenges will come from others who are seeking to adopt a version of the "Irish model".' Peter Sutherland said he was not as optimistic about the future as some. He said we face some hard decisions and we are not good at taking hard decisions.

Joe Macri of Microsoft was optimistic about the future, holding that the country has great potential, but 'we have to address some issues around competitiveness, around infrastructure, health services and the education system' and the efficiency of the public service. Gary McGann was optimistic but warned that we must not 'give up trying to have a strong manufacturing base' and 'social progress has got to be a core part of the game plan of our economic success and not a by-product of it'.

David Begg believed that if the international economy remains stable, then Ireland should too, but we need to make and 'execute well considered and consensual plans to stabilise the economy for the transition to a mature democracy'. He warned that we 'must avoid the exaggerated reliance on market forces to solve all problems while avoiding a reversion to economic autarkism' and insularity.

'There is a sense of hope in Ireland now that is contagious,' Olivia O'Leary said. 'But we still behave as though all the good times might disappear tomorrow. So we go on a mad spending spree instead of investing our wealth in the things that will make life better for the long term – better education and health services, better public infrastructure, better planning, and a country which is shaped as we wish it to be, not as others have decreed we must have it.' There are many areas which we need to address, and 'we have not decided what the core values of being Irish are'.

As economic growth slows, there should be a new emphasis on economic and social development, on reducing traffic congestion, stress and on slowing the pace of life a little and on ensuring all are sharing in the new affluence, especially those at the bottom. So the slowdown could be good, provided there is some growth. If the slowdown is gradual, then there will not be major problems.

Economic policy has been remarkably successful for twenty years, but it must now be further refined to shift the emphasis to education, training, and on building productivity. Continuing reliance on low company and personal taxes, on construction, on domestic demand, on personal borrowing, has to move to creating a process where building productivity in all areas becomes natural, through improved education and innovation. Productivity growth will come less from manufacturing in the future but through education, training, constant upskilling of all workers at all levels; from the shift from ICT-production to ICT-use in all areas, including services and importantly, public services.

In conclusion, Ireland's rapid economic success has been remarkable compared to other countries. Compared to its own sad economic history, the progress since 1987 has been truly amazing. The economic changes over the past twenty years have seen this small island become one of the highest-income countries in the world. Ireland is well placed to maintain its high standard of living. As well as ensuring that there is continued economic progress, people need to consciously decide what kind of society they wish to build. There is a strong economic base which enables choices to be made. As Ireland continues to be transformed, the Irish people can afford to determine their own core values.

APPENDIX 1

Total Irish employment, manufacturing employment and unemployment 1983–2008

	Total employment (x 1000)	Change	Manufacturing employment	Unemployed (x 1000)	Percentage (x 1000) %
1983	1,124	−22	202.2	183	
1984	1,103	−21	195.6	204	
1985	1,079	−24	186.9	226	
1986	1,081	2	184.2	227	
1987	1,090	9	182.4	232	
1988	1,111	0	182.8	217	16.3
1989	1,111	0	187.0	197	15.0
1990	1,160	49	191.9	172	12.9
1991	1,156	-4	195.1	199	14.7
1992	1,165	9	198.0	207	15.1
1993	1,183	18	199.3	220	15.7
1994	1,221	37	204.8	211	14.7
1995	1,282	61	217.0	178	12.2
1996	1,329	48	221.8	179	11.9
1997	1,380	50	234.6	159	10.3
1998	1,495	95	241.3	126	7.8
1999	1,591	115	239.6	97	5.7
2000	1,671	97	248.6	75	4.3
2001	1,717	80	251.0	65	3.6

	Total employment (x 1000)	Change	Manufacturing employment	Unemployed (x 1000)	Percentage (x 1000) %
2002	1,750	46	239.3	77	4.2
2003	1,778	33	230.0	82	4.4
2004	1,836	28	223.2	84	4.4
2005	1,929	58	220.0	86	4.2
2006	2,039	110	224.0	93	4.4
2007	2,117	78	223.4	105	4.8
2008	2,150	33			

Source: CSO, ESRI and own forecast. New series from 1988 on.

APPENDIX 2

GNP and GDP volume change, 1980–2008

	GNP	GDP
1980	2.6	2.9
1981	1.8	2.5
1982	−1.3	1.5
1983	−1.9	−0.7
1984	1.1	3.2
1985	0.2	1.9
1986	0.1	0.4
1987	3.7	3.6
1988	1.7	3.0
1989	4.7	5.6
1990	6.5	7.7
1991	2.0	1.6
1992	2.5	3.6
1993	3.0	2.3
1994	6.5	5.9
1995	8.0	9.6
1996	7.8	8.3
1997	10.3	11.7
1998	7.7	8.5
1999	8.5	10.7
2000	12.3	11.8

	GNP	GDP
2001	3.8	5.7
2002	2.8	6.0
2003	5.5	4.3
2004	3.9	4.3
2005	4.9	5.9
2006	6.5	5.7
2007	4.4	4.7
2008	2.9	2.7

Sources: CSO and ESRI for later years

This table shows the economic growth rates each year measured by both Gross National Product (GNP) and Gross Domestic Product (GDP) against the previous year. Both figures are given as they diverge in Ireland (see explanation for the difference in Ireland given in Chapter 10). It can be seen that economic growth was very high in the late 1990s and 2000 but the economy actually shrank in 1982 and 1983, when measured by GNP.

APPENDIX 3

The Irish public finances 1983–2007

	Exchequer balance	Gross current government revenue			Current government spending		Ireland's national debt	
	%	Overall total €m	% of GNP	% Increase on previous year	Overall total €m	% of GNP	% increase year on year	% of GNP
1983	12.20	8,641	45.3	16.9	9,402	49.3		95.8
1984	11.30	9,145	44.2	5.8	10,130	49.0	7.7	103.3
1985	−12.3	9,640	43.5	5.4	11,029	49.8	8.9	106.0
1986	−11.4	10,160	42.6	5.4	11,699	49.1	6.1	115.1
1987	−9.1	10,992	43.0	8.2	12,173	47.6	4.0	117.6
1988	−3.1	11,830	44.0	7.6	12,296	45.7	1.0	116.2
1989	−2.2	11,943	40.4	1.0	12,395	42.0	0.8	106.8
1990	−1.9	13,001	40.6	8.9	13,213	41.2	6.6	99.4
1991	−0.9	13,941	41.5	7.2	14,333	42.7	8.5	96.0
1992	−2.6	14,849	41.7	6.5	15,429	43.3	7.6	93.9
1993	−2.3	16,042	41.6	8.0	16,528	42.9	7.1	93.5
1994	−2.0	17,450	41.8	8.8	17,412	41.8	5.3	89.0
1995	−1.7	18,009	38.6	3.2	18,570	39.5	6.7	82.3
1996	−1.7	19,844	38.2	10.2	19,504	37.6	5.0	73.1
1997	−1.1	22,369	37.5	12.7	21,537	36.1	10.4	65.4
1998	−0.5	25,202	36.7	12.7	22,338	32.5	3.7	54.6
1999	1.4	28,938	37.6	14.8	24,121	31.3	8.0	51.7

	Exchequer balance	Gross current government revenue			Current government spending		Ireland's national debt	
	%	Overall total €m	% of GNP	% Increase on previous year	Overall total €m	% of GNP	% increase year on year	% of GNP
2000	2.0	33,460	37.6	15.6	25,918	29.1	7.4	41.0
2001	3.6	35,344	36.1	5.6	29,936	30.6	15.5	37.0
2002	0.7	38,925	36.6	10.1	33,033	31.1	10.3	34.2
2003	0.1	41,085	35.1	5.5	36,299	31.0	9.9	32.1
2004	−0.8	45,238	36.4	10.1	39,131	31.5	7.8	29.7
2005	0.0	50,005	35.8	10.5	43,297	31.8	10.2	27.4
2006	1.5	57,365	38.5	14.7	47,611	31.9	10.4	25.1
2007	−0.9	61,123	38.1	6.4	53,074	32.9	11.5	24.0

Sources: Department of Finance and Budget Statement 2007

APPENDIX 4

Changes in consumer prices, 1980–2007

	Percentage change
1980	18.2
1981	20.4
1982	17.1
1983	10.4
1984	8.6
1985	5.4
1986	3.9
1987	3.2
1988	2.1
1989	4.0
1990	3.4
1991	3.2
1992	3.0
1993	1.5
1994	2.4
1995	2.5
1996	1.6
1997	1.5
1998	2.4
1999	1.6
2000	5.6
2001	4.9
2002	4.6

Percentage change

2003	3.5
2004	2.2
2005	2.5
2006	4.0
2007	4.8

APPENDIX 5

House prices and completions 1982–2007

	House Completions		Dublin house prices (€)	
	Total	Percentage change	New	Second-hand
1982	26,798	−7.3	48,886	45,912
1983	26,138	−2.5	48,169	48,249
1984	24,944	−4.6	48,819	50,936
1985	23,948	−4.0	49,166	50,382
1986	22,680	−5.3	50,891	51,450
1987	18,450	−18.7	50,864	49,139
1988	15,654	−15.2	57,994	54,077
1989	18,068	15.4	68,393	63,148
1990	19,539	8.1	80,749	74,833
1991	19,652	0.6	78,715	76,075
1992	22,464	14.3	79,200	77,490
1993	21,391	−4.8	75,539	76,814
1994	26,863	25.6	81,993	82,772
1995	30,575	13.8	86,671	88,939
1996	33,725	10.3	97,058	104,431
1997	38,842	15.2	122,036	131,258
1998	42,349	9.0	160,699	176,420
1999	46,512	9.8	193,526	210,610
2000	49,812	7.1	221,724	247,039
2001	52,602	5.6	243,095	267,939

	House Completions		Dublin house prices (€)	
	Total	Percentage change	New	Second-hand
2002	57,695	9.7	256,109	297,424
2003	68,819	19.3	291,646	355,451
2004	76,954	11.8	322,628	389,791
2005	80,957	5.2	350,891	438,790
2006	93,419	13.3	405,957	512,461
2007 (Q2)	38,708	−11.2	426,900	473,749

Source: DELG

APPENDIX 6

The major FDI companies in Ireland

Today there are almost 1,000 foreign multinationals in operation in Ireland, employing 153,000 directly and more indirectly. IDA Ireland is a successful state body which has been encouraging firms to invest here for many decades. It originally targeted leading companies in the following sectors for investment: pharmaceuticals, ICT, medical technologies, international financial services, engineering, international services, and consumer products. Over the years, IDA in co-operation with key national partners has set out to reposition Ireland as an advanced knowledge-driven economy reflecting global changes in business and Ireland's evolving capabilities.

Today Ireland has over 170 companies employing 35,000 people in the pharmaceutical/chemical, biopharmaceuticals, medical devices and diagnostics sectors. There has been foreign direct investment in the pharmaceutical sector in Ireland for more than forty years. The first major corporation to invest was Squibb (now Bristol-Myers Squibb) in 1964. Currently thirteen of the top fifteen companies in the world have substantial operations in Ireland. The pharmaceutical cluster in Ireland is well developed and the country is now one of the world's largest exporters of pharmaceuticals.

Pharmaceutical companies in Ireland include Schering-Plough, Wyeth Merck, Pfizer, Amgen, Genzyme, Allergan Wyeth, Takeda, Novartis, GlaxoSmithKline, Eli Lilly, Bristol-Myers Squibb and many more. Six out of ten of the world's top-selling drugs are produced in Ireland including Lipitor and Zocor.

Today there are 210 overseas companies engaged in many areas of information and communications technologies. Seven of the world's top ten ICT companies have a substantial base in Ireland. The ICT sector in Ireland employs over 43,000 people and is a 'who's who' list of global leaders such as IBM, Dell, Apple, Intel, HP, Microsoft, Analog Devices,

Oracle, Ericsson and many more. Ireland's position as a leading location for ICT investment was reinforced by investments by Cisco, Netgear, Trend Micro and Sandisk.

IDA continues to support core competencies in manufacturing; high-level manufacturing and engineering is undertaken in Ireland by market leaders such as ABB, Kostal, Liebherr, Lufthansa, Intel, GSK, Abbott and many more.

Ireland is a leading location for medical technology investment and has attracted eighy-three companies, including eight of the world's top ten companies. Multi-facility companies include Abbott, Becton Dickinson, Boston Scientific, Johnson & Johnson, Stryker, and Tyco Healthcare.

In consumer products the big names in Ireland include Black & Decker, Bose, Colgate Palmolive, Hasbro, Oakley, Braun Oral B, Whirlpool, Procter & Gamble, and Yves Rocher.

The government established the International Financial Services Centre (IFSC) in 1987. Ireland's position in the international financial services industry has evolved from an industry serving local market needs into one of the world's leading financial hubs. Top global financial institutions with companies such as Citigroup, State Street, Depfa Bank, JP Morgan, HSBC, Merrill Lynch, XL, Hartford and ABN Amro manage European and global functions from Ireland. Ireland is now home to half of the world's top fifty banks and one of the main European locations for insurance and for the funds industry. The success of the IFSC has led to the growth of non-regulated financial services activities, expanding into locations throughout Ireland such as IFS, BISYS, PFPC, Sun Life, State Street Bank and MBNA who all have regional operations. Up to 24,000 professionals work directly in the industry.

Ireland has also emerged as a leading location in Europe for digital media, with Amazon, Google, eBay and Yahoo all locating operations over the past few years.

APPENDIX 7

The pay agreements of the eight national agreements 1987–2006

Pay is only a small, albeit an important, part of the Agreements. For example Towards 2016 is 139 pages long, covering the economy, competitiveness, globalisation, social and economic development, issues through the lifecycle framework, the workplace and employment rights and conditions.

8   Towards 2016

Pay increases under this programme were:
- 3 per cent of basic pay for the first six months of the agreement as it applies in each particular employment or industry;
- 2 per cent of basic pay for the next nine months of the agreement as it applies in each particular employment or industry – except for those employees on an hourly basic rate of €10.25 per hour or less on commencement of the second phase, where a 2.5 per cent increase will apply;
- 2.5 per cent of basic pay for the next six months of the agreement as it applies in each particular employment or industry; and
- 2.5 per cent of basic pay for the next six months of the agreement as it applies in each particular employment or industry.

7   Programme for Sustaining Progress April 2004 to October 2005 (18 months)

Pay increases under this programme were:
- Phase One: 1.5 per cent for six months as it applied in each particular employment or industry – except for those employees on an hourly basic rate of €9 per hour or less on commencement of the first phase, where a 2 per cent increase applied;

- Phase Two: 1.5 per cent for six months as it applied in each particular employment or industry;
- Phase Three: 2.5 per cent for six months as it applied in each particular employment or industry.

6 Programme for Sustaining Progress January 2003 to April 2004 (18 months)

Pay increases under this programme were:
- 3 per cent for nine months
- 2 per cent for six months
- 2 per cent for three months.

Benchmarking awards kicked in for public sector workers in the second year of the agreement, that is, from 2004.

5 Partnership for Prosperity and Fairness April 2000 to December 2002 (33 months)

Pay increases under this programme were:
- Phase One: 5.5 per cent for twelve months
- Phase Two: 5.5 per cent for twelve months
- Phase Three: 4 per cent for nine months.

There was a minimum increase of £12, £11 and £9 respectively.

4 Partnership 2000 January 1997 to March 2000 (39 months)

Pay increases under this programme were:
- Phase One: 2.5 per cent for twelve months
- Phase Two: 2.25 per cent for twelve months with a minimum increase of £3.50
- Phase Three: 1.5 per cent for nine months with a minimum increase of £2.40
- Phase Four: 1 per cent for six months with a minimum increase of £1.60.

3 Programme for Competitiveness and Work June 1994 to December 1996 (42 months)

Pay increases under this programme were:
- Phase One: 2 per cent for twelve months
- Phase Two: 2.5 per cent for twelve months with a minimum increase of £3.50

- Phase Three: 2.5 per cent for six months with a minimum increase of £3.50
- Phase Four: 1 per cent for the remaining six months.

2 Programme for Economic and Social Progress January 1991 to December 1993 (36 months)

Pay increases under this programme were:
- Phase One: 4 per cent with a minimum increase of £5.00
- Phase Two: 3 per cent with a minimum increase of £4.25
- Phase Three: 3.75 per cent with a minimum increase of £5.75.

The agreement also allowed for a local bargaining clause which provided for a maximum of 3 per cent to be negotiated locally.

1 Programme for National Recovery July 1987 to December 1990 (36 months)

Pay increases under this programme were:
- 3 per cent on the first £120.00 per week
- 2 per cent on the balance for each of the three years of the agreement.

There was a minimum increase of £4.00 per week for each of the three years.

BIBLIOGRAPHY

Allen, Kieran, *The Celtic Tiger: The Myth of Social Partnership in Ireland*, Manchester: Manchester University Press 2000.
— *The Corporate Takeover of Ireland*, Dublin and Oregon: Irish Academic Press 2007.
Barry, Frank, John Bradley and Eoin O'Malley, *Indigenous and Foreign Industry*, in F. Barry, ed., *Understanding Ireland's Economic Growth*, London: Macmillan Press 1999.
Boyle, Richard, 'Evaluation Capacity Development in the Republic of Ireland', Washington: World Bank Operations Evaluation Department, *ECD Working Paper* No 14, June 2005.
Cassidy, Mark and Derry O'Brien, *Ireland's Competitiveness Performance*, Central Bank of Ireland Quarterly Report Q2, 2007.
Cech, Zdenìk and John Macdonald, 'The "Celtic Tiger" Learns to Purr' in *Ecfin Country in Focus*, Brussels: EU Commission, November 2004.
Central Bank of Ireland *Quarterly Reports*, various.
CORI, *Socio Economic Review 2007: Addressing Inequality*, Dublin: 2007.
CSO, *Industrial Earnings*, Dublin: various years.
— *Regional Population Projections 2006–21*, Dublin: 2005.
— *EU Survey on Income and Living Conditions*, Dublin: 2006.
— *Measuring Ireland's Progress 2006*, Dublin: 2006.
— *Quarterly National Household Survey*, Dublin: 2007 and various years.
— *Statistical Yearbook of Ireland 2006*, Dublin: 2007.
Economic Policy Institute, *State of Working America 2006/07*, Washington: 2007.
ESRI, *Medium Term Review*, Dublin: 2005.
— *Quarterly Economic Commentary*, Dublin: Economic and Social Research Institute 2007.
European Commission, *Employment in Europe*, Brussels: 2006.
— *The EU Economy Review: Adjustment Dynamics in the Euro Area*, Brussels: November 2006.
— *European Economy*, Brussels: Autumn 2006.

— *The European Economy*, statistical appendix, Brussels: 2007

Eurostat, various data sources: Queen Tree 2007.

Fahey, Tony, Helen Russell and Chris T. Whelan, *The Best of Times? The Social Impact of the Celtic Tiger*, Dublin: IPA 2007.

FÁS, *Quarterly Labour Market Commentary*, Dublin: various.

Finance, Department of, *Economic Development*, Dublin: 1958.

FitzGerald, Garret, *Reflections on the Irish State*, Dublin: Irish Academic Press 2003.

FitzGerald, John, 'The Story of Ireland's Failure – and Belated Success' in B. Nolan, P. J. O'Connell and C. T. Whelan, eds, *Bust to Boom? The Irish Experience of Growth and Inequality*, Dublin: IPA 2000.

Forfás, *Science and Technology Indicators*, Dublin:

— *Enterprise Statistics 2006*, Dublin: 2006.

Frieden, Jeffry A., *Global Capitalism: Its Fall and Rise in the Twentieth Century*, New York: W. W. Norton & Company 2006.

— 'Will Global Capitalism Fall Again?', Presentation for Bruegel Essay and Lectures Series, Brussels: June 2006.

Future Skills Group, *Tomorrow's Skills: Towards a National Skills Strategy*, Dublin: Forfás 2007.

Garretsen, Harry and Jolanda Peeters, *Capital Mobility, Agglomeration and Corporate Tax Rates: Is There a Race to the Bottom for Real?*, CESifo Economic Studies, Oxford: OUP 2007.

Garvin, Tom, *Preventing the Future: Why was Ireland So Poor for So Long?*, Dublin: Gill & Macmillan 2004.

Geary, John, *Employee Voice in the Irish Workplace: Status and Prospect* in Peter Boxall, Peter Haynes and Richard Freeman, eds, *Employee Voice in the Anglo-American World*, New York: Cornell University Press 2006.

Gibbon, Edward (1776–1788), *The History of the Decline and Fall of the Roman Empire*, London: Penguin Books 2000.

Gray, Alan, ed., *International Perspectives on the Irish Economy*, Dublin: Indecon 1997.

— *The Need for a Balanced Perspective on the Structure, Performance and Prospects for US Foreign Investment in Ireland*, Dublin: Indecon, May 2007.

Gunnigle, Patrick, M. O'Sullivan and M. Kinsella, 'Organised Labour in the New Economy: Trade Unions and Public Policy in the Republic of Ireland' in D. D'Art and T. Turner, eds, *Irish Employment Relations in the New Economy*, Dublin: Blackhall Press 2002.

Hardiman, Niamh, *Partnership and Politics: How Embedded is Social Partnership?*, Geary Lecture, UCD, Dublin: 2005.

Hasting, Tim, Brian Sheehan and Padraig Yeates, *Saving the Future: How Social Partnership Shaped Ireland's Economic Success*, Dublin: Blackhall Publishing 2007.

Haughton, Jonathan in John O'Hagan and Carol Newman, *The Economy of Ireland*, Dublin: Gill & Macmillan 2005.

Honohan, Patrick and Brendan Walsh, 'Catching Up With the Leaders: The Irish Hare', in *Brookings Papers on Economic Activity*, Washington, DC: Brookings Institution 2002.

Hughes, Ian, Paula Clancy, Clodagh Harris and David Beetham, *Power to the People? Assessing Democracy in Ireland*, Dublin: tasc/New Island 2007.

IDA Ireland, *Annual Report* and website http://www.idaireland.com/home/index.aspx?id=3

Indecon, *Survey of US firms in Ireland*, Dublin: 2007.

Irish Congress of Trade Unions, *The Jobs Crisis*, Dublin: Irish Congress of Trade Unions, Sept. 1984.

— *Tax Cuts Did not Create the Celtic Tiger*, Dublin: Irish Congress of Trade Unions, Autumn 2004.

— *Life Long Learning Everybody Wins*, Dublin: Irish Congress of Trade Unions, 2005.

— *A New Governance Structure of State Companies*, Dublin: Irish Congress of Trade Unions, Summer 2005.

— *Offshore Outsourcing: The Implications for Ireland*, Dublin: Irish Congress of Trade Unions, Spring 2006.

— *The Coming Challenges of Productivity*, Dublin: 2006, also http://www.ictu.ie/

Kavanagh, C. and E. Doyle, 'Human Capital and Productivity in the Irish Context' in C. Aylward and Ronnie O'Toole, eds, *Perspectives on Irish Productivity*, Dublin: Forfás 2007.

Kennedy, K. A., T. Giblin and D. McHugh, *The Economic Development of Ireland in the Twentieth Century*, London: Routledge 1989.

Kennedy, K. A., ed., *From Famine to Feast: Economic and Social Change in Ireland 1847–1997*, Dublin: IPA 1998.

Kennedy, Paul, 1989, *The Rise and Fall of Great Powers*, London: Fontana 1989.

Kirby, Peadar, *The Celtic Tiger in Distress: Growth and Inequality in Ireland*, Hampshire: Palgrave 2002.

KOF, *Index of Globalisation 2007*, Zurich: Swiss Federal Institute of Technology.

Krugman, Paul in Alan Gray, ed., *International Perspectives on the Irish Economy*, Dublin: Indecon 1997.

Landes, David, *Wealth and Poverty of Nations*, London: Little, Brown 1998.

Marx, Karl, *Das Kapital*, London: Lawrence and Wishart 1887 and 1957.

MacSharry, Ray and Padraic White, *The Making of the Celtic Tiger*, Cork: Mercier 2000.

McWilliams, David, *The Pope's Children: Ireland's New Elite*, Dublin: Gill & Macmillan 2006.

National Competitiveness Council, *Annual Competitiveness Report*, Dublin: Forfás 2006.

— *Benchmarking Ireland's Performance 2007*, Dublin: Forfás 2006.

— *The Competitiveness Challenge*, Dublin: Forfás 2006.

— *Cost of Doing Business in Ireland*, Dublin: Forfás 2006.

—*Education and Competitiveness*, forthcoming, 2007.

NESC, *NESC Strategy 2006: People, Productivity and Purpose*, Dublin: 2005.

— *Migration Policy*, Dublin: 2006.

Nolan, Brian and Bertrand Maître, 'Economic Growth and Income Inequality: Setting the Context' in Tony Fahey, Helen Russell and Chris T. Whelan, eds, *The Best of Times? The Social Impact of the Celtic Tiger*, Dublin: IPA 2007.

O'Connell, Philip J., *Astonishing Success: Economic Growth and the Labour Market in Ireland*, Geneva: 1998.

O'Donnell, Rory and Damian Thomas, 'Ireland in the 1990s: Policy Concentration Triumphant' in S. Berger and H. Compston, eds, *Policy Concentration and Social Partnership in Europe*, New York: Berghahn Books 2002.

OECD, *ICT and Economic Growth – Evidence from OECD Countries, Industries and Firms*, Paris: 2003.

— *Growth Study*, Paris: 2003.

— *Education at a Glance*, Paris: 2005.

— *Growth in Services: Fostering Employment, Productivity and Innovation*, Paris: 2005.

— *Working Paper No 1 on Alternative Measures of Well-Being*, Paris: October 2005.

— *Employment Outlook*, Paris: 2006.

— *Report on Ireland*, Paris: March 2006.

— *Taxing Wages*, Paris: 2006.

— *Economic Survey of Spain*, Paris: 2007.

— *Employment Outlook*, Paris: 2007.

— *OECD Factbook*, Paris: 2007.

Ó Gráda, Cormac, *A Rocky Road*, Manchester: Manchester University Press 1997.

— 'What Have We Learned from the "Celtic Tiger" Phase of Irish Economic Development?' in *ESRI Quarterly Economic Commentary*, 2002.

O'Hagan, John and Carol Newman, *The Economy of Ireland*, Dublin: Gill & Macmillan 2005.

O'Hearn, Denis, 'Macroeconomic Policy in the Celtic Tiger: A Critical Assessment' in C. Coulter and S. Coleman, eds, *The End of Irish History: Critical Reflections on the Celtic Tiger*, Manchester: Manchester University Press 2003.

O'Leary, Olivia, *Party Animals*, Dublin: O'Brien/RTE 2006.

Oxford Economics, *Regional Contributions to UK Public Finances in 2007*, Oxford: Oxford Economics 2007.

Plutarch, *Fall of the Roman Republic*, London: Penguin Books 1972.

Roche, W. K. and J. F. Geary, 'Collaborative Production and the Irish Boom: Work Organisation, Partnership and Direct Involvement in Irish Workplaces', *The Economic and Social Review* 31/1 (2000), 1–36.

Roche, William K., *Accounting for Social Partnership in Ireland*, Dublin: UCD 2003.

Roche, W. K. and T. Cradden, 'Neo-Corporatism and Social Partnership' in Maura Adshead and Michelle Millar, eds, *Public Administration and Public Policy in Ireland: Theory and Methods*, London: Routledge 2003.

Roll, Eric, *A History of Economic Thought*, London: Shenval Press 1966.

Sexton, Gerry, 'Trends in Output, Employment and Productivity in Ireland 1995–2005' in Ciaran Aylward and Ronnie O'Toole, eds, *Perspectives on Irish Productivity*, Dublin: Forfás 2007

Social and Cultural Planning Office, *Public Sector Performance: An International Comparison of Education, Healthcare, Law and Order and Public Administration*, The Hague, Holland: September 2004.

Sweeney, Paul, *The Politics of Public Enterprise and Privatisation*, Dublin: Tomar 1990.

— 'Employment in Ireland' in Peter Shirlow, ed., *Development Ireland*, London: Pluto Press 1995.

— *The Celtic Tiger: Ireland's Economic Miracle Explained*, Dublin: Oak Tree Press 1998.

— *The Celtic Tiger: Ireland's Continuing Economic Miracle*, Dublin: Oak Tree Press 1999.

— 'Globalisation' in Maura Adshead and Michelle Millar, eds, *Public Administration and Public Policy in Ireland: Theory and Methods*, London: Routledge 2003.

— 'La Reforma Economica de Irlanda. Obstaculos y Logros' in *Globalisación Economica: Desafios Para un Nuevo Consenso*, Dialogo Politico, Julio, Buenos Aires: Konrad Adenauer Stifung AC 2003.

— 'Corporation Tax: Leading the Race to the Bottom' in B. Reynolds and S. Healy, eds, *A Fairer Tax System for a Fairer Ireland*, Dublin, CORI Justice Commission 2004.

— *Selling Out? Privatisation in Ireland*, Dublin: tasc/New Island, 2004.
— *The Workplace of the Future: A Colloquium Celebrating Ireland's Presidency of the European Union*, Montreal, May 2004, Dublin: ICTU.
Tansey, Paul, *Productivity: Ireland's Economic Imperative*, Dublin: Microsoft 2005.
Teague, Paul, 'Monetary Union and Social Europe', *Journal of European Social Policy*, 8, 1998.
Tonra, Ben, *Global Citizen and European Republic: Irish Foreign Policy in Transition*, Manchester: Manchester University Press 2007.
US Bureau of Labour Statistics, 2006.
Walsh, John, *The Falling Angels*, London: Flamingo 2000.
Watson, Dorothy, Christopher T. Whelan and Bertrand Maître, *Validating the European Socio-Economic Classification: Cross-Sectional and Dynamic Analysis of Income Poverty and Lifestyle Deprivation*, ESRI Working Paper No. 201, Dublin: June 2007.
Whelan, C., Brian Nolan and Bertrand Maître, 'Consistent Poverty and Economic Vulnerability' in Tony Fahey, Helen Russell and Chris T. Whelan, *The Best of Times? The Social Impact of the Celtic Tiger*, Dublin: IPA 2007.

NOTES

Introduction

1   *The Economist,* in a cover article titled 'Europe's Shining Light' (17 May 1997), said that 'Ireland's transformation is so dazzling . . . one of the most remarkable economic transformations of recent times: from basket case to "emerald tiger" in ten years,' quoted in Sweeney, *The Celtic Tiger: Ireland's Economic Miracle Explained,* Oak Tree Press, 1998. While this book, written in 1987, was the first one on the Celtic Tiger and the first book with the now over-used term Celtic Tiger in its title, the term was actually coined by Kevin Gardiner of Morgan Stanley in 1994 in a review of the Irish economy.

2   OECD, *Report on Ireland,* Paris: March 2006. The Organisation for Economic Co-operation and Development has a membership of thirty of the richest countries in the world. It undertakes excellent statistical analysis and data, but has a fairly conservative outlook, like most international economic organisations.

3   See Appendix 1 for employment and Appendix 2 for growth data including forecasts. The GNP forecast was for 2.9 per cent for 2008 at time of writing.

4   For a critical view of the Eircom ESOT see Chapters 3 and 6 of Sweeney's *Selling Out?*

5   W. B. Yeats, 'Easter 1916', written 25 September 1916.

Chapter 1

1   Kennedy *et al., Economic Development of Ireland.*

2   The IDA was originally set up in 1949 to examine tariffs and quotas, but was given the job of attracting foreign investment and encouraging Irish firms in 1952. The Shannon tax-free zone was set up in 1947, and SFADCo was set up in 1959. An Foras Tionscail was also set up in 1949 to give grants to firms in the West and South West.

3   Kennedy *et al., Economic Development of Ireland,* 81–2.

4   The economic war with Britain was sparked off by a dispute over which government, the Irish or British, should receive the land annuities paid by Irish tenant purchasers. De Valera had made it an election promise

in 1932 that Ireland would keep them.
5   Fahey *et al.*, *The Best of Times?* 2007.

Chapter 2
1   Interview with the author, 24 February 2007.

Chapter 3
1   Interview with the author, 8 January 2007.
2   ICTU, 2006, *The Coming Challenges of Productivity.*
3   Frieden, 'Will Global Capitalism Fall Again?'

Chapter 4
1   Interview with the author, 19 February 2007.
2   The Tallaght Strategy was the decision by Alan Dukes, leader of the
    main opposition party, not to oppose fiscal reform by the government
    in a speech made in Tallaght, Co. Dublin in 1987.
3   There was zero tax on profits of manufacturing exports for many years,
    which was extended to exported services later, when the nominal
    corporation tax rate was 50 per cent. The 50 per cent rate which
    applied to all other companies was progressively reduced to just 12.5
    per cent from January 2004 and many tax allowances were
    simultaneously reduced.

Chapter 5
1   Interview with the author, 23 April 2007.
2   Tansey, *Productivity: Ireland's Economic Imperative.*
3   NESC, *People, Productivity and Purpose.*

Chapter 6
1   Interview with the author, 19 April 2007.

Chapter 7
1   Interview with the author, 10 January 2007.

Chapter 8
1   Interview with the author, 19 April 2007.

Chapter 9
1   Sweeney, *The Celtic Tiger: Ireland's Economic Miracle Explained,* and
    The Celtic Tiger: Ireland's Continuing Economic Miracle.
2   Ian Traynor, 'Wealth Gap Grows and Solidarity Fades as Rebellion of
    Rich Spreads across EU', *The Guardian,* 11 June 2007.

3 Sexton, 'Trends in Output, Employment and Productivity in Ireland 1995–2005'.

4 Bertie Ahern, Taoiseach, Irish Management Institute Annual Conference, Killarney, 23 April 2004, quoted in Sweeney, *The Workplace of the Future*.

5 There had been national pay agreements in earlier decades.

6 Bill Attley, interview with the author, 31 May 2007.

7 Peter Cassells, interview with the author, 25 June 2007.

8 Jack O'Connor, President of SIPTU, Ireland's largest trade union, in interview with the author, 10 May 2007.

9 The CSO estimated unionisation at 35 per cent in 2004 (QNHS, *Union Membership*, 7 Sept 2005) based on a survey of households. It found membership totalled 521,400. However, the actual paid-up membership of trade unions in Ireland in 2004 was 577,000 in Congress alone. In 2006 Congress' membership was 603,000 with another 29,000 (PNA and NBRU, unions which are outside Congress and those in the army and guards' unions), which gave a total union membership of 632,000 out of 1,700,000 employees (which includes proprietorial directors, i.e. really self-employed in their own small companies, rather than employees, and who number between 70–110,000) giving a 37.2 per cent density in 2006. Fifty-five per cent of Congress' membership is in the private sector, contary to the opinions expressed by some.

10 Allen, *The Corporate Takeover of Ireland*, 11.

11 *Ibid.*, 62.

12 Kirby, *The Celtic Tiger in Distress*.

13 OECD, *Employment Outlook* 2007.

14 Teague, 'Monetary Union and Social Europe'.

15 Jim O'Leary, *Irish Times*, 11 June 2004.

16 OECD, *Taxing Wages*.

17 Fitzgerald, 'The Story of Ireland's Failure – and Belated Success'.

18 Hardiman, 'Partnership and Politics: How Embedded is Social Partnership?'

19 O'Donnell and Thomas, 'Ireland in the 1990s'.

20 Social and Cultural Planning Office, *Public Sector Performance: An International Comparison of Education, Healthcare, Law and Order and Public Administration*, The Hague.

21 It will be seen below that an academic study found that core economies can maintain higher company tax rates, but it is more difficult for peripheral ones to do so with the pressure of tax competition between nation states.

22 Garretsen and Peeters, *Capital Mobility, Agglomeration and Corporate*

Tax Rates: Is There a Race to the Bottom for Real?

23 Sweeney, *The Politics of Public Enterprise and Privatisation* and *Selling Out? Privatisation in Ireland.*

24 Social and Cultural Planning Office, *Public Sector Performance: An International Comparison of Education, Healthcare, Law and Order and Public Administration.*

25 OECD, *Education at a Glance.*

26 Eurostat, by Int. Standard Classification of Education (ISECED), 2007.

27 *The Guardian,* 11 June 2007.

28 Kavanagh and Doyle, 'Human Capital and Productivity in the Irish Context'.

29 You have to watch the educational comparators; they can be confusing as the age comparisons may differ, e.g. some compare those of young cohorts and others the whole working population etc.

30 Future Skills Group, *Tomorrows Skills: Towards a National Skills Strategy.*

31 *Irish Times,* 20 March 2007: Parents face a waiting game to get their children into fee-paying schools. Some will have to wait until 2019. 'Since the abolition of third-level fees, parents have used the college fund for secondary schooling, and the private sector has become synonymous with academic success, at least in the public mind.'

32 NIMBY – *Not In My Back Yard.* These can be insiders who oppose development close to themselves. With increased incomes in Ireland, new reactionary Anti groups are emerging – the NOPEs – *Not On Planet Earth!*

33 Barry, *Understanding Ireland's Economic Growth.*

34 Barry *et al.,* 'Indigenous and Foreign Industry'.

35 Cech and Macdonald, 'The "Celtic Tiger" Learns to Purr'.

36 Honahan and Walsh, 'Catching Up with the Leaders: The Irish Hare'.

37 Boyle, 'Evaluation Capacity Development in the Republic of Ireland'.

38 Gray, *International Perspectives on the Irish Economy.* Contributors include Paul Krugman and Jeffery Sachs.

39 FitzGerald, 'The Story of Ireland's Failure and Belated Success'.

40 FitzGerald cites Paddy Geary in *How Fianna Fáil's Economic Policies Cannot Get This Country Moving Again,* 1978.

41 Ben Tonra, 'Foreign Policy and Who We Are', *Irish Times,* 20 January 2007 and *Global Citizen and European Republic: Irish Foreign Policy in Transition.*

42 Ireland ceded its monetary policy to the European Central Bank when it joined the Euro.

43 World Trade Organisation in *ESRI Quarterly*, Summer 2007, in a section on services.

Chapter 10

1 Of the twenty-six counties which make up the Republic, population fell from 6.5m in 1841 to 3.2m in 1901 (CSO census).

2 Though unemployment in 1989 actually fell slightly by 2 per cent on two years earlier, to 15 per cent, helped no doubt by the emigrants.

3 Future Skills Group, *Tomorrows Skills: Towards a National Skills Strategy*. Its recommendations are to take actions to improve the skill base especially for those with lowest educational attainment.

4 Philip O'Connell and Helen Russell, 'Employment and the Quality of Work' in Fahey *et al.*

5 European Commission, 'Employment in Europe', *Statistical Appendix*, 2006.

6 Employment rate is the percentage of the *population* aged 15–64 that is employed.

7 OECD, *Employment Outlook* 2006.

8 The participation rate is the number of persons in the *labour force* expressed as a percentage of the total population aged fifteen or over.

9 OECD, 'Labour Markets in the BRICs', *Employment Outlook* 2007.

10 European Commission, 'European Economy', *Statistical Appendix*, Autumn 2006.

11 Central Bank of Ireland, 'Indices of Relative Wage Cost in Manufacturing', *Quarterly Report*, April 2007.

12 For those single people on twice the average industrial earnings, the rise in net disposable incomes was higher at 91 per cent but it was less for those on only half of industrial earnings, whether single or married. Source: Department of Finance net tax calculations undertaken for Congress in May 2007.

13 Economic Policy Institute, *State of Working America 2006/07*, Washington: 2007. See http://www.stateofworkingamerica.org/news/SWA06Facts-Wages.pdf

14 Larry Summers, quoting a study done by him and others for the Hamilton project in *Financial Times*, 25 June 2005. Summers believes that income inequality is not just continuing but also growing – and that 'something quite fundamental is at work' in these English-speaking countries, clearly excluding Ireland. He says that economic growth, the solution in the past, 'is no longer credible' and his suggested response appears to be government action which goes with the grain of the market.

15 OECD, *Employment Outlook* 2006.

16 US Bureau of Labour Statistics, 2006.

17 Such as *Taxing Wages* from the OECD which shows the net and gross cost of hiring workers. As well as low overall earnings, the wedge is helped by the low income taxes paid by Irish workers, and by the low social contribution paid by their employers. Alternatively, *The Cost of Doing Business* from the NCC sets out international comparison for hiring different categories of workers and Ireland is still not too high in Europe, but earnings are rising faster than many countries.

18 ICTU, *Tax Cuts Did Not Create the Celtic Tiger.*

19 CSO, *EU Survey on Income and Living Conditions.*

20 CSO, *Measuring Ireland's Progress.*

21 KOF, *Index of Globalisation.*

22 *The Economist,* 6 April 2006.

23 Cassidy and O'Brien, *Ireland's Competitiveness Performance.*

24 European Commission, *The EU Economy Review: Adjustment Dynamics in the Euro Area,* 210.

25 Forfás, *Enterprise Statistics 2006.*

26 ESRI, *Medium Term Review.*

27 Indecon, *Survey of US firms in Ireland.*

28 *Ibid.*

29 Forfás, *Science and Technology Indicators.*

30 Forfás, *Enterprise Statistics 2006.*

31 The European Central Bank. Its mission is to curb inflation and wider economic issues are not part of its remit. Ironically, in order to curb inflation in the larger economies in 2006 and 2007 by raising interest rates, it pushed Ireland's Consumer Price Index up significantly – by twice the normal rise in periods. European consumer prices are measured by the Harmonised Index of Consumer prices, which conveniently does not include interest rates. Thus the HICP would not be entertained by the property-owning and mortgage-burdened Irish citizens!

32 *Rational* in the sense of broadly maintaining a government balance between revenue and expenditure over time. There can still be great argument/debate about the level of spending and taxation, sources and levels of taxes, etc. which is the essence of political debate in most countries, though it has been relatively absent in Ireland for some years, perhaps due to the economic boom.

Chapter 11

1 Philosophers and thinkers have been intrigued by this since time immemorial. For example, Plutarch, who lived in the first and second centuries AD, focused on leaders and the influence of birth and education in his *Fall of the Roman Republic.*

2   Landes, *Wealth and Poverty of Nations.*
3   Kennedy, *The Rise and Fall of Great Powers.*
4   For much more on this area see Hughes *et al., Power to the People?*, the excellent book from the Democracy Commission.
5   The first wave of globalisation was from the mid-1880s to 1914 with the outbreak of the First World War. It was followed by the rise in protectionism, depression, war and genocide until the end of the Second World War, and then by the second wave of globalisation.
6   Like John Walsh's father in *The Falling Angels* who only wanted to 'retire home to Galway and celebrate the community that should always have been theirs . . . just as he had left the place thirty three years earlier'. (Flamingo 2000, 225.)
7   Imports from Germany doubled in under ten years and our exports to there, which are much higher than imports, peaked in 2001, but are still high.
8   'Cutting Up the Union Poses Challenges', *Financial Times*, 25 April 2007.
9   OECD, *Economic Survey of Spain.*
10 Oxford Economics, 'Regional Contributions to UK Public Finances'.
11 FitzGerald, *Reflections on the Irish State*, Chapter 8.
12 OECD, *OECD Factbook.*
13 The main thrust of a chapter which I wrote in 2003 was that globalisation is not inevitable and when it failed, there was a depression, poverty, mass unemployment, the rise of fascism and mass genocide. While globalisation has its critics, it has greatly benefited Ireland. 'Globalisation', in Maura Adshead and Michelle Millar, eds, *Public Administration and Public Policy in Ireland: Theory and Methods*, London: Routledge 2003.
14 This was an international agreement by the great powers agreed in 1944. The Bretton Woods System was a system of governance over monetary relations among independent nation states. The IMF and World Bank were established under it. It was effective until the 1970s.
15 'Berlin Looks at Vetting Acquisitions by Foreign State Owned Funds', *Financial Times*, 26 June 2007.
16 ING study quoted in a worried *Financial Times* editorial on these funds on 23 July 2007.
17 Francesco Guerra and James Polti, 'Blackstone Pays a Heavy Price to Come to Market', *Financial Times*, 22 June 2006. The price was rigorous disclosure of financial information, of its low taxes, its aggressive accounting and the staggering pay to the top managers. Blackstone owns companies in virtually every sector and every continent.

18 *Financial Times,* editorial, 20 June 2007.
19 OECD, *Employment Outlook* 2007.
20 '"Dangers of Globalisation Overblown" Says OECD in Move to Calm Fears', *Financial Times,* 20 June 2007.
21 Fahey *et al., The Best of Times?*
22 *Ibid.,* 10.
23 Watson *et al., Validating the European Socio-Economic Classification.*
24 Whelan *et al.,* 'Consistent Poverty and Economic Vulnerability' in Fahey *et al.*
25 Nolan and Maître, 'Economic Growth and Income Inequality', 41.
26 *Ibid.,* 41.
27 It is not known whether the income tax data used took into account the gross incomes of the high earners who avoided paying income tax through the use of the tax shelters, such as the property-based schemes, the business expansion schemes or pension-related schemes, etc.
28 *Irish Independent,* 31 May 2007, reporting on IL&P establishing such a division.
29 *Irish Times,* 12 May 2006.
30 Fujita, Krugman and Venables, 'The Spatial Economy', quoted by Haughton in O'Hagan and Newman, *The Economy of Ireland.*

INDEX